✴ *The Turks*

The Turks

DAVID HOTHAM

JOHN MURRAY

Printed Offset Litho in Great Britain by
Cox & Wyman Ltd
London, Fakenham and Reading

0 7195 2725 2

❋ Contents

✻ Illustrations

*Photos: Ara Güler

†Photos: Turkish Ministry of Tourism and Information

❋ *Author's Note*

I STARTED this book in 1965, but in July 1966 was appointed to a good job as staff correspondent of *The Times* in Bonn. The book was only half finished at the time. Being immersed for three years in the ponderous intricacies of German politics, I found it quite impossible to concentrate on the Turks. The book was laid aside, and only finished after I left Bonn in 1969.

Although I have tried to deal with events in Turkey up to the moment of going to press, the point of this book is not primarily to recount events, but to introduce the Turks as a people. My qualifications for this are that I lived for eight years among them, and my knowledge of their language enabled me to talk with every type and class of Turk. I have read quite widely in Turkish, including as much as I could of modern Turkish literature, and have travelled, at one time or another, to most parts of Turkey.

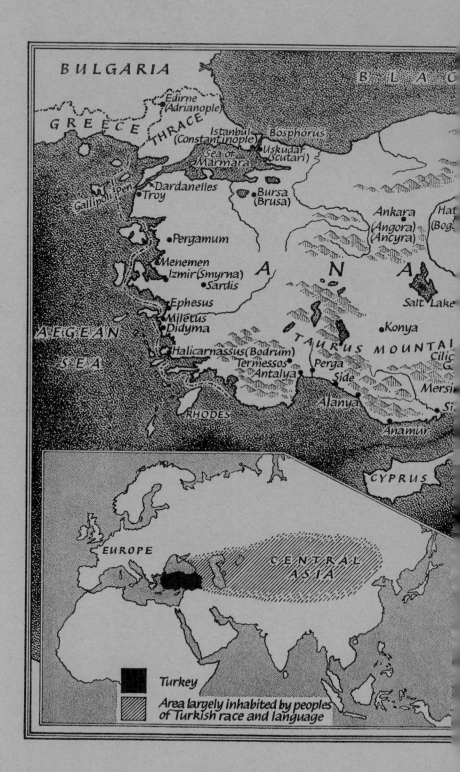

S E A

SOVIET
UNION

...sun

Trabzon
(Trebizond)

Zigana Pass

Erzurum

River Araxes

Mt.
Ararat

Sivas

PERSIA

O L I A

Malazgirt

...yseri

Keban
Dam

Mush

L.
Van

Van

Diyarbakir

Mardin

Gaziantep

Urfa

...na

Iskenderun

Antioch

River Euphrates

S Y R I A

River Tigris

Z

I R A Q

Miles

| 0 | 50 | 100 | 150 | 200 | 250 | 300 | 350 | 400 | 450 | 500 |

| 0 | 80 | 160 | 240 | 320 | 400 | 480 | 560 | 640 | 720 | 800 |

Kilometres

1 ✳ *The Turks and Europe*

IS A TURK a European? Many people would instinctively say No, but they might be wrong. The Turks are members of the Council of Europe. There are no Arabs, Africans, Indians, or Japanese at Strasbourg, but there *are* Turks. Nobody has asked the Turks to leave, nor have they themselves shown the slightest inclination to do so. Can one sit in the Council of Europe and not be a European?

Our question may seem academic. Who cares today about classifying people as 'westerners' or 'orientals'? The world is one world. But *is* the question so academic? Europe is gradually uniting, and in course of time, if this process goes on, will ultimately emerge as some kind of single federative state. Will not the question arise – is it not already arising – as to which peoples should be included in the new Europe? In other words: Who is a European?

The point about the Turks is that they want to be in this process. Of all the 'debatable' peoples they seem to me the most interesting, because they alone, in our time, have made an all-out effort to transfer from one civilization to another. They were Asiatics; they are Europeans. *Are* they Europeans? For many centuries they were resident in Europe, but not really part of it. Now they are members of the Council of Europe. Is that the inner sanctum?

The Turks are not only members of the Council of Europe, which is a purely deliberative and fairly ineffective body, but have applied to be permanent citizens of a United Europe, if and when such an entity comes into being. For them it is not merely a matter of exporting their figs and tobacco to the West; they want to be integrally, once and for all, part of Europe.

There is no obvious reason why this should not be so. Geographically, it is perfectly feasible. It would be absurd for a Japanese, a Chinaman, or an Indonesian, to call himself a European. Obviously you cannot extend Europe, like a sort of concertina, to include the

I

whole world. But the Turks lived in Europe, geographically, for some six hundred years, and are contiguous to it. Turkey was the 'Sick Man of Europe', not the 'Sick Man of Asia'. If we can stretch our Continent from the Atlantic to the Urals and include the Russians, why should we not stretch it from the Atlantic to the Caucasus and include the Turks?

Turks are Muslims, undoubtedly, and have been for a thousand years, whereas it is true that most Europeans are, or were, Christians. Moreover the Turks, historically, were the ferocious opponents of Christendom, during the Crusades and at other times. Would this prevent them being Europeans today? Can one make religion the touchstone in such a matter? Are we still fighting the Crusades? A Jew can be a European, so why not a Muslim?

Muslims are polygamous; Christians monogamous, and most Jews also in practice. Does this mean that one cannot be a European and have four wives? Many people might say Yes. A European may have a wife, a mistress, and a girl-friend, all running concurrently, as it were; but it is a matter of the system. A European may be polygamous by nature, but in Europe there is not polygamy as a *system*. The European candidature of the Turks might depend on the extent to which they have abolished polygamy, not only in name but in fact.

On a less earthy level, we should remember that Muslims are monotheists. They may have four wives, but they worship one God. Monotheism is a strong bond between Christians, Muslims, and Jews. If 'East is east and west is west, and never the twain shall meet', as Kipling decided for us, it is perhaps between monotheists and polytheists, rather than at some other point, that the 'divide' comes. Theologically speaking, this would make Muslims part of the West.

The argument is perhaps a little tortured. Christianity and Islam, historically, have developed as profoundly different, if not mutually exclusive, worlds. Admittedly the Albanians are Muslims, and are also Europeans; but Albania is not representative of any aspect of the European civilization, or, for that matter, of Islam. It is different for the Turks, who were the foremost champions of Islam, and for a thousand years were virtually submerged by the

Islamic culture. Thus the drama of the Turks, in their long love-affair with Europe, is essentially the drama of *religion*. Is a Turk a European? For the moment let's leave the question open.

* * * * *

For centuries the Turks were the scourge of Christendom and the standing menace to Europe. During the Middle Ages, pestilences, floods, earthquakes, Turks, Tartars and comets were listed as the traditional punishments reserved by the Almighty for sinners. In the sixteenth century Martin Luther prayed to be delivered from 'the world, the flesh, the Turk, and the Devil'. Few peoples in history have been put in such company as this. The word 'Turk' came to be a symbol in western languages for everything that was violent or savage:

> When she is by, I leave my work,
> (I love her so sincerely),
> My master comes like any Turk
> And bangs me most severely.

My own childhood memories are punctuated by the menacing dictum of a series of formidable nannies: 'Don't behave like a little Turk!'

In 1949, when the Turks asked to become members of the Council of Europe, there was opposition in the West, on grounds that the Turks were not, and never could be, a European people. *The Times* argued portentously that the Turks could not possibly be admitted because they wrote in the Arabic script – a fearful gaffe, of course, because Turkey had adopted the Latin script twenty-one years before. A prominent Turkish politician, Mr. Kasim Gulek, wrote a letter of protest to the editor, which was published.

In the end the Turks were admitted to the Council of Europe, and later to NATO and other western organizations, but this was done largely because of the cold war. The Americans wanted a brave, staunch people like the Turks on their side. The Turks owned Constantinople,* the Straits, and the highly strategic peninsula of Anatolia, and in a possible conflict with the Soviet Union all these were vital. Thus it was more for military than other reasons

* Istanbul being the modern name for the city, Constantinople is only used where the context, for historical or other reasons, seems to demand it.

that the Turks were received into Europe. Many Europeans were hesitant about having the Turks with us in any capacity other than that of temporary allies.

It would be interesting to know what the word 'Turk' really means today to an average west-European mind. If the collective subconscious is formed by history, as to a large extent it must be, the fact that the Turk was for hundreds of years the enemy of Christendom and Europe must colour our thoughts and feelings. 'Modern history begins under the stress of the Ottoman conquest', wrote Lord Acton. Many of us doubtless have a deep-rooted prejudice against the Turks, and a feeling that the Turk cannot be 'one of us'. Conversely the Turk, in his heart, may think the same about us.

One of the tangible issues which aroused these feelings in recent years is the Cyprus crisis, or rather the series of Cyprus crises of the 1950's and 60's. This was essentially a conflict between Turks and Greeks, and, as such, revived issues going back in history as far as the Crusades, and even beyond. How many of us, during the Cyprus troubles, were instinctively anti-Turkish and pro-Greek, on grounds that the Greeks were Christians and Europeans, whereas the Turks were not? Some organs of the western press, which I could name, showed gross anti-Turkish prejudice; others were remarkably fair to the Turks.

Of course we have so much which binds us to Greece, because we think of the age of Pericles and Socrates and Athenian democracy as the 'dawn of the western civilization'. These feelings were revived in the nineteenth century by the exploits of Byron. There is a tremendous amount of romantic Hellenism still latent in Britain.

It is equally clear that relatively little binds us historically to the Turks. Most people still consider the fall of Constantinople in 1453 as an unmitigated disaster. I have the feeling that many Philhellenes nourish in their hearts the hope that some day, somehow, the Greeks will recapture the city, and even win back parts of Anatolia, as they tried to do in 1919. But this is romantic nonsense. The Turks asserted their right to these places by military conquest – the way in which all peoples in history have asserted their right to be anywhere – and it is unlikely that they will ever relinquish them.

Many westerners, perhaps unconsciously, see the question in

almost Manichaean terms: the Greeks are the blue-eyed boys, the Turks the villains. But we should remember that some of the greatest European historians, not least Gibbon, admired the qualities of the Turks, and deplored the degeneracy of the Greeks in the Middle Ages, and the squabbles and jealousies between Rome and Byzantium which led to the loss of Constantinople. Gibbon begins chapter 64 of *Decline and Fall of the Roman Empire*: 'From the petty quarrels of a city and her suburbs, from the cowardice and discord of the falling Greeks, I shall now *ascend** to the victorious Turks . . .'. Of course one cannot read too much into one Gibbonian verb, but other historians have admired the Ottoman system: the remarkable religious toleration, and the astonishing practice of the principle of the 'career open to talent', under which a slave could rise to be Grand Vizier (roughly Prime Minister) in that strange and interesting realm.

Historical attitudes are gradually breaking down, no doubt, as the Turks mix with us in the Council of Europe, NATO, and the organizations of the West. Some people still have extraordinary ideas about the Turks: that they are Negroes with fuzzy hair, who eat their children, wear turbans, or sit crosslegged on divans with innumerable wives and concubines in the background. A Turkish delegate to the Council of Europe told me that when he first went to Strasbourg in 1949 a member of one of the western delegations said, apparently seriously, that he had always understood that Turks had *tails*. . . . I must add that it is not clear to me how he reassured himself that they didn't.

In the last eight years some 600,000 Turks have flooded into western Europe (mainly West Germany) in search of jobs. This is an altogether remarkable event, because it is the first time in history that large numbers of Turks have entered western Europe (in their military conquests they never got beyond the outskirts of Vienna). This is something completely different to a few highly educated and westernized Turkish diplomats or officials going to Strasbourg or Brussels, because it means that hundreds of thousands of ordinary Turks from remote Anatolian villages are penetrating to the heart of the western civilization.

* My italics.

The Turks

Can an oriental people become western? What exactly is involved in this strange process? 'East is east and west is west'. Was Kipling right? Can a Turk, who undoubtedly *was* an Asiatic, become a European?

What did Kipling mean? We all know the famous verse so well that we seldom stop to think out its real significance. There is some truth in it, of course, as everybody who has lived in the East knows, but it was a thought highly coloured by Kipling's own strongly imperialist viewpoint. Kipling's experience of the East was mainly in India, at the height of the British Raj. For him the 'East' probably meant the Indian coolie, the incomprehensible oriental who masked his true feelings about his imperial masters.

Things have changed since Kipling's day. The East is no longer incomprehensible to us. All those countries which were once part of the British empire, or somebody else's empire, have achieved their independence. We know better now what they think and feel. We know far more than we did about the religions and philosophies of the East. Something of the mystery and glamour of the East has gone, and a great deal of cross-fertilization between East and West is going on. While orientals are becoming 'westernized', long-haired European youths dress like Gurus and go and meditate in the foothills of the Himalayas. Kipling's verse, though still famous, seems a little out-of-date.

It is worth noting that Mustafa Kemal Atatürk, the man who more than anybody else tried to make Turkey part of Europe, specifically denounced Kipling's idea that East and West were watertight compartments; he claimed (perhaps rightly) that this was a notion conceived by Europeans to help keep non-European peoples in subjection. Atatürk was later hailed by many eastern peoples as the pioneer of the Asian revolutions against the West.

The Turks are not, of course, the first people in history to move from Asia into Europe. This was done over a thousand years ago by the Hungarians, Finns, and Bulgars, all of whom emerged from the Eurasian Steppe in the eighth or ninth centuries A.D. and settled roughly into their present habitats. I don't think anybody would today deny these three peoples the name of Europeans. But the Hungarians, Finns and Bulgars were all three converted to Christianity, and this fact made it much easier for them to become 'western'. It is far more difficult for the Turks.

Nevertheless the Turks, though not actually regarded as a European people, did live for some six hundred years within the boundaries of Europe. They had what one might call a ringside seat at the spectacle of European history. By capturing Constantinople, and inheriting most of the Byzantine empire, they drank in much of the Greek and Roman culture. It is interesting to note that in the Middle Ages, though we thought of Turkey as the East, people who lived to the east of Turkey thought of it as the West. The country which the Turks mainly inhabited, Anatolia, was traditionally known by people further east as 'Rum', meaning 'Rome'. That was only natural, because for centuries Anatolia had been part of the Roman empire.

*   *   *   *   *

This brings us finally to a very interesting and peculiar problem; who *are* the Turks? The question may seem an odd one, but it is not quite so odd as it sounds. It should be phrased a little more precisely, thus: who are the people who today live in Turkey, and whom we call the Turks? I am not, of course, referring here to the Turkish peoples of the Soviet Union or China, because it is only the Turks of Turkey who are claiming to be Europeans, and who are members of the various European organizations.

Who are the Turks? The ethnic history of Anatolia, which forms the bulk of modern Turkey, is an amazingly complex one. The Hittites, now believed to be a people who came from the west or north, and who spoke an Indo-European language, established a great empire in Anatolia in the second millenium B.C. After them came the Phrygians, Lydians, Persians and many others. Alexander the Great conquered the whole Anatolian peninsula in the fourth century B.C., giving it the Hellenic culture, at least down to a certain level. There were large influxes of Celts and Jews into Anatolia in the period leading to the beginning of the Christian era. Then the whole of Anatolia was part of the Roman empire, and later of the Byzantine empire. There were Armenians living in the east of the country, and Kurds in the south-east. The Turks did not arrive on the scene till the eleventh century A.D. Later, the picture was further complicated by the Mongol invasions.

The Turks

One of the most puzzling episodes in history is the 'Turkification' of Anatolia after the arrival of the Turks. It is a problem which historians have not fully solved to this day. The puzzle is that only a comparatively small number of Turkish invaders from central Asia entered Anatolia: they filtered in in smallish bands over the next two hundred years. There was some fighting, of course, but there were no massacres or deportations of the native population. Yet after a time the whole population of Anatolia, which up to then had been Greek- or Armenian-speaking, and Christian, became Turkish and Muslim.

There are various theories about what happened in Anatolia in the centuries following the Turkish conquest, and the extent to which the invaders intermarried with the local populations. One thing seems reasonably clear. The pre-Turkish inhabitants of Anatolia, who, roughly speaking, were a glorious amalgam of all the races which had gone before – pre-Hittites, Hittites, Phrygians, Lydians, Celts, Jews, Greeks, Romans, Armenians, Kurds, Mongols, and Heaven knows what else – were *not replaced* by the Turks. A handful of Turks from Asia added themselves to the stock, so that the 'Anatolian mixture' went on being more or less what it was before. The difference was that, instead of the indigenous mixture assimilating the Turks, the relatively few Turkish conquerors were strong enough to impose their stamp on the native peoples, so that the latter became Turkish-speaking and Muslim, and were from now on known as 'Turks', living in a country called 'Turkey'.

This means that the inhabitants of modern Turkey, whom we call the Turks, and who of course *are* the Turks, in the sense that they compose the modern Turkish nation, are really a people formed over many centuries out of a mixture of the races mentioned in the last paragraph. Racial theories can, of course, be used to prove almost anything, and the fact that the Turks are an even more complex mixture than the British leads at first sight to no obvious conclusion. But it is germane to the question we are discussing: whether the Turks are Europeans. This 'Anatolian mixture' of Hittites, Phrygians, Greeks, Romans, Armenians, Celts and others which is what the modern Turks appear to be, is not a particularly 'Asiatic' mixture. If one examines the origins of the peoples involved, one can argue that the Anatolian stock is as much 'western' as 'oriental'. The Turks of Turkey have a better claim to be considered Europeans, on purely ethnic grounds, than most people would suppose.

These theories are borne out by the complete difference in appearance between the Turks of Turkey and the Turkish peoples of the Soviet Union and western China, who look far more oriental. These Asiatic Turks have slanted eyes, high cheek-bones, and yellowish skins, whereas the Turks of Anatolia are classified by ethnologists as a white race, and physically speaking are indistinguishable from most of the peoples of Europe. One rarely sees a Mongoloid face in Turkey today, and if one does, it is usually the face of a Turcoman nomad, or a refugee from central Asia.

When one crosses the border from Greece or Bulgaria into Turkey, the oriental appearance of the country comes not from the physique of the people, or from their clothes, which for the last forty years have been western, but rather from the mosques and minarets, the symbols of a different world, Islam. The fact that the Turks are Muslims makes Europe, in the literary *cri de coeur* of a modern Turkish writer, 'keep up that deaf wall against us'. But can Europe reject the Turks because of religion?

2 ✲ The Religious Question

THERE is one important difference between the Turks and other peoples traditionally regarded as outside the pale of Europe: whereas the others wanted to imitate or in some way adapt the western civilization, the Turks actually wanted to *be* the West. As I have said, Turkey's aim is to be part of Europe, and the aim of the Turks, or a powerful minority of them, to be Europeans. This being so, anybody writing a book on Turkey is bound to get involved in a discussion about Christianity and Islam.

The Turks, or the great majority of them, are Muslims. Most of Europe is, or was, Christian. Christianity and Islam are not only different religions, but to a large extent mutually exclusive worlds. It is not merely that we go to church, they to the mosque, we believe in the Gospels, they in the Koran, we are allowed one wife, they four. Certain doctrines regarded as fundamental by Christians are rejected, in fact abominated, by Islam: the divinity of Christ, for example, or the Trinity.

The Trinity is particularly abhorred by Muslims because it blurs the One-ness of God – for them the essential feature of the Deity. There are ferocious passages in the Koran condemning those who 'associate partners to God' (which is how Muslims conceive the Trinity), and enumerating the painful chastisements reserved for them in the life hereafter. During my travels in Turkey, in remote villages and in conversation with illiterate peasants, I have often been rigorously cross-questioned about Christian dogmas, and asked in particular to explain how one God can be three persons. Turkish peasants are very interested in religion, and are often quite well-versed in matters of doctrine. I advise anybody who visits a Turkish village to have at his fingers' ends a satisfactory explanation of the Trinity in simple Turkish.

Obviously it is not for me to embark on any deep consideration of the differences and similarities between Christianity and Islam. All I can say is that I lived for eight years in a Muslim country and did my best to observe what went on there. I found Islam, as religions go, an attractive religion, not least in its outward manifestations and architecture. There are many exceedingly fine mosques in Turkey. Turkish minarets are particularly tall and slender. I grew to appreciate the call of the muezzin, and in course of time almost to prefer it to the Christian peal of bells. (Church bells are offensive to a Muslim ear.)

Unfortunately in much of Turkey today, and in other Muslim countries, the call to prayer is relayed by amplifiers fixed to the minarets. As a result the beautiful chant of the muezzin resembles a raucous summons to prayer rather than an invitation, and can be so deafening that it drowns the sound-tracks of outdoor cinemas, and can even break windows. The idea of the amplifiers is to give the muezzin a greater coverage of his flock. Some unbelievers claim that lazy muezzins record their cry on tape, and that the early-morning call, 'Prayer is better than sleep', is switched on from bed. These tales are indignantly denied by the Faithful.

A remarkable sight in a Muslim country is that of simple people saying their prayers in public, something one seldom if ever sees in Europe. A gardener in a park, a worker on a jobsite, a peasant in a field, even a burocrat in his office, at the hour of prayer, will start performing the ritual prostrations Islam prescribes.* His prayer may last fifteen minutes or so. He kneels and presses his forehead to the ground, then stands with his head bowed in a reverent posture, kneels again, or sits for minutes on end apparently rapt in contemplation of the Ineffable. He is quite unembarrassed. These public prayers by simple people make one feel that Islam, whatever its merits or defects, permits a directness of relationship with the Almighty equal if not superior to that achieved by any other religion.

Impressive too is the annual observance of the Ramazan fast, one of the five duties which make a Muslim a Muslim. Between dawn and dusk, for thirty days, not only must nothing be eaten or drunk, but nothing material must pass the lips or enter the body. The good Muslim may not smoke a cigarette, enjoy a pinch of snuff, take medicine, or even, according to some extremists, receive an injection.** If he swallows a fly, it is a grave sin; though if he does

---

* Muslims may worship on any piece of ground, provided it is clean.

** There is a controversy about this. Some hold that intravenous injections break the Fast, but intramuscular ones do not.

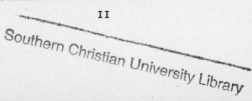

so inadvertently, it is no doubt venial. The keeping of the Fast is a meritorious act of abstinence which can be a severe physical strain, especially if (since Ramazan is a moveable month) it falls in summer.

The fast begins at dawn, and at dusk, when it ends, good Muslims can make up for their hours of strenuous abnegation, if they feel like it, by having a good blow-out. Some cynics irreverently maintain that the Faithful put on weight in Ramazan.

Ramazan in Turkey ends with a festival called the Sugar Bayram, a most agreeable occasion, rather like our Christmas, when the children dress up, presents are given, and vast quantities of sweets are consumed. Everybody feels very pleased with themselves after the long fast, people make visits and are kind to one another, and there is a general atmosphere of peace and goodwill. Two months later comes the Kurban, or Sacrificial, Bayram.

For those who are not used to it, this latter festival is a horror, because every family in the country which can afford it kills an animal, usually a sheep (the poorer families a goat). One sees the unfortunate creatures for weeks beforehand, being fattened up for the occasion. On the morning of the great festival, one can hardly find a piece of ground where knives are not flashing, blood flowing, and woolly limbs twitching in the death agony. This important but ghastly festival is based on the story of Abraham and Isaac. It is said that some 300,000 animals are sacrificed yearly in Turkey. It is not an occasion for children. In fact one wonders what the effect is on small children to be taught to associate their religion with so horrific a slaughter at so early an age.

There is a considerable difference between the Christian and Muslim attitudes to life and to other people. Muslims have a greater sense of the community, help each other more, and are more conscious of one another's needs. At the same time they give greater importance than we do to the observance of rituals and rules, and have a much stricter accountancy as to which acts are meritorious and which sinful. They seem on the whole to be more given to contemplation than we are.

This is perhaps linked to the famous fatalism which is so much associated with Islam. Muslims do not deny free will, but have deep in them the feeling that everything which happens in the Universe is predestined by God, down to the smallest detail, and that 'what is written is written'. The moment of death, for every man, is fore-ordained, and nothing can change it. The very word 'Islam' means 'submission' to the will of God. This attitude led orthodox Islam to reject such things as insurance: if people are killed in accidents, or property is burnt or destroyed, it is God's will. Insurance is an expression of mistrust in the Divine power.

It has often been said that fatalism has been responsible for keeping Islamic countries economically backward, because people who feel that everything is 'written' are less likely to struggle for material progress and will be resigned to their lot. There has been no movement in Islam similar to the Reformation in Europe, mainly because, while Luther could revolt against the Pope and remain a Christian, the only real authority in Islam is the Koran. One cannot revolt against the Koran and remain a Muslim.*

Muslims have an interesting relationship to the Koran, different to that of Christians to the Bible. They believe it descended from God and was dictated to the Prophet in Arabic, via the Archangel Gabriel. For Muslims the sight and sound of the Koran has a magic about it, rather than a precise sense. It can never be criticized or changed; it cannot be translated. One of the holiest acts for a Muslim is to become a *Hafiz*: that is to be able to repeat the whole Book by heart. Professor W. Cantwell Smith has suggested that the real Christian equivalent to the Koran is not the Bible but the person of Christ.

Carlyle described the Koran as 'a wearisome, confused jumble', which no European could be expected to read except out of a sense of duty, and so it seems to most non-Muslims who read it for the first time. But it is important to remember that the Koran is adored by Muslims not only for its content, but even more for its symbolism and for the sheer sensuous sound of the Arabic words, which have an incantatory, almost magical, effect. It is more like a majestic musical composition than a book. For Muslims it is as impossible to translate the Koran as it would be for us to translate Beethoven's fifth symphony.

There are many other contrasts between Islam and Christianity:

---

* The Sunni-Shia split in Islam was not a Reformation but resulted from a dispute about the succession to the Caliphate.

but the main practical difference is in their attitude to women. The Koran expressly sanctions not only polygamy but male superiority. Mahomet openly liked women, and had a great many wives, while limiting the Faithful to four; and the story told by Muslim apologists that he married only the ugly ones in order to be kind to them seems hardly to correspond to the truth. Certainly the personal example of Mahomet on this question was very different to that of Christ; but then Mahomet never claimed to be divine. In fact the obvious humanity of the Prophet makes him an unusually engaging figure.

A physical description of Mahomet by William Bolitho, in his book *Twelve against the Gods*, gives a vivid picture of the founder of Islam:

Though there was never any portrait of the Prophet, the minutest peculiarities of his appearance have been piously preserved by the Faithful. He was a small man, but he caught the eye. Usually he was taciturn, and more and more subject to fits of abstraction, when he heard or saw nothing. But he could be agreeable, rather boisterous, company. When he spoke, he turned his whole body and not only his head; when he laughed, which was not seldom, he opened his huge mouth, like a crocodile, so that his gums and all his teeth were visible, and his eyes disappeared. These were piercing but bloodshot; he used to paint his eyes with kohl and antimony to make them appear more lustrous. He dyed his beard, some say red, some yellow, and was fond of loudly-coloured linen clothes, though he abhorred silk, which 'was invented so that women could go naked in clothes'. He had a great shout; both his anger and his mirth were explosive. He had a curious gait, very important, as if he was descending a steep and invisible hill.

I have often tried to imagine the manner of the Prophet's walk, in accordance with this description, but have never quite succeeded in doing so.

Despite their differences Christianity and Islam have a good deal in common. Most authorities agree that in matters of doctrine, apart from the Trinity, much less separates them than one would suppose. The historic enmity between the religions came not so much from their origins or teaching as from exaggeration of differences by ferocious exegetists on both sides, from the Crusades and religious wars and reciprocal anathemas of the 'Infidel'. Some historians maintain that there is no fundamental antithesis between the doctrines, and that the eastern Christian sects, such as the Nestorians and Monophysites, which broke away early from the main body of Christendom, were as near to Islam as to their own church.

Christians, Muslims, and Jews, the 'People of the Book', as Mahomet called them, have scriptures, prophets, even doctrines, in common. All three are monotheistic faiths, and monotheism is an important bond. One can almost put a ring round the monotheistic religions, it has been suggested, to mark them off from the polytheistic and non-theistic religions of the further East – Hinduism, Buddhism, Taoism, Shinto, and so on – so that the monotheistic faiths would fall on the western side of Kipling's 'great divide', putting Christians, Muslims, and Jews together in the same camp.

How far such arguments are valid I do not know. Personally, having lived for some years in the Far East, as well as the Middle East, I found that the Far-Eastern religions were much stranger to me than Islam. I can pray in a mosque, whereas I would hesitate to do so in a Hindu or Buddhist temple, perhaps because in the mosque I feel I know who I am praying to, and for me the Muslim Allah is the same as the Christian God; whereas in an oriental pagoda I should have no very clear idea to whom, if anybody, I was praying. I suppose that is what being a monotheist means. For the moment I shall leave it at that. Let's get back to the Turks.

* * * * *

The Turks had an interesting religious history before they were converted to Islam about a thousand years ago. Before that they had lived for the most part somewhere north-west of China, and were for a long period in the orbit of the Chinese civilization. Most of the Turkish peoples at that time were Shamanists, that is worshippers of the sun, the 'sky-god', and other peculiar deities. Shamanistic practices have been preserved in Turkish customs and religious rites to this day. For example, in parts of Turkey peasants still beat drums and fire off guns during an eclipse of the sun – a relic of the Shamanistic belief that the sun-god had constantly to struggle against malign forces. The Turkish national flag, the star and crescent, is a Shamanistic symbol.

In about the ninth century A.D. most of the Turkish peoples living in central or eastern Asia begun to come under the influence of a number of competing world religions. These included Christianity, Buddhism, Taoism, Manichaeism, and Islam. One Turkish people, the Uigurs, established a brilliant civilization in the ninth century A.D., in which four different religions – Buddhism, Christianity, Manichaeism, and Shamanism – were all practised side by side. Quite a few Turks, in that early period, were converted to Christianity. It is amusing to speculate what might have happened if all the Turks had become Christians. Presumably history would have been very different, and the Turks, along with the Hungarians, Finns, and Bulgars, would have long ago been part of Europe.

Not much research has yet been done, so far as I know, to discover traces of the Chinese civilization among the Turks. Yet it is reasonable to suppose that, as they lived in the Chinese sphere of influence for thousands of years before their conversion to Islam, there must be a large residue of that civilization in the Turkish culture. Some authorities have solemnly asserted that the early use of the handkerchief among the Turks was a relic of Chinese influence, since apparently handkerchiefs were unknown in Europe before the fifteenth century. The Karagöz shadow-plays, a most popular feature of the life of the common people of Turkey until quite recently, are known to have originated in the Far East – either India or China. Chinese designs have been detected in Turkish carpets. The Turkish thinker Ziya Gökalp, who lived at the beginning of this century, maintained that traces of Taoism are to be found in Turkish folk-poetry and in the practices of the Turcoman nomads who roam much of Anatolia to this day. If so, it seems a fascinating field for research.

At one point, it appears, the Turks were very nearly converted to Buddhism. There is a record in early Chinese sources of an occasion when the Emperor of China offered to build a Buddhist temple for the Turks, but the Turkish Khan of the day refused the offer after being advised that Buddhism, being a passive religion, might adversely affect the warlike qualities of the Turks. For anybody who knows the Turks today, it is rather difficult to imagine them as Buddhists.

In the end, however, the vast majority of the Turkish peoples of central Asia adopted Islam, partly, it seems, because this energetic religion better suited their martial nature. Despite this, the Turks have never been very orthodox Muslims, and there are many things in the Turkish culture today which are pre-Islamic, non-Islamic, or downright anti-Islamic. I shall say more about this later. Turkish Islam has always been full of heterodox practices which are looked at askance by the pundits of el-Azhar.* Some go so far as to suggest that the Turks picked the wrong religion, and that Islam, or at least orthodox Islam, was not really suited to them at all.

* * * * *

Turkey has had nearly two hundred years of gradual 'westernization', but the greatest westernizer, as I have mentioned, was Mustafa Kemal Ataturk, who lived about forty years ago. Ataturk's aim, and that of the men around him, was to make the Turks part of the western civilization and part of Europe. He sensed well enough, however, that the main barrier between Turkey and Europe was religion. Whatever scholars might write, it was plain that most people regarded Europe as roughly co-terminous with Christendom, or what had been Christendom in the past. The world of Islam was a non-western and non-European world.

Thus, in attempting to 'Europeanize' Turkey, most of Ataturk's extraordinary changes of the 1920's and 30's were concerned, directly or indirectly, with the religion. He went a long way towards separating Turkey from Islam and the Islamic background. He abolished the Muslim Caliphate. He did away with religious education in the schools. He closed down the Dervish orders which had been such a feature of Turkish life in Ottoman times. He prohibited the fez and replaced it by the European hat. This was a symbolic blow at Islam, because the brimless fez made it possible for the Muslim to press his forehead to the ground in ritual prostrations, whereas the hat was abominated as the headgear of the 'Infidel'.

But he went much further than this. He swept away the Arabic

---

* The University in Cairo which is the fount of Islamic orthodoxy.

alphabet, in which the Turks had written their language for a thousand years, and replaced it by the Latin alphabet of Europe. Now the Arabic script, to an extent which it is difficult for us to imagine, is deeply linked with the religion. Not only is it the script of the Koran, but of all the holy literature, and of the calligraphy which adorns the mosques and monuments of Islam. Being in itself beautiful, the script plays an important role, because of the strict Muslim taboo on painting and sculpture. Much love of beauty was expressed in the calligraphy which is such a feature of Islamic art.

In most Muslim countries Arabic texts scribbled on pieces of paper have the power of magical charms, and are used to cast or exorcise spells; whereas for pious Muslims the very sight and shape of the Latin alphabet smells of the Infidel. It is interesting to speculate how far this pious revulsion from the Latin letters has prolonged illiteracy in Turkey, which, forty years after the reform of the script, seems more widespread than it should be.*

To complete the break with Islam Ataturk strongly encouraged painting and sculpture, both forbidden by the religion as a form of idolatry. He also started to erase from Turkish the vast number of Arabic and Persian words which had inundated the language, replacing them by Turkish words taken from Turkey's pre-Islamic past. This reform has altered the language to such an extraordinary degree that Turkish today is more different to that of 1920 than modern English to that of Chaucer – a process of six hundred years crammed into forty.

In fact in the last fifty years the language has so changed that people today cannot understand the early speeches of Ataturk, the originator of the reform, and one sees the strange phenomenon of Turkish writers 'translating' their own books from the old Turkish into the new. There are even Turkish-Turkish dictionaries.

The change of script, together with the purification of the language, has had the effect of detaching the under-forty generation of Turks almost completely from the Islamic cultural background, while opening up (at least scriptwise) the whole of the literature of the West. As far as westernization is concerned, the change of the script is one of the most important things of all. Travellers arriving

* About 60%.

in Turkey from Persia or the Arab countries, and seeing the Latin letters, tend to say to themselves: 'This is Europe!'

One might think this was enough for one man to do in a brief fifteen years of rule, but Ataturk went further. Even he, though a complete autocrat, could not convert the whole Turkish people to Christianity; but he did the next best thing. He abolished the Koranic law, and replaced it by codes of law taken from western Europe. A few changes were made in these western codes to adapt them to the rather different character of the Turkish people, but broadly speaking they were adopted as they stood – lock, stock, and barrel.

This was an astonishing thing to do in a Muslim country, because the most sacred part of Islam is the law. It is more important than theology or doctrine, and is really the essence of the religion. To abrogate the Koranic law (the *Sheriat*, as it is called in Turkey), and to substitute for it codes of law taken from infidel Europe, was for devout Muslims an unthinkable affront. No other Muslim country has abolished the Koranic law, though some of the more progressive ones have modified or modernized it to suit present-day conditions.

Finally Ataturk erased from the Turkish constitution all reference to Islam, and made Turkey into a 'secular' state. There has been some argument as to the exact meaning of this word 'secular'; we shall discuss this later. But its meaning in the Turkish context was clear: it meant 'non-religious', consequently, in this case, 'non-Islamic'. Turkey, by becoming a secular republic, withdrew officially from the world of Islam.

But the Turks themselves are still as Muslim as ever, if not more so, that today there is a curious distinction between Turkey as a state, and the Turks as a people. The Turks are Muslims, but Turkey is no longer an Islamic state. Here again, what Ataturk did was unique. No other Muslim country has 'gone secular' in the way Turkey did. Orthodox Muslims regard the secularization of Turkey as an apostasy from Islam, and Ataturk as a heretic.

It would be interesting to know, in parenthesis, how far the fact that Turkey is no longer part of Islam has sunk into the consciousness of the western world. Perhaps Turkish membership of NATO and the Council of Europe, changing the Turks from old enemies into new friends, has made us forget the religious differences of the past. In Cyprus, how many people saw the struggle between Turks and Greeks as one between Muslims and Christians?

I had an interesting talk not long ago with a well-known Turkish diplomat, in which he mentioned that when he recently told a London press conference that he was a Muslim, his statement was received with surprise, almost disbelief. Perhaps those present did not expect so sophisticated a man to have any religion at all; but it may also have meant that they no longer expected a Turk to be a Muslim. Many modern Turkish intellectuals, the products of forty years of Kemalist secularism, are more or less atheists, at least in outward appearances. Between them and Europeans there is no visible barrier of religion. In this sense Turkey has come nearer to Europe than ever before.

3 ✳ Kemalism and Reaction

ONE of the finest works of modern architecture is the mausoleum in Ankara which houses the tomb of Ataturk. It is built of yellow limestone in the form of a colonnaded temple, and stands on a low hill in the centre of the city. It is vast and austerely simple. By day its walls glisten in the Anatolian sunlight, while after dark, skilfully illuminated from within, the tomb glows through the night like the soul of modern Turkey. For the Kemalists this mausoleum is a kind of secular Mecca. Adjoining the tomb is an immense courtyard, usually silent but for the tramp of sentries or the bark of an occasional command.

Nobody who has attended a formal ceremony in that colossal arena can fail to be impressed. The most extraordinary example I remember was the massive rally of army officers which filled it to overflowing a few days after the military revolution of May 1960. This was something far more than a mere ceremonial occasion: it was a concourse of votaries to a shrine. The words written that day in the book of honour by General Gursel, the revolutionary leader; 'Great Father, approve us, and permit us to follow in your footsteps', had both the tone and phraseology of a prayer. The words express something of the unique relationship between the Turks and the dead Ataturk.

All nations have their great men: but I doubt whether anything quite resembles the cult of Ataturk in modern Turkey. He is the 'Eternal Leader'. Written references to him use the Turkish equivalent of He with a capital H, as though he were divine. Turkish schoolchildren are taught to offer their lives for his, to leap into the tomb themselves so that he may rise again. On the anniversaries of his death, at five minutes past nine on November 10th 1938, all traffic stops and a two-minute silence is observed. Newspapers appear in black-fringed mourning editions, and a torrent of articles record every aspect of the Great Man's life, many of them reading like paeans of praise to the Deity.

It is a strictly monotheistic cult. Ataturk, like Allah, is One, and none can be associated with Him. ('The One Man' is the title of the best biography of him in Turkish, almost as if no other had lived.) Today, thirty-four years after his death, worshippers still speak with bated breath of his steel-blue eyes, his piercing glance, his savage energy, and his iron resolve. He was indeed a very extraordinary man. His disciples, disgusted with the course of events since his death, seem to be waiting for a second coming.

Mustafa Kemal* was the timely giant who stepped into the anarchic flux at the end of the first world war and literally changed the fate of Turkey. He turned military defeat into victory, restoring to his demoralized and dismembered country its independence and pride. Basically he was a successful general, and everything he did later became possible because he had the army solidly behind him. He sprang to fame during the Gallipoli campaign, where he, more than any other single man on the Turkish side, prevented the capture of Constantinople by the Allies. It was at Gallipoli that he gave that tremendous command to his men: 'I do not order you to attack: I order you to die!' – no more extraordinary in being given than in being obeyed.

The great moment in Kemal's life came in May 1919. Greece, backed by Britain, had invaded Anatolia. This led to one of the most critical struggles of modern history. The Greeks fought to recapture the Anatolian provinces of the Byzantine empire, the Turks to hold what for eight hundred years had been Turkish soil. Kemal defeated the Greeks at the battle of the Sakarya in August, 1921 (said to be the longest pitched battle in history), then drove them savagely and irreversibly into the Aegean sea. Admittedly the Greek generals were not much good (one of them suffered from the illusion that his legs were made of glass, so that he was unable to walk) and they were up against military genius. Having won the war of Turkish independence, Kemal achieved absolute power in his country, and later, in a few brief years, carried through the astounding series of westernizing changes we have recounted in the previous chapter.

* Throughout this book I have referred to the founder of modern Turkey sometimes as Ataturk, sometimes as Mustafa Kemal, sometimes simply as Kemal, as the context seemed to demand. The important thing to realize is that all three are the same person.

~~Ataturk was an attractive dictator~~, as dictators go. He was a pleasing contrast to his contemporaries, the manic Hitler, the vainglorious Mussolini, the crafty, ruthless Stalin. He was more civilized, more human. He killed far less people. He had a sense of humour, he liked women, he drank (though he was never drunk on the job). He could carouse all night with cronies, yet be at his desk by eight. His physical resistance was amazing. But he died of cirrhosis of the liver at the age of fifty-seven. His early death was a tragedy for Turkey.

Other points distinguish Ataturk from less agreeable autocrats. He made no attempt to conquer territory or invade other peoples' countries. Having established the limits of the new Turkey, which included Constantinople and the Straits, he was content to leave it at that. In this respect he was a formidable realist. His foreign policy slogan, hardly fashionable in the 30's, was: 'Peace at home, peace in the world'.

Ataturk expressed ~~two fundamental needs of the Turks~~, at the point they had reached in their story: the need for national ~~independence~~, and the need for ~~civilization~~. The first of these involved a struggle against the West: Ataturk is still regarded in Asia as the first of the great Asian liberators who revolted against the domination of Europe. Of the two aims, this was the more banal. But the distinguishing hallmark of the Turkish revolution was the ~~drive of the Turks to acquire civilization~~. This was ~~'Kemalism'. It was the inner conviction that the secular civilization of the West was higher than the religous civilization of Islam.~~ The word 'civilization' rings through Ataturk's innumerable speeches like a bell tolling in a high wind:

> We shall follow the road to civilization and get there. Those who halt on the road . . . will be drowned by the roaring flood of civilization.
>
> Civilization is so strong a fire that he who ignores it is burnt and destroyed.
>
> We shall be civilized, and be proud of it.
>
> We must prove that we are capable of becoming active members of the society of civilized peoples.
>
> We shall live as a progressive, civilized nation. We shall be part of civilization.

Our great struggle is to lift ourselves to the level of the most civilized and prosperous nations.

Ataturk described the fez, the headgear which he abolished, as 'a badge of ignorance, indifference, backwardness, and hostility to civilization and progress' – a phrase which incidentally was hardly relished by the Arabs, who wore the fez, and still do so.

This obsessive emphasis on civilization distinguishes the Turkish revolution from other revolutions. The aim was not to overthrow an *ancien régime* or colonial rule, not even primarily to raise the standard of living of the people; the aim was to 'civilize' the Turks, and by doing so to change their image. The Turks were associated with barbarism and war: they should from now on be associated with civilization and peace. The Turks had many enemies in the world. Ataturk said in a speech in 1921:

History is based less on intelligence, logic and judgement, than on sentiment. It is a radical error to suppose that what we are doing now [i.e. defeating the Greeks] can wipe out the animosity our enemies have had for us for centuries. It is not by military victories that we shall do this, but only by attaining to everything which modern knowledge and civilization demand, and by actually reaching the cultural level realized by all civilized peoples.

The civilization in question was that of the West: this was Kemalism.

Kemalism in Turkey is a quasi-religion, with its true believers, its crypto-sceptics, its horde of lip-servers, and its secret enemies. The cult of Ataturk is official and universal; but it would be idle to pretend that it is sincere. The true Kemalists are the army officers and the intellectual élite; a potent combination – but they have against them the tremendous power of reactionary Islam. As for the popular view of Ataturk, it is really a mixed one: the people see him as part-saviour, part-monster. Turks of all classes venerate the leader who squelched the Greeks and drove them into the sea; but most fail to understand the man who passionately admired a civilization anathematized for centuries as the enemy of Islam. The Kemalist myth that every Turk loves Ataturk is like the Christian myth that every church-goer loves God.

24

I had an interesting example of this when I first arrived in
Turkey. I had asked a taxi-driver in Ankara to drive me to the
tomb of Ataturk, but in doing so I made a linguistic error. Instead
of the Turkish word normally employed for a secular tomb, I
used one which means the shrine of a Muslim saint. The use of this
latter word caused a violent explosion from the driver, the gist of
which was that Ataturk was the enemy of Islam. He had made a
fine job of the Greeks, but then had ruined the country by importing the degenerate western culture. He had harmed Turkey's
traditions and corrupted her morals. He was the 'Infidel'. Through
a *lapsus linguae*, I had had an interesting revelation. I soon found
that my taxi-driver was no exception.

Kemalism is not a precise doctrine. In Turkey today parties and
politicians of every shade and colour shelter under its broad
umbrella. Conservatives and revolutionaries, communists and
fascists, socialists and capitalists, liberals and radicals, even people
opposed – root and branch – to the whole concept of Kemalism –
all march under Ataturk's banner. They are enabled to do this
partly because of the extreme vagueness of doctrine. The so-called
'six principles' of Kemalism are Republicanism, Nationalism,
Etatism, Secularism, Populism, and Reformism. These principles
are inscribed in the political programme of the Republican Peoples'
party – the party founded by Ataturk himself in 1923 – and are
always known in Turkey as the 'Six Arrows'.

Except for Republicanism, all these six principles are sufficiently
ambiguous to be adopted by all parties. Etatism has been defined
as anything from state socialism to state capitalism, Secularism as
anything from mere 'freedom of conscience' to the fiercest atheism.
Nationalism is a principle subscribed to by all Turkish parties,
indeed by every individual Turk. Reformism could be claimed
equally by the extreme left or the extreme right. Populism is a
peculiar Turkish concept, hardly razor-sharp in precision, the
meaning of which we shall learn later. Thus, while it is universally
accepted in Turkey that the 'Six Arrows' are of the utmost
importance, there is no agreement whatever about the ideological
direction, if any, in which they are pointing.

*   *   *   *   *

In fact the key principle of the Turkish revolution was *secularism*, and one cannot understand modern Turkey unless one knows what this word meant. In the Christian West secularism merely means a separation between the spheres of authority of Church and State; but it was something far more drastic in a Muslim country, because in Islam religion and state are fused. The Koranic Law permeates every aspect of men's lives. No other Muslim country has 'gone secular' in the way Turkey did, and when Turkey did so it came as a profound shock to the rest of the Muslim world.

Kemalist secularism has been compared to Marxist atheism, but it did not go quite so far as this. It did not try to suppress religion altogether. Its real aim was to release the Turkish people from the grip of fanatical men of religion, the so-called 'hodjas', into whose power the Turks had fallen, due largely to the fact that the ordinary Turk had no knowledge of the Arabic language.

There is no ordained priesthood in Islam, but in Turkey something very similar to a priesthood had grown up – an especially conservative and bigoted one – which could always keep the simple Turk in terror by quoting Koranic texts, and whose religious practices were mixed with magical and barbaric rites. Ataturk was convinced that the Turks were basically a reasonable and not a fanatical people, and could be civilized if they were released from the clutches of 'doctors of religion'. He hoped to do this by striking at the source of the hodjas' power – their knowledge of Arabic.

Ataturk described as 'the greatest act of the revolution' his attempt to get a first-class literary translation of the Koran in Turkish. He wanted the Turk to read the scriptures in his own language. He changed the call to prayer from the traditional Arabic into Turkish, and wanted to go further and have the services in the mosque in Turkish too. But he ran into such terrific opposition in the orthodox Muslim world that in the end, except for the call to prayer, he abandoned these projects.

He invited one of the leading poets of the day, Mehmet Akif, to translate the Koran into a beautiful simple Turkish that every Turk could understand. But the poet, under the influence of the fanatical opposition to Ataturk, persistently shirked the task. This was a tragedy, as he would have been an ideal man for the job. There have been various unofficial translations of the Koran in Turkish, but none approaching the beauty of the Arabic original.

There was another interesting and more far-reaching idea behind Turkish secularism. The Turks had come to Islam, only about a thousand years ago, from other religions such as Shamanism, Manichaeism, even Christianity, and as Muslims they had never been very orthodox. This implied that, as a people, they were capable of moving on to other religions, and were not, as it were, forever committed to Islam, at least not orthodox Islam. Ataturk said boldly that the Turks, throughout their history, had 'respected all beliefs', not merely Islam, adding that the religion of the Turks was 'neither this nor that particular religion'.

Professor Niyazi Berkes, in his book *The Development of Secularism in Turkey*, describes the Turks as 'perhaps the only people to have multifarious experiences with all the great religions of the world', and claims that the Turks 'had passed successively through Shamanism, Buddhism, Judaism, Christianity, Manichaeism, and Islam', carrying traces of all these religions alive in their national culture.

This idea has been quietly forgotten under the influence of the Islamic revival in Turkey since Ataturk's death. Even Ataturk, in the last years of his life, gave up the struggle in face of massive opposition. But he never ceased to believe that the ordinary Turk was tolerant and progressive, if only the hodjas and fanatics would allow him to be so. The idea of secularism was not to abolish religion, but to allow the reasonable, humanizing element in Islam to operate on the Turks. For the Kemalists, secularism is the most important of all principles, indeed the key to civilization itself.

* * * * *

The other idea behind secularism was to end the conflicts between the various religious sects and Dervish orders, so that the Turks could be welded into a single homogeneous nation. The numerous Dervish orders in Ottoman Turkey – the Bektashi, Mevlevi, Rufai, Nakshbendi, Kadiri, etc. – each with its peculiar rituals and forms of worship – had arisen because the Turks, as we have seen, were not orthodox Muslims. Turks have a mystical, romantic side to their nature which made orthodox Islam – the five prayers in the mosque, prostrations and repetition of formulae – seem rather stuffy and dull. Their nature craved for something more exciting, colourful, and aesthetically pleasing.

Many of these famous Dervish orders – the *Tarikat*, as they were called – used music and dancing in their religious rites, both of which were frowned on by orthodoxy. The Mevlevi believed that by spinning round and round continuously in the same direction with arms outstretched, to the music of pipes and drums, their 'adepts' could achieve a mystical union with God. This is the dance of the Whirling Dervishes, a beautiful and extraordinary spectacle. The Bektashi, for their part, had enormous popularity and prestige because of their connection with the Janissaries, and were celebrated for their sceptical and irreverent attitude to religion. There were *Tekkes*, or Dervish convents, all over Turkey under the empire, where the common people really enjoyed their religion. They went to the mosque out of duty, but to the *Tekke* for inspiration.

Ataturk simply abolished these Dervish orders on grounds that they were nests of fanaticism and a source of disunity for the nation he was trying to create. But the abolition of the *Tekkes* was a tremendous blow to the common people, and one which they have never quite got over. There is not the slightest doubt that the banned Dervish orders continue in secret today in many parts of Turkey. From time to time people are arrested on the curious charge of 'being caught in the act of performing a religious rite'. One of the most intriguing mysteries of present-day Turkey is the extent to which these secret activities of the Dervish orders continue.

Very important also for the understanding of Turkey is the large unorthodox sect of the Alevi, which probably numbers some six to eight million (out of a population of thirty-five million), and whose members live mainly in the east and south-east of Anatolia. Most Turks are Sunni Muslims, but the Alevi are linked to the Shi'i of Persia, the other great branch into which Islam split soon after its foundation. The Alevi are not really pure Muslims, but syncretist: their religion is a mixture of Islam, Shamanism, and Christian cults taken over from peoples who inhabited Anatolia in the past. They are connected with the Bektashi, who in turn had a link with the Janissaries, and the Janissaries, as we know, were recruited from Christian children in the Balkans.

The Alevi live in their own villages and seldom intermarry with the Sunni. Tension between the two religious groups is one of the important social realities in present-day Turkey. According to the

~~Sunni the Alevi are heretics, who drink wine, do not go to the mosque, commit incest and other nameless sins, and (horror of horrors!) even believe in the Trini~~ty. They are said to indulge in mass sexual orgies in large halls where the lights are put out. But in my experiences the Alevi are usually enlightened, tolerant, and liberal people. As a minority, they are discriminated against in various ways by the Sunni majority. Secularism was supposed to end all this discrimination between the sects. For this reason most Alevi are keen supporters of Ataturk. Some are said to believe that Ataturk was a Mahdi, or religious leader.

* * * * *

Kemalism was a strong force in Turkey in the 1920's and 30's, deployed with all the concentrated power of single-party rule against a reluctant people. The advent of the democratic regime in 1945 inevitably weakened that force. Pressure from above was relaxed, that from below increased. It is difficult, perhaps impossible, to combine democracy with a revolution. Revolution usually means rule by a minority, a self-styled élite, whereas democracy, by definition, is majority-rule. There is only one way in which the two things can be reconciled: if the majority itself supports the aims of the revolution. This was not the case in Turkey.

Most Turks disapproved, misunderstood, or opposed Kemalism, which they saw primarily as an assault on Islam. When democracy came in 1945, there was a popular reversion to the religion and its traditions. Instead of the leaders leading the people, the people were now leading the leaders, and, so it seemed to the Kemalists, leading them backwards. This popular movement is known in Turkey as the 'Reaction'.

The Kemalists hate the Reaction like a mongoose hates a snake. They also fear it. They fear the deep, well-authenticated power of fanatical Islam. Their fear is kept alive by a number of terrifying events from the past: the so-called '31st March incident' in 1909, when troops of the Turkish army mutinied against the Young Turk revolutionaries, and nearly staged a successful counter-revolution; or the Sheikh Said rebellion in south-east Turkey in 1925, which was partly an expression of Kurdish nationalism, and also had social causes, but was mainly a religious revolt against the secular policies of the Kemalist state.

The most gruesome of these reactionary outbreaks was in 1930 in the town of Menemen, in western Turkey. Some Muslim fanatics killed a young army officer in a peculiarly horrible way: they held him down on the ground and slowly sawed his head off with a rusty saw, chanting 'Allah is great' the while. Having severed his head from his body, they scooped up the blood in their hands and drank it, while a number of townsfolk stood round and applauded. The victim of this ghastly deed, whose name was Mustafa Kubilay, is revered today as one of the chief martyrs of Kemalism.

There have been other fanatical outbreaks in the last forty years, though nothing quite of this blood-curdling order. Despite the explosion of extreme leftism in the last few years, it is still the religious Reaction which is the terror of the Kemalists. They see it as a dark sinister force dragging Turkey back out of Europe into Asia, threatening to undo everything Kemalism stood for.

In a situation like this, small things become intensely symbolic. Any political act which seems a concession to the Reaction, is abominated by the revolutionary élite. A good example is what happened over the call to prayer. Traditionally, in all Muslim countries, the call is chanted from the minaret in Arabic. Ataturk changed it into Turkish. It was one of his most unpopular reforms. The Democrat party, which came to power in 1950, changed the call back into Arabic. This was popular with the electorate, but raised immediate doubts about the new party's attachment to the secular reforms. Many Kemalists turned against the party from this moment.

The Democrat party was not a counter-revolutionary party, but was gradually led astray by the almost irresistible temptation to exploit the power of popular Islam for its own political advantage. It was just too easy. To promise to build a mosque in a village, to evoke the name of Allah in a political speech, to give money to help Turkish pilgrims to go to Mecca, even to make a timely genuflection – all these things were worth thousands of votes at election time. This the Democrat party did in the 1950's, and its successor, the Justice party, is doing today.

Highly symbolic of the Reaction, in the eyes of the Kemalists, is the black headscarf worn by women, known as the *Charshaf*. This is not the same as the veil; one hardly any longer sees the veil itself in Turkey. But women in backward parts of the country use the black headscarf to cover their faces, almost as if it were a veil. The habit is most often seen in the provincial towns of Anatolia, rather than among the peasantry. The towns in Turkey are, on the whole, more reactionary than the villages. For the Kemalists, the black headscarf is a concrete symbol of the Reaction, and any increase in its use is morbidly noted.

Another significant item is male headgear. Ataturk banned the fez and brought in the hat. The fez, as we have seen, was convenient for the observance of Islam, because it had no brim, whereas the hat did. It is interesting to see the compromise, perhaps unconscious, by which this strange problem has been resolved. Extremely few Turks today wear brimmed hats. The bulk of the people, and the entire peasantry, wear cloth caps of an identical pattern. These, having brims only in front, can be reversed during prayer, enabling the forehead to meet the ground. In this way the Turk can render unto Ataturk that which is Ataturk's, and unto Allah that which is Allah's.

One thing which most alarms the Kemalists is the revival and expansion of religious education. It was completely stopped by Ataturk in the schools, with the idea that all Turks should henceforth have one single uniform secular education. This reform was the coping-stone of the secular regime. Before the time of Ataturk there were religious colleges and secular colleges, producing two opposed streams of westernized and non-westernized Turks. The idea of unifying education was to eradicate this duality, and create a single stream of secular westernized youth.

Since 1949 all forms of religious education have crept back under popular demand, and are enormously expanding. In primary schools religion is once again virtually a compulsory subject. Tiny children all over Turkey are memorizing the words of the Koran, with no idea of what they mean, and often at the expense of any kind of secular education. The Kemalist objection to the Koran classes is that it puts the children from the earliest age in the grip of fanatical or bigoted hodjas, whose level of education is abysmally low.

The imam schools, in the eyes of the Kemalists, are even more dangerous. The idea of these was to replace the ignorant type of old imam by 'enlightened men of religion'. The programme of the schools, though it makes a gesture to western science and languages, is concentrated mainly on Islam and the Islamic culture. The result is that a constant stream of young theological students is pouring out of these colleges, and out of the revived institutes of divinity, in such a way as to make a nonsense of the principle of unified education. Far from being secular and western, these theological graduates are almost bound, by their training as professional men of religion, to be fundamentally opposed to the Kemalist aim of making Turkey part of Europe.

This is the basic struggle. Many Turks see the issue as a straight fight between the West and Islam, Kemalism and Reaction, Europe and Asia. They note with horror the ever-increasing number of Turkish pilgrims who go yearly to Mecca, the expanding circle of people who keep the Ramazan fast, the vast number of new mosques which have been built in Turkey in recent years (said to be more than in all the Arab countries put together), and wonder angrily what has become of Ataturk's 'secular state'.

Many identify Islam with backwardness and the East, the two things modern Turks are trying to get away from. This makes them indulge in bitter exaggeration. 'Every minaret is a tombstone under which a Turkish village lies buried', said a prominent Kemalist recently. Another, with a bizarre flight of fancy, suggested that Turkey's best hope was to convert all mosques into factories, all minarets into factory chimneys.

The extreme leftists, being Marxists, see the picture with different eyes. For them the West-versus-Islam issue is superficial, a red herring, and the real drama is the class struggle. The guns trained by the Kemalists on bigots, sheikhs, hodjas, and religious fanatics are trained by the Marxists on 'middlemen, usurers, compradors, imperialists, and conservative forces'. For them the issue is not cultural, but social, revolution.

4 ❋ The 1960 Coup

THE MAIN EVENT in Turkey's recent past is the army coup of May 27th 1960. To understand Turkey, it is important to know what the causes of this event were, what actually happened, and what the consequences of the army's seizure of power have been.

The course of events was an unusual one. Two rival factions quickly appeared in the National Unity Committee, (NUC), the group of thirty-eight officers which seized power. One, headed by General Gursel, nominal leader of the revolution, favoured an early return to democracy; a smaller group, of which the most prominent figure was a certain Colonel Turkesh, was for prolonging military rule to carry out 'radical reforms'. Many observers, with the Egyptian parallel in mind, assumed that elderly Gursel would prove the Turkish Neguib, Turkesh the Turkish Nasser. In fact the opposite happened. In November 1960, in a 'second coup' as dramatic as the first, the radical group (known as the 'Fourteen') was ousted and sent into exile.

The remainder of the N.U.C. promised to hold free elections and transfer power to an elected parliament. It kept this promise. After seventeen months of military rule, during which the Turkish seats at the Council of Europe remained discreetly empty, the Committee returned power to a new parliament. Gursel became head of state, but the other military leaders melted modestly into semi-oblivion as life-members of the Senate. Not Jacobins but Girondins, not Bolsheviks but Mensheviks, came out on top in this strange Turkish 'revolution'.

The Turks have the remarkable faculty, at critical moments, of doing something absolutely unexpected. There are at least three examples of it in the present century. In 1919, after Turkey had been officially defeated, the Turks fought back and turned defeat into victory. In 1945, President Inönü changed a dictatorship 'overnight' into a democracy. In 1961, the soldiers who had seized power the year before restored a full parliamentary regime. In

33

each case what was confidently predicted on all sides was the contrary of what happened. Quite a good rule-of-thumb for Turkey-watchers is to think out, in any given situation, what the most likely course of action is, and then to expect the opposite. It is not infallible, but it often turns out right.

Another point about the 1960 coup is the remarkable strain of characteristic Turkish legalism which runs through it. The soldiers, as almost their first act after seizing power, turned to university professors to justify the coup on grounds of *democratic principle*. The professors obligingly did so, not because they were afraid of the army, but because they were even more in favour of the coup than the army itself. This led to the extraordinary fiction that the National Unity Committee was the 'legitimate successor' of the abolished parliament, and inherited its sovereign powers. The coup was presented, in the most impressive professorial language, as merely an episode in democratic politics.

The same scrupulous attention to legal nicety was shown in the trials of the deposed leaders. These were held, not under special revolutionary law, but under the penal code. It is true that Article 146 of the code prescribed the death penalty for 'violation of the constitution', and under this vague clause it was easy to sentence any of the former leaders to death. Three men were in fact executed – a serious blot on the 'bloodless revolution'. Yet the Turks, to do them justice, strove hard to preserve the appearance of democratic procedures. There was a baffling casuistry about the trials, to which I shall return later. Meanwhile I must briefly discuss the causes of the coup.

*   *   *   *   *

The story of Adnan Menderes, the Turkish Prime Minister brought to power in the 1950 election, is an unusual one. He was born in 1899, son of a family of landowners in western Turkey. In 1930, at the age of thirty-one, he entered politics, and became a member of parliament. For fifteen years he was virtually unknown. In 1945, when single-party rule was ended, he joined the new Democrat party, and leapt immediately to the fore. When he became Prime Minister in 1950, astonishingly enough, it was the first office he had ever held in the state. He ruled Turkey for ten years amid ever-increasing controversy and uproar, was then overthrown by the army, tried, and hanged. After his death, he became a legend and a mystique among the common people of Turkey, many of whom still regard him, quite wrongly, as the source of everything good that was ever done in their country.

Menderes was a man of great energy, exuberance, eloquence, and genuine goodwill, to which was added something of the spoilt charm of a son of the upper class. He sincerely believed he had a mission to develop Turkey. He embarked simultaneously on a vast number of projects: factories, roads, ports, oil refineries, hydroelectric schemes, irrigation, grain storage plants, and the complete re-planning of cities. But his enthusiasm was not matched by a knowledge of finance. He committed almost every mistake known to the science of economics. Soon, despite a huge influx of American aid, there were unbalanced budgets, falling exports, massive inflation, and enormous foreign debts. When criticism swelled, he repressed it by illiberal acts. He tried to suborn the judiciary and muzzle the press. He imprisoned journalists.

In particular, he did two fatal things: he antagonized the army and exploited the religious reaction. The officers were anyway chafing under civilian rule. Under Menderes, a new class, that of business and commerce, rose to power and prestige. There were capitalistic developments all over Turkey. Great fortunes were made. Menderes announced the curious ideal of 'a millionaire in every district'. But as the capitalists and merchants came up, the soldiers and bureaucrats went down. Many officers were hard hit by the inflation. Some, almost ruined, retired from the forces. Nothing was done, as was done by a later Prime Minister, Demirel, for the welfare of the army. The salary of a Turkish general was hardly more than that of a resident American sergeant. All this made the soldiers angry and out of joint. As far back as 1954, it was later revealed, cells in the forces began plotting the government's downfall.

The key issue was religion. This above all was the red rag to the army bull. Menderes, by restoring the Arabic call to prayer, expanding religious education, making political use of fanatical Muslim sects, and in other ways encouraging the dreaded Reaction, ultimately reaped the whirlwind. He alienated all the Kemalist forces – army, intellectuals, writers, youth – who in the last resort were the strongest. Above all, as leader of the Opposition, was the formidable person of Ismet Inönü ('Ismet Pasha'), Ataturk's lieutenant, and focus for all the forces of the Republic which regarded it their sacred trust to maintain intact the secular ideals of the revolution.

But with the masses Menderes was immensely popular. In their eyes he was the first 'man of the people' to become Prime Minister of Turkey. He had the gifts of the demagogue: charm, eloquence, an easy manner, and not too much scruple about how to please the voters. He descended to their level. Inönü, though a brilliant intellect, had never been good with the masses. They saw him as a general – olympian, unbending, and remote. Menderes was genuinely loved. Above all, in the eyes of the populace, he was a 'good Muslim'. Indeed, he was a man favoured by Allah.

There was a strange event in 1959, when I was in Turkey. During one of the Cyprus crises, Menderes flew to London at the head of a Turkish delegation. His plane, landing in fog at Gatwick, crashed in flames with the loss of fourteen lives. Menderes himself had a remarkable escape from death. On his return to Turkey there were scenes of extraordinary enthusiasm. I myself was at Ankara station when his train pulled in. The platform was lined on both sides with hundreds of sacrificial animals, which were slaughtered in a ghastly carnage as the train stopped. Amid the dying groans of innumerable expiring beasts, Menderes stepped from his carriage. More creatures – sheep, oxen, even camels – were sacrificed in the streets as the Prime Minister's cortège drove by. Blood ran in torrents down the main boulevard, lapping the tyres of the smart limousines. The Prime Minister had been preserved from death by divine intervention.

The last months before the coup was a massive confrontation between the two main parties, seemingly without issue. The whole country was divided into hostile camps. Villages were rent between the rival factions. There were Democrat coffee-houses and Republican coffee-houses, Democrat grocers and Republican grocers, Democrat and Republican mosques. Such a situation can easily arise in countries where two big parties confront each other. A degree of sophistication in democratic practice is needed to make the regime work. This was not yet available in Turkey. It was said later that there was nothing wrong with Turkish democracy, except that the Turks took it too seriously.

In the final weeks the Democrat leaders behaved with extraordinary imprudence. It was obvious from March onwards that the army, or a large part of it, favoured the opposition, in particular the venerable person of Inönü. It was equally obvious that if unrest and disorder started and continued, the army, the only possible arbiter, might intervene. But Bayar and Menderes refused to believe, up to the very last minute, that the army could strike. There seems no question, in retrospect, that they could have saved themselves by holding elections (which they might well have won), or even by the resignation of Menderes. Menderes, it is said, was personally inclined to resign; but hesitated from day to day, and from hour to hour, until finally he was lost.

One officer who took part in the revolution has since said that if the government had resigned and called elections at any time up to the eve of the coup, the coup would not have happened. It was a matter of days, almost of hours. If only Menderes could have made that fateful decision to resign. But he did not, perhaps could not. He was hampered by a proud, hypersensitive, and at the same time vacillating, character. How bitterly he must have regretted this later. And what a warning to the irresolute! That little indecision cost the whole difference between the normal respect due to a retired (if controversial) Prime Minister – and a rope round his neck.

Celal* Bayar, the President, was a different type. He was a man of great obstinacy, durability, and courage. He refused to resign when the officers, after the coup, suggested that by doing so he could save his life. He never admitted the legitimacy of the coup. He is said to maintain to this day that he is legally President. At the age of seventy-seven he sat like a lion through the eleven-months trial. Like Charles I he rejected the right of the court to judge him. As I had to report on the trial, I often saw this indomitable old man at close quarters. In the end his courage was rewarded. He was sentenced to death by the court, but the Committee changed the sentence to life imprisonment. He was reprieved from the edge of the gallows.

One of the facts which aggravated the confrontation of the 1950's was the personal antipathy between Bayar and Inönü, which dated back to the time of Ataturk. The fires of conflict were stoked, as it

* Pronounced 'DJELAL'.

37

were, from the top. There was never any real hope of a meeting of leaders and a reconciliation. The clash of these two remarkable old men, both today nearing ninety, has been one of the determining factors of Turkish politics in the last twenty-five years. Their spectacular reconciliation, in May 1969, though an impressive event, came ten years too late.

Among unanswered questions in Turkey is whether there was collusion, before the coup, between the army and the Republican Peoples' party, of which Ismet Pasha was chairman. Inönü, at a crowded press conference immediately after the military takeover, emphatically denied that he had been in any way privy to the plot. His party has always strenuously rejected such suggestions, which were widely believed by supporters of Menderes, and have been repeated recently, in a newspaper interview, by Bayar himself. There is no conclusive evidence either way, though it is known that in December 1957 a number of revolutionary officers had approached Inönü and invited him to collaborate with them in action against the Menderes government. Inönü very properly had refused.

Circumstantial evidence, for what it is worth, tells rather against the Peoples' party. The party had been out of office for ten years. It had lost three general elections running, and, due to a peculiarity of Turkish politics which I shall explain later, seemed unlikely to win one for many years to come, if ever. Ismet was getting old. As a former general, and Ataturk's right-hand man, he was popular with the army, though not, as it turned out, with all the officers who made the coup.

Bayar's personal convictions on this point are expressed in an amusing story, no doubt apocryphal, which did the rounds after the coup. Bayar and Menderes, under heavy guard, were sitting together in an armoured bus which was to take them to prison. It was their first meeting since their fall from power. Menderes, deeply demoralized and in fear for his life, was bemoaning his fate: 'It's Kismet', he kept repeating. 'Kismet! Kismet!'* 'Don't you believe it', snorted old Bayar, 'it's not Kismet, it's Ismet!'

Ismet Inönü, having been in Turkish politics for sixty odd years, and knowing every move in the game, is one of those men whose every act is ascribed by his enemies to Macchiavellian motives. It

* Kismet = fate.

is said of him that 'forty foxes go round in his head, and the muzzle of one fox never touches the tail of the next'. This is a picturesque Turkish way of saying that Ismet is a very crafty old man. He is certainly a very experienced old man. He has enormous power and influence in Turkish politics, and one of the biggest of all questions is what will happen in Turkey when Ismet goes.

* * * * *

No official account has been published about the secret planning of the coup, but there have been a number of unofficial versions. The best of these is *The Inside Story of the Revolution*, written by two Turkish journalists* in 1965. It is hardly likely that this account is the whole truth; some of it is probably what the chief actors in the drama would like people to think was what happened. This does not mean that a lot of it is not true so far as it goes.

According to the *Inside Story* there were rumblings in the army from the moment of the 1950 elections, when a group of young officers wanted to intervene and restore Inönü to power, but were discouraged from doing so by a senior general. From 1954 dated the first revolutionary cells in the armed forces. At first they were isolated, unaware of each other's existence, but by 1956 a number of secret committees, having contacted one another by chance, united to form what later became the main revolutionary nucleus.

It is fascinating, in the graphic pages of the *Inside Story*, to study the anatomy of a military coup: the secret meetings, the passwords, the hairs-breadth escapes when the expanding plot was on the brink of exposure. Interesting too is the gradual ripening of the political situation, which alone enabled the coup to be successful. If the political and economic situation inside Turkey had not deteriorated to the extent it did by May 1960, it is doubtful whether the coup could have succeeded. Another essential factor was the need for a senior general as leader. In so vast an army as the Turkish, with 30,000 active officers, a coup by colonels or majors stands very little chance. In the planning of the 1960 coup one of the chief preoccupations of the conspirators was to find a leader. They found one; but the risks they took in doing so were considerable.

Incredible though it seems, an offer to lead the coup was made

* Abdi Ipekçi and Omer Sami Coşar of the Istanbul newspaper *Milliyet*.

by a member of the secret revolutionary committee, Lt.-Col. Faruk Guventurk, to the Minister of Defence in person. Guventurk, according to his own account, proposed the leadership in the Minister's office in Ankara. The scene is straight out of Dumas. Having broached the subject, the colonel drew his revolver, laid it on the Minister's desk, and remarked: 'Sir, my revolver and I are at your service'. Why the Minister did not have him arrested is not recorded. Instead, he is said to have replied meekly: 'I am only a simple lawyer, not the sort of man to lead a revolution. I cannot get mixed up in something like this'. Other offers were made to various generals, including General Cevdet Sunay, the present Head of State, but they all declined, on one ground or another. Finally an approach was made to General Cemal Gursel, C-in-C Land Forces, the most senior active officer below the level of the chiefs of staff.

The approach to Gursel, who ultimately headed the coup and later became head of state, was made by one of the plotters, Major Sadi Koçaş,* in a motor-car during a military exercise, under the very noses of two American officers who happened to be in the same vehicle. In order to find out whether the Americans knew Turkish or not, Koçaş turned sharply to them and asked in Turkish 'What is the time?'. He banked on anybody who knew the language being unable to refrain from looking instinctively at his watch. The trick worked. The Americans stared blankly back. One of them said 'Excuse me?'. Koçaş then turned to General Gursel and got down to business. Very circumspectly, in the days that followed, he began to unfold the situation in the country leading up to the offer to head the coup. It took him about a week to get to the point. When finally he did so, Gursel immediately accepted.

The last weeks before the coup were touch-and-go for the plotters. On May 3rd 1960 a bombshell exploded among them when General Gursel was suddenly retired by the government without warning. There was a frantic search for a new leader. The man chosen this time was Major-General Cemal Madanoglu, chief of logistics at HQ Land Forces. Though two grades lower than Gursel, he ranked as a 'Pasha', and was considered senior enough for the job. Madanoglu accepted the assignment. Then the Commandant of the Ankara War School, Brigadier Sitki Ulay, and the

* Pronounced 'KOCHASH'.

Photo: *Ara Güler*

Istanbul street merchant

Making bulgur in south-eastern Anatolia

Commander of the Guard at the President's palace, Colonel Osman Köksal, were co-opted.

One of the most curious relationships in the final weeks was that between President Bayar and the Commander of the Presidential Guard, Colonel Köksal. Köksal was a key man in the plot, whose job was to ensure the surrender of the President, if possible without bloodshed. About twelve days before the coup the colonel had an extremely narrow squeak. An anonymous informer wrote to Bayar saying that the Commander of the Presidential Guard was implicated in a plot against the regime. Bayar immediately summoned Köksal and said: 'Colonel, I hear rumours that members of the Presidential Guard have been got at by the People's party. What have you got to say about that?' Köksal replied that he had no information to confirm such rumours, adding coolly: 'Sir, some people even say that I am plotting against you. The idea is to get me transferred, so that the People's party can put their own man in my place'.

Astonishingly enough, this reply seems to have satisfied Bayar, who made no further enquiries. Yet it is hardly conceivable that the President had no suspicions. Inspecting the Guard one morning Bayar said to the soldiers: 'If there is an attack on the Palace, will you defend me?' The men replied in chorus: 'Sir, if the colonel orders it, we shall do so'. Bayar can hardly have liked this reply, but he took no action.

The actual coup was executed with great brilliance early in the morning of May 27th, with the loss of only one life. Zero hour had to be delayed by twenty-four hours at the last minute because of two unexpected hitches. The first of these was the sudden departure of Menderes to western Turkey and the need to make special arrangements for his capture. Secondly, the infantry units in the Ankara area, which had been given the job of taking over most of the city, refused at the last minute to act without instructions from a four-star general. The retirement of Gursel had deprived the revolutionaries of their only full general, and no such order could be given. It was therefore decided to move the infantry units out of Ankara, and cadets of the Ankara War School were used instead to take over many parts of the capital.

It is not clear with what purpose Menderes set forth on that last journey to western Turkey. It was said later that he had had

41

some vague idea of rousing the peasantry. There were rumours that large stocks of arms had been distributed to the Anatolian villages, and to the inhabitants of the shantytowns on the fringes of the big cities. This was used later to argue that the fallen government had brought Turkey to the verge of civil war. Yet it is difficult to imagine Menderes and Bayar leading a peasant rabble against the Army.

Menderes's car was picked up by a spotter plane and he was finally captured at the west Anatolian city of Kutahya. He made a last desperate attempt to telephone to the governors of the eight provinces of western Turkey which had always been his political stronghold; but the line was dead. Menderes gave up the struggle. With an ashen face, he leaned back in his chair, awaiting capture. Shortly afterwards the officers arrived to take him. The time was 8 a.m. The coup had achieved complete control of Turkey in a few hours.

5 ✳ *Trials and Aftermath*

THE TRIAL of the deposed leaders was held on the small barren island of Yassiada (the 'flat island'), twelve miles by sea from Istanbul, and was a great human and dramatic spectacle, as all such trials must be. I covered much of it as a foreign correspondent.

The trial had a bad press in the outside world. It was assumed by most people that it was a tedious comedy, the result of which was a foregone conclusion. It was said then, and has been said since, that summary execution of the deposed leaders would have been better than death sentences pronounced sixteen months later. This might seem a cleaner job to outsiders, but how many of the accused themselves would have preferred this solution? Most of them, eleven years later, have not only regained their freedom, but have had all civil and political rights restored to them.

In staging the trial, the Turks were caught between the contradictory motives of democracy and revolution. There were two ways, if one wanted to be objective, of looking at the matter. The trial was certainly more unfair than a normal democratic trial; but it was fairer than a normal revolutionary trial. People looking at the trial in the light of the British principle that a man is innocent till he is proved guilty, saw it simply as a revolutionary tribunal rigged up as a penal court. Others, who argued that a trial held immediately after a military coup could not, by the nature of things, be indistinguishable from the proceedings of the Old Bailey, felt that the procedure adopted had the effect of moderating the course of justice. If one remembers that at the time of the trial many bloodthirsty people were demanding up to fifty executions, there is perhaps something to be said for this viewpoint.

There were two unusual features about the trial. The first was that, not just a few leaders, but the entire parliamentary majority of the ruling Democrat party, nearly five hundred men and women, was put in the dock. This was perhaps logical. In the days when monarchs were absolute, one could arraign the monarch. But

43

in a regime where a parliamentary majority is absolute, one must logically arraign that majority. The result at Yassiada was that the prisoners in the dock often outnumbered the spectators.

The second unusual feature has already been mentioned. The trial was held, not under revolutionary law, but the normal penal code. Article 146 of the code, as we have seen, prescribed the death penalty for 'violation of the Constitution'.* That was fortunate for the revolutionaries, because it meant they could send any of the accused they could convict of this exceedingly vague offence, quite democratically as it were, to the gallows. This enabled the prosecutor at the trial to demand 107 death sentences. Of these 15 were passed. There were 3 executions.**

The revolutionary aspects of the trial were obvious enough. The court was packed with soldiers. The judges lived, together with the prosecutors, behind a barbed-wire entanglement in obviously close contact with the leaders of the military regime. Defence counsel, though there were many of them, and though they often spoke. eloquently and at length on the main issues, were clearly handicapped and cowed. Yet, given the facts of power, and seeing that the opposition to the coup of a large section of the population made a counter-revolutionary movement a possibility which had to be taken into account, it is difficult to see how things could have been much otherwise. These were political facts, not legal procedures.

The weakness of the trial, it seems to me, was that an offence under Article 146, which alone could lead to death sentences, was hardly susceptible of proof in a court of law. Whether there had been a violation of the constitution was a question of Byzantine subtlety, still discussed to this day, and dependent on the testimony of 'experts' of whom none could be impartial. Listening in court, it seemed grotesque that men's lives should depend on such refinements.

My own view is that the Menderes government, by exploiting the Islamic reaction, may well have infringed the spirit, if not the letter, of Ataturk's constitution. But few today doubt that the executions, because of their effect both on internal politics and

---

* The death penalty for this offence was not in the Italian Zanardelli code, on which the Turkish penal code is based, but was added in the time of Ataturk.

** Adnan Menderes, Prime Minister; Fatin Zorlu, Foreign Minister; Hasan Polatkan, Finance Minister.

outside opinion, were a serious error. Furthermore, the fact that Bayar and the other Democrats were all released from prison only four years later, and have since got all their former civic rights back, makes the three hangings seem more than ever a gross injustice – an act, not of reason, but emotion.

* * * * *

I shall not go into the details of the long proceedings, but only mention one or two scenes which have remained fixed in my memory. One is the opening day. The sight of Bayar, Menderes, and the others being brought into court still stays with me as one of the most extraordinary I remember. The last time we had seen these men had been at some official function in Ankara, surrounded by acolytes and toadies, wearing that sated look of those long in power, with yes-men leaping to satisfy their idlest wish, condescending to speak to a few favoured guests. Suddenly they were simply prisoners, facing judgement, possibly death. One had an intense, almost physical, sensation of what a violent change of power is, of the fragility and mutability of human affairs, so well expressed in the words of Lear:

'Who loses and who wins; who's in, who's out'.

One thing was certain: these men were out; others, for the time being, were in.

The trial opened with a case which was little better than a farce. Bayar was accused of selling a greyhound given him by the King of Afghanistan, for a sum of £800, to the Ankara zoo. The charge was misuse of public money, in that Bayar had forced the zoo to purchase the animal out of state funds. The purpose of the 'dog-case', as it came to be known, was probably to discredit Bayar, not only because of the money involved, but because dogs are not very popular animals in Turkey, as opposed to cats, which were loved by the Prophet Mahomet (the Prophet is said to have once cut off a part of the cloak he was wearing rather than disturb a cat which was sleeping on it). In fact the 'dog-case' merely had the effect of making the start of the trial ridiculous in the eyes of the world.

Beginning with this farce, the drama gradually deepened as the trial went on. There were nineteen different cases, carefully graded in intensity and importance, culminating in those carrying the death penalty. The atmosphere now became increasingly heavy and oppressive. A strange relationship grew up between Menderes, the principal accused, and the presiding judge, Salim Bashol, a majestic figure in robes of scarlet and gold. Menderes, in the later stages, as the strain told on him, grew pale and thin, and at times his voice hardly rose above a whisper. He still kept something of the eloquence which had made him, in his day, one of the best speakers in Turkey, but his spirit appeared broken, and at times he seemed to be pleading with Bashol for his life. He heaped elaborate courtesies and oriental titles on the judge, addressing him even as 'Your Majesty'. It was like some terrible comedy. But nothing could save Menderes, and probably he knew it.

What was very striking at the end of the trial was the impassivity of all the accused, especially when the death sentences were passed. None of those condemned showed any trace of emotion. One incident remains vividly in my mind. Zorlu, the deposed Foreign Minister, was one of the fifteen sentenced to death. A friend in the row behind had escaped with a lighter penalty than had been expected. Having heard his own death sentence, Zorlu turned coolly round to congratulate his friend in the row behind. Coming at such a moment, it was an extremely impressive gesture. Zorlu was at all times very brave.

Menderes was not in court on the final day. He was said to have attempted suicide by an overdose of sleeping-pills, and was too ill to be present. His execution had to be delayed. Zorlu and Polatkan were hanged early next day, and gruesome photographs of their sheeted corpses swinging from the tripod gallows were published in the morning papers. Zorlu, by all accounts, died very bravely. He is said to have joked with the hangman up to the very last minute, and to have kicked the chair away from under him with his own feet, always a mark of courage at Turkish hangings. He wrote a moving last letter to his family, which was later published, beginning with the words: 'I am now about to mount to the presence of God . . .'. He was offered, and received, the last ritual ablution of the Muslim faith. He was fifty-one.

As for the unfortunate Polatkan, the confirmation of his death sentence must have come as a fearful shock, where so many more notorious figures had been reprieved. Indeed it is difficult to understand on what grounds he was singled out. He left a pathetic two-line note: 'My wife and family must be told that I am innocent; my mother and brothers also'.

The fate of Menderes was more macabre. As he was ill, a panel of doctors was detailed to attend him. Bulletins on his state of health were issued every few hours. Official photographs appeared, showing him putting his tongue out, having his chest tapped, or his pulse-rate measured. He recovered quickly. Soon he was pronounced healthy enough to be hanged, and this was accomplished. Very little is known about the details of the execution, except that a great storm was raging, highly unusual at this season in the Marmara. This has of course been added to the Menderes legend. It is said that the unseasonable storm blew for the passing of Menderes.

The 36-hour delay which separated the hanging of Zorlu and Polatkan from that of Menderes is perfectly explicable by the alleged suicide attempt of the former Prime Minister. Some have suggested, however, that there was another reason. Menderes was the only member of the fallen regime whose popularity in the country was such that his execution might have caused widespread disorders. It has been claimed that the 'suicide attempt' was stage-managed to enable the military leaders to test the reaction to Menderes's death sentence, while striking terror with the sensational photographs of Zorlu and Polatkan swinging in their nooses.

During the period of the executions, extreme precautions were taken throughout Turkey. But, so far as is known, nobody made the faintest protest against the hanging of Menderes, one of the most popular prime ministers Turkey ever had. I find this one of the most astonishing non-events of Turkish history. Admittedly the army was in power, and there was little anybody could safely do. But one would have thought that somebody, somewhere, in a population of thirty million, would have lifted a finger or raised a shout. The Turkish people sustained the blow in a massive silence, perhaps swearing in their hearts revenge. Thus it was that Turkey's renewed democracy was founded on a blood-feud.

The result has been that the 'Menderes mystique' is an important fact of Turkish politics. Much of the population refuses to believe that Menderes is really dead. He is said to ride nightly on a white horse from the prison-island to the mosque of Eyub in

Istanbul. The Justice party, which today rules Turkey, has adroitly cashed in on this mystical belief. By adopting as its symbol a white horse, it has said to the population, in so many words: 'We are the party of Menderes the martyr'. The population has responded, in election after election, by voting large majorities to the Justice party. How long will this strange motive continue to determine Turkish elections?

Ultimate responsibility for the executions lay with the National Unity Committee, which under the provisional constitution had to confirm the death sentences. The voting in the Committee was thirteen to nine. Many interventions had been made, both inside and outside Turkey, to try to prevent the hangings. The Queen, among foreign heads of state, appealed for clemency. She and the Duke of Edinburgh stopped for an hour at Ankara airport on their way to London from Teheran, and spoke to General Gursel.

Inönü, in particular, wrote an impressive letter to Gursel, arguing that in civilized countries people were no longer executed for political offences. It was said later that a majority of the Committee might well have commuted all the death sentences, had not irresistible pressure been brought to bear on the Committee, on that dramatic night of 15th September 1961, by revolutionary elements in the armed forces. Finally, as a result of negotiations, a grisly bargain was struck at three.

The fact is that by September 1961 the Committee was no longer master of Turkey. Power had passed months earlier into the hands of a body of officers behind the scenes popularly known as the 'real junta'. These officers, the romantic element in the forces, wanted blood, and they got it. They forced the Committee into unwise action. One of the leaders of the 'real junta' was a certain Colonel Talat Aydemir. It is perhaps poetic justice that Aydemir himself, three years later, was to end his life on the scaffold.

* * * * *

The story after this, put briefly, was one of the rapid return to democracy, and the maintenance of the regime, not without difficulty, against all revolutionary pressures. The 'Fourteen', the radical group in the NUC, had been expelled nearly a year before. But in 1962 and 1963 two military revolts had to be beaten off.

This was possible because the democratic impulse in the army overcame the revolutionary. Many officers had a genuine distaste for such adventures. 'Turkey is not Syria', 'Turkey is not Patagonia', are phrases often heard there.

The two revolts, in February 1962 and May 1963 had one peculiar feature in common: both were led by the same man, Colonel Talat Aydemir. Such a thing must be rare. Most people who make putsches against established governments don't get a second chance. After the 1962 putsch (the closer shave of the two), the Inönü government agreed to pardon Aydemir and sixty-nine other officers, who were merely retired from the forces. This explains how Aydemir lived to strike again.

Aydemir was a strange man. After the failure of the first revolt he went about saying openly that he was going to make a second. He gave interviews to the foreign press, and issued lists of persons who were to be ministers in his government. I spoke to him twice during this period. One might have thought he was unbalanced, but he did not seem so. He was calm and rational – idealistic in his way. He denied that he would instal a military dictatorship, or even that he would take power himself. His line was that pure Westminster democracy was the wrong regime for Turkey. As practised, it was corrupt, and got nothing done.

Aydemir was a Circassian. Circassians are famous for their unruly temperament, but noted more for their courage than their brains. There were also psychological reasons behind his repeated attempts to bring off a successful coup. Aydemir had been leader, back in 1956, of the first secret committee in the forces which ultimately made the 1960 revolution. But in 1960 he had been in Korea, and the coup was made without him. He bitterly resented this. He had a strong personal urge to stage a coup of his own.

But he made gross blunders. Neither of the two insurrections was properly prepared, especially the second. In neither was the political situation in the country ripe for such an event. Secondly, there was no high-ranking officer to head the coup. Aydemir wanted to do everything himself. Thirdly, he made no serious attempt to co-opt the airforce, which turned against him, with decisive effect, on both occasions.

Aydemir made the fatal error, on the night of the 1963 attempt, of declaring over the radio that he personally had taken over the country. It is conceivable that if he had not done this he might have succeeded. But a number of senior officers who were sitting on the fence on that dramatic night, some of whom were certainly sympathetic to the general aim of a military seizure of power, backed out when they heard the name of Aydemir. This was not because he was personally unpopular, but because he was of too junior a rank. In fact at this time he was even retired. The generals had had enough of being ordered about by colonels and majors during the period of the NUC.

One incident on this violent night should be mentioned, because it is one of the most extraordinary single-handed exploits on record. Lieutenant-colonel Ali Elverdi, an active officer, was sitting quietly at home in Ankara, when he heard Aydemir's first radio announcement that he had taken control of the country. Elverdi leapt to his feet, dressed, rushed out in his Jeep, met Aydemir's tanks in the street, forced the tank-crews at pistol-point to give him the password, and then, armed with the password, drove through three insurgent barricades to the radio building. He entered the building unopposed, climbed two flights of stairs, and arrived at the studio where a rebel officer was actually in process of reading Aydemir's revolutionary declaration. Threatening the officer with his revolver, Colonel Elverdi pushed him out of the studio, seized the microphone, and made his own announcement saying that the revolution had been check-mated.

At this moment some rebel officers broke into the studio and captured Elverdi, but not before the latter, with truly amazing presence of mind, had telephoned to the transmitting station at Etimesgut, twenty miles from Ankara, telling it to cut the wires connecting the station with studios in the city. This was done. The revolutionaries were unable to continue their broadcasts. The units waiting outside the capital, some of which might have joined Aydemir if they had thought he was winning, were led to suppose that the putsch had failed.

Colonel Elverdi was taken to a studio where he was told to stand face to the wall, with his arms above his head. He expected immediate execution. But by some miracle he got away with it. Aydemir, who arrived at that moment, for some reason (perhaps because he already saw failure staring him in the face), spared

Elverdi's life. Aydemir admitted at his trial that the failure of the putsch had been mainly due to Elverdi's singlehanded action. Colonel Elverdi later received the highest Turkish award for bravery and resolution.

The second Aydemir putsch was more serious than the first, because it involved bloodshed. Two officers and six other ranks were killed. This time Aydemir and his followers were jailed and tried. The secret military trial lasted three months. Aydemir and his second-in-command, Major Fethi Gurcan,* a cavalry officer, were sentenced to death. But the sentences were only carried out after prolonged delay. Clearly the rebels had enough adherents in the armed forces to make their execution a delicate matter.

Both Aydemir and Gurcan, in their defence at the trial, claimed that the type of democracy introduced by Inönü was unsuited to Turkey, and had caused the country to deviate from the spirit and principles of the Kemalist reforms. Both spoke with eloquence and idealism in their own defence, especially Major Gurcan, who was younger than Aydemir. Both claimed, in particular, that the main effect of democracy had been to divide the country into bitterly hostile camps, thereby destroying the national unity which was the precondition of social and economic progress.

Gurcan's last words are moving, and reveal something of the minds and feelings of Turkish officers in their country:

> It is my belief that Ataturk is not a mere symbol whose vitality and function are exhausted, who is hung on walls and talked about on holidays and anniversaries; nor is he merely a great man to be remembered with feelings of gratitude. He represents an ideal, a doctrine, a Weltanschauung, a developing system of government, which can and must be applied to our society. . . .
>
> In the face of death, and in the presence of God and justice, my conscience is as clear as that of a poet who takes up his pen to write in praise of Ataturk. I believe that our cause will live more strongly through having found men who are ready to die for it. And I say this: Ataturk is dead, but he has not ceased to exist. I shall now die, but Ataturk's ideals, through my death, will acquire yet higher value.

* Pronounced Gurjan.

With these fine words, Major Gurcan joins the select company of those who have died for their beliefs.

Aydemir's last words were more personal:

> There comes a time when a leader who believes in himself must show to those who come after how to die, so that his idea and ideal should not fade but should take stronger root . . . I have engaged since 1956 in the most perilous enterprises for the welfare of Turkey. . . . I braved all dangers, but I failed. . . .

These ideas are certainly still strong among the younger officers, but the fate of Colonel Aydemir and Major Gurcan had the effect, for some years, of cooling off ardent spirits. Since 1963, though there have been occasional rumblings, there have been no further putsches.

In March 1971, the army, by threatening direct intervention, ousted the Justice party government under Mr. Demirel and installed a national coalition under Professor Nihat Erim. There is martial law in several Turkish provinces, and Dr. Erim governed in collaboration with the army. Despite this, the forms of parliamentary government are preserved. Since then Dr. Erim himself has been put out of office.

6 ✳ *The Turkish Army*

THE ARMY is the strongest organized Kemalist force in Turkey, and, as it is a somewhat special army, something should be said about it. I shall not go over its conquering exploits from the past. We all know how it captured Constantinople, occupied large tracts of eastern Europe, and reached the gates of Vienna. We know about the famous corps of the Janissaries, recruited from Christian children in the Balkans, taken young by the Ottomans and turned into Muslims and Turks.

The Janissaries in the later years of the empire became an unruly force which made and unmade monarchs. When the Janissaries 'overturned their cauldrons' (the symbol of revolt), the Sultan trembled, for he knew who would be overturned next. Finally, in 1826, one particularly energetic Sultan, Mahmud II, challenged the Janissaries, and in a few sanguinary hours terminated their existence forever. All that is left today of this famous corps is the Janissaries' band, which is trotted out on festive occasions, with its peculiar march, two steps forward and one step back, performed to sinister music.

Turkish children are taught to feel pride in the glorious past of the army, whose exploits started long before the foundation of the Ottoman realm. The first regular army in Turkish history is said to have been organized by the East Hun empire in 200 BC: surprise attacks by the already famous Turkish cavalry kept the Chinese on the run. Incidentally it is interesting to note that Turkish military historians usually take it for granted that the hordes of Attila and Jenghis Khan were 'Turkish' armies. (The word 'horde' is derived from 'ordu', Turkish for army).

Turkish armies were linked from the earliest times with high moral and spiritual conduct. A military manual written nine hundred years ago in Kashgar tells us that a Turkish commander 'needs to be strong to stand against evil, and must have love and respect for good'. The four most important qualities of a general are listed as 'honesty, generosity, courage, and sound military

53

knowledge', in that order. With these traditions, it is hardly surprising that in Turkey today the army is regarded, by others and by itself, as a moral as well as a physical force.

Turkey's modern army is a conscript force, and an enormous one: 30,000 officers, and nearly half-a-million men under arms. It is the biggest army in NATO. This is a heavy burden for a backward country. But the army's prestige is such that few if any Turks advocate a reduction in size. It is possible that the army, which makes Turkey the most powerful country in the Middle East, to some extent assuages crypto-imperialist longings in a people which for so long governed so vast an empire.

In the last years of the empire, with bloody and exhausting wars on many fronts, military service was raised to twenty years. The Turkish soldier served in the forces and died in God-forsaken places like the Yemen. Even today, fifty years after the end of the empire, the Yemen is still a sad joke in Turkey, a subject for mournful poetry and songs, something which has forever entered the romantic Turkish soul.

In Turkey the army is more than a branch of the state, it is a part of life. It is a unifying, in a sense a civilizing, force. Every Turk, unless physically or mentally unfit, does military service. For most of them it is an important educative experience. The army takes peasants from remote villages, feeds them, clothes them, teaches them to read and write, instructs them in a trade, brings them to the cities. Most Turks seem to enjoy military service, and to profit by it.

I remember once giving a Turkish conscript a lift in my car, somewhere on a road near Istanbul. He was a peasant's son from the east. When I asked him what he felt about army life, he replied with great seriousness: 'It brings you in touch with three important things: discipline, humanity, and civilization'. A striking reply from a raw recruit! Still, the Turkish soldier has a hard life, and occasionally suffers rough treatment.

I once saw an extraordinary example of the latter in a military headquarters in Istanbul. I was waiting in the hall of the building, and some soldiers were loafing about nearby. I don't know what they had done wrong, but suddenly an officer rushed downstairs from the floor above, his face purple with rage, and laid about those men with appalling ferocity. He used his outstretched arm, with the fist clenched, as a sort of battering-ram, with which he struck the soldiers repeatedly on the sides of their heads. Any one of his blows would have killed me. But the soldiers remained absolutely impassive, like blocks of wood. When it was over they drifted sheepishly away, while the officer walked calmly upstairs again in high good humour.

Despite this, Turkish officers have a reputation for intelligence, enlightenment, and awareness of social problems. They also regard themselves as the natural élite of the nation, and as keepers of the social conscience. All reformist movements in modern Turkey came from the army: the Young Turk revolution of 1908, Ataturk's movement after 1919, the 1960 coup. The reason is that Turkish officers are not drawn, as in many other armies, from the upper class, but from much lower social backgrounds, including even the peasantry.* For this reason the army has almost always been a radical, rather than a conservative, a left-wing rather than right-wing, force. As it is the army which makes revolutions in Turkey, this is a fact of obvious importance.

I have often been struck by the dignity and moderation of Turkish officers. They are also remarkably articulate. I remember a curious conversation I once had with a group of officers in an army club in Ankara: a strangely dry and intellectual conversation, mainly about political theory and constitutional law. Such abstract questions as the separation of powers in democracies, the pros and cons of second chambers in parliamentary government, figured in the conversation. They were well informed about British history and politics. I left the meeting impressed.

There is a good deal of romantic radicalism among the officers. The members of the 1960 Committee, asked after the coup what literature had most influenced them in their youth, almost all replied that they had been inspired by a book called *The Country of the White Lilies*, by a Bulgarian called Grigori Petrof, which had been made compulsory reading by Ataturk in the 1920's. It is a romantic, idealistic account, vaguely leftist in tone, of reforms carried out in Finland in the nineteenth century under the aegis of the Finnish philosopher and writer, Johan Snellman. Several officers also expressed reverence for Nietzsche.

* Of the thirty-eight officers who seized power in 1960, only two came from a social background of any degree of prosperity.

The Turks

The Turkish army has played an important role in most stages of recent Turkish history. As I said, it was behind the various reform movements. The unchallenged position Ataturk achieved in Turkey was the direct result of his military victory over the Greeks. Though he, and Inönü after him, both resigned their commands and became civilian presidents, in top hat, white tie, and tails, they never ceased, in the eyes of both the people and the army itself, to be generals. Thus, though the democratic principle of the supremacy of the civil over the military power was theoretically established during the presidencies of Ataturk and Inönü, it was not fully established in fact. The people continued to imagine, rightly, that the army was in power.

What made the 1950 election such an extraordinary event in Turkish history was that the Democrat party, brought to power in that year after Inönü had started the multi-party system, was a genuinely civilian government, the members of which had no connection with the army. Bayar, the president, was a banker; Menderes, the Prime Minister, a farmer. It was partly this aspect of the matter which made the population regard the election as an occasion for rejoicing, and made Menderes such a popular figure. The traditional rule of army and bureaucracy had been broken.

It is important to understand the value attributed by the Turkish army to the democratic ideal. The army is strongly Kemalist: Kemalism equals westernization: westernization, in its political expression, means democracy. The army is thus impelled by a double, perhaps contradictory, motive. It is the watchdog of Kemalism; but it has a genuine passion for democracy. These two motives make it oscillate constantly between intervention and refraining from intervention.

The Menderes period (1950–1960) was the first in which the army was genuinely out of politics. During these ten years, though they were to end in disaster, the principle of the dominance of the civil over the military power was really applied. This of course did not please some officers, who were constantly itching to take over, or put Inönü (as an old general) back in power. Menderes and Bayar, of course, behaved in the unwisest possible fashion in their relations with the army, encouraging the religious reaction, neglecting the welfare of the officers, and ignoring all signs that a military intervention was imminent until the eve of the coup.

56

Milking sheep in Anatolia
Three peasants from Antalya

Photo: Ara Güler

Isak Pasha Sarayi, Dogubayazit

Demirel, Prime Minister from 1965 to 1971, with the fate of Menderes as a warning, has been a more astute performer. At his first political meeting, in 1965, having ended a speech amid the rapturous applause of his supporters, he was handed an anonymous note from the audience, which read: 'We hanged Menderes, and we shall hang you!' This gives something of the flavour of Turkish politics.

But Demirel, from the beginning, was much cleverer with the army than his predecessor, going out of his way to cultivate good relations with the generals, and spending lavish amounts of money for the welfare of the dangerous middle-and lower-rank officers – the ones who make revolutions. The officers had their salaries increased, and were provided with cheap lodgings, PX's, and many other facilities. But it was uncertain how long these tactics could last. One cannot buy off rebellious officers forever.

Though Menderes got the name of a dictator, through his foolish attempts to suborn the judiciary and muzzle the press, the Menderes period was, in a sense, more genuinely democratic than the present regime. As we have seen, the army was subordinated to the civil power. In the present system this is not so. There is a civilian government; but the body which really decides all important questions is a joint civilian-military body called the National Security Council. This meets once a month under the chairmanship of President Sunay, who was so recently Chief-of-Staff that he is universally regarded as a soldier (like Ataturk and Inönü). The other members are the Prime Minister, three members of the cabinet, the Chief-of-Staff, the commanders of the three services, and a number of other generals. It virtually amounts to joint civilian-military rule.

Since March 1971, the army has moved nearer the forefront of the political scene. But despite the system now in force – a sort of interlocking arrangement in which the government consults the generals on all important decisions – the generals seem against an open seizure of power. The last thing the Turks want is to be confused with the Arabs, or with banana republics where military coups follow one another with distressing frequency. The Turks are a people of altogether different calibre, who governed for six hundred years an empire as large as the Roman and much more durable than the British. For these reasons the army is restrained.

The Turks

The influence of Inönü, the champion of democracy, has weighed strongly with the senior ranks of the army. How much it counts with the middle and lower ranks is less sure. Many of the colonels and below are radicals of one kind or another, by all accounts mainly leftist, some perhaps doctrinaire socialists. That there are real communists among the officers, though not impossible, seems less likely.

The size of the officers' corps has an important bearing on the making of military coups in Turkey. It is difficult, if not impossible, for colonels to stage a successful coup against the tremendous upper crust of generals in the Turkish army. There are as many generals in Turkey as there are colonels in Egypt.

The two putsches by Colonel Aydemir failed partly because the colonel omitted to observe this rule. The generals were reluctant to envisage the prospect of being ordered about by a colonel. The first of the two putsches, in particular, was a close shave. But on the night when all hung in the balance the senior commanders turned against the audacious colonel, who ended up, not in the President's palace, but on the scaffold.

7 ❉ Democracy

THE QUESTION of the political regime is more important
in Turkey than in most other countries which have adopted
democracy because of the Turkish desire to be part of
Europe and the Western civilization. Western democracy is prized
in Turkey as an end in itself, as being the political expression of
the civilization Ataturk and his successors aimed at. In the minds
of idealistic Turks it is for this reason valued more highly than even
industrial progress or social reform.

Turkey is a member of the Council of Europe, and the statutes
of that body make a democratic regime a condition of membership.
That is why neither Spain nor Portugal are members, and why
Greece for the time being has been suspended. It is strange that
Turkey, so long the country *par excellence* of despotic rule, should
today be a democracy, while Greece, where political freedom was
more or less invented, is a military dictatorship.

Many people assume that Turkish democracy cannot possibly
last, because the Turks have no democratic tradition, and are
inured to authority and obedience. T. E. Lawrence, no lover of
the Turks, once said that if in a crowded Turkish railway station
one shouted 'Sit down' in a loud enough voice, everybody would
do so, without asking why. The historian H. A. L. Fisher dismissed the Turks (wrongly in my opinion) as 'a nation of private
soldiers'.

It should be put on record, however, that the struggle to achieve
democracy in Turkey is a long and extremely stubborn one, dating
back at least a hundred years to the time of the constitutional
reformer Midhat Pasha and other liberals. Turkish history during
the last century, from the point of view of the regime, has roughly
been the story of constitutional rule alternating with dictatorial
relapses. The brief democratic period ushered in by Midhat in
1876 was terminated two years later by Abdul Hamid II, who had
Midhat strangled in a dungeon in Arabia, then ruled despotically
for thirty years.

Abdul Hamid's regime got Turkey a bad name in the West. The Sultan's repression was pushed to absurd lengths. Newspapers were closed down for making a passing reference to the French revolution. The press was forbidden to mention that foreign monarchs had died. by assassination: the violent death of the Empress Elizabeth of Austria was ascribed to 'pneumonia', those of the King and Queen of Serbia to 'indigestion'. Even schoolbooks were affected. The chemical formula $AH=O$ was proscribed: it could be construed to mean 'Abdul Hamid equals nothing' – a clear case of *lése majesté*.

The Young Turk revolution of 1908 overthrew Abdul Hamid in the name of Freedom, but the Young Turks themselves quickly degenerated into an odious dictatorship. Next came Ataturk, whose regime was an interesting one of what might be called dictatorship with democratic features. In 1945 Inönü inaugurated a regime of multi-party democracy on the Western model, which, with a brief interval of military rule after 1960, has lasted to the present day.

The parliament building in Ankara is a very fine one. It is enormous, and said to be proof against earthquakes. Its vestibules are adorned with twenty-five varieties of Anatolian marble. The debating chamber, vast and beautiful, makes the House of Commons look puny. It is panelled in mahogany, and hung with sixteen massive chandeliers, said to represent the sixteen Turkish states which have existed since time began. The building, designed by the Austrian architect Holzmeister, took twenty-one years to construct, and was completed in 1960, oddly enough the very year in which an army coup abolished the parliamentary regime. But the sight of so stupendous a building standing empty may well have encouraged the soldiers to restore democracy more quickly than they might otherwise have done.

The adoption of democracy, and the struggle to maintain it in Turkey, is most closely associated with the name of Ismet Inönü, the 87-year-old statesman who was President of the Republic in 1945, and is today leader of the opposition. Inönü, single-handed, made the historic decision to change the monolithic regime of the People's party into a democratic system. The new opposition born in that event, the Democrat party, won the 1950 elections and ousted Inönü and his party from power. Inönü thus established democracy at the cost of his own downfall – a remarkable, if not unique, act.

The influence of Inönü was also the main factor which induced the army to restore democracy so quickly after 1960. Many people, especially in the last few years, have expressed doubts about whether Westminster democracy is suited to a country like Turkey, where much of the population is illiterate, and there is widespread ignorance. But Inönü has constantly expressed his personal conviction that it is the best regime for Turkey. Yet the struggle to establish the regime is a hard one, and five men, including a Prime Minister and a Foreign Minister, have so far been hanged in the process.

*   *   *   *   *

The course of Turkish democracy is an interesting one, and may even be instructive for students of political science. Despite great traumas and upheavals, the regime has stuck, and the experiment (for such it is) is still going on today. It needs faith. Those five corpses are a grim reminder of how difficult it is to transplant this particular form of political regime into what is nearly, though not quite, alien soil.

Ataturk, having defeated the Greeks (and indirectly the British), governed Turkey for fifteen years till his death in 1938. He imposed a series of spectacular reforms on a reluctant people. Despite this, Ataturk had a genuine passion for democracy. If he didn't practise it, he laid the basis for it. He enounced the principle, revolutionary in Turkey at that time, that 'sovereignty belongs to the people'. He abolished the Sultanate, the symbol of absolutism, and made parliament, at least in theory, supreme in the state.

Twice in his lifetime an opposition party existed. This is better than most dictators achieve. The first of these, the Progressive Republican party of 1924, was the more genuine of the two. It was formed in the days before Ataturk had established his absolute mastery over Turkey, and was composed mainly of prominent figures who had fought with him in the war of independence. This was a real political struggle, from which Ataturk emerged the victor. The Progressive party was found, mysteriously, to have connections with the great Kurdish rebellion in south-east Turkey.

61

Whether it really had such connections is uncertain. At all events Ataturk suppressed the party, and ruled unchallenged.

The second opposition, the Free Republican party of 1930, was more of a deliberate experiment in democracy. Ataturk invited one of his friends, Fethi Okyar, to form an opposition to the ruling People's party, which was headed by the Prime Minister Inönü. The People's party, after seven years of power during which Ataturk had carried out his sensational and unpopular reforms, was much criticized. Ataturk's intention, it seems, was partly to siphon off popular discontent: partly to pull the rug from under the feet of Inönü, with whom he was at loggerheads on questions of economic policy.

The result was nearly disaster. What Ataturk had not foreseen was the immediate success of the new party. People rushed to support it from all over Turkey, including many religious fanatics. A colossal new band-waggon was set rolling in an unpredictable direction. There were tumults and disorders. The ordinary Turk could not grasp that there could be a legal opposition to the established power. If there had been an election, the new party would probably have won it. It was soon clear that democracy was premature, and the party was dissolved after three months. The experiment was not tried again in Ataturk's lifetime.

The lesson of the Free party was that there was a fundamental popular opposition to the Kemalist reforms. This came in part, though not entirely, from the religious interest. It was also a massive popular protest against the military-bureaucratic class, represented by Ataturk and Inönü, which traditionally had governed Turkey. Ataturk was appalled by this outburst of opposition to his rule. He judged that if the Free party came to power, the whole secular edifice he had established by the reforms might be destroyed, and his work undone. It would amount to a legal counter-revolution.

Many people have questioned how it was that Inönü, only seven years after Ataturk's death, felt able to introduce democracy, when the great Kemal had failed. There have been various explanations of Inönü's motives in 1945. The allies had won the war. Democracy as a political system had defeated dictatorship (at least the Fascist variety of it). Turkey needed American aid. In 1945 Stalin was making territorial demands on eastern Turkey. Others say that Inönü, for internal reasons, deliberately courted political suicide.

But Inönü's own explanation is a different one. He has said on several occasions that he merely did what Ataturk himself had intended, and would have tried again if he had lived. Ataturk had always wanted Turkey to be a democracy. The reasons for introducing democracy, according to Inönü, were not political, but ideological. He was merely realizing an important, perhaps the most important, aim of the Kemalist revolution. The question is still debated: was Inönü right?

* * * * *

In my view there is a fundamental contradiction at the root of modern Turkey: I would call it the 'dual legitimacy' problem. What I mean is that there is a conflict as to what the basis of the state really is. According to Kemalism, it is the principles of Ataturk, above all secularism; but according to democracy, it is the will of the people. 'Sovereignty belongs to the people', said Ataturk. The people were represented by parliament, and in practice, by the majority in parliament. But what happens if this same majority, representing the people, acts against Kemalist principles? It means that one legitimacy conflicts directly with the other. If it has never been decided which of these two principles has priority, there is bound to be a series of crises, conflicts, and upheavals.

Essentially, it is the conflict between Democracy and Revolution. The reforms, by their nature, were the work of an élite. Whether the reforms were or were not a 'revolution' is a matter of dispute. Certainly they were not a social revolution. They have been described as a 'revolution from above', though it is uncertain whether such a phrase is not a contradiction in terms. A revolution is usually a movement which challenges the established order from below. However this may be, the modern Kemalists interpret Kemalism in terms of revolution. For them democracy, if it reflects the wishes of a conservative people, is merely a pretext for maintaining the status quo.

The 'dual legitimacy' problem means that since 1945 there is no consensus in Turkey as to what body in the state really represents the nation. Is it the intellectual élite (which includes the army)?

Or is it the majority in parliament? The House of Commons, in the well-known phrase, can do anything but 'change a man into a woman, or a woman into a man'. But the question of a 'dictatorship of the majority' is one which, so far as I know, has not been completely solved in political theory. What would happen in England if a parliamentary majority was bent, say, on restoring the personal power of the Monarch, thus acting against the Revolution Settlement? Would some other body in the state have the right, in the name of the people, to resist the majority of the ruling party?

This was the problem the Turks were up against after 1945, and which led ultimately to the 1960 coup. The Menderes period illustrated very clearly the double legitimacy problem. Bayar and Menderes stood for the supremacy of the popular will, which, roughly speaking, was against the reforms. Tempted by the ease with which they could win votes, they slid into exploiting religion. The army stood for the legitimacy of the Kemalist revolution. The army, as we have seen, was not impervious to democracy; quite the contrary. But it held that in the last resort, in a direct conflict between the revolution and the popular will, the revolution must come first.

Menderes and Bayar, theoretically speaking, were right: their parliamentary majority, in principle, could do no wrong. But justification by Locke and Montesquieu was of no help to them when it came to the showdown. Convinced of their democratic rectitude, they ignored obvious warnings about where their course was leading, and in the end found it useless to be theoretically right when confronted with the facts of power. Furthermore the army, by its own logic, was justified. The revolution had to be protected. It was one of those arguments which in the event is decided by the strongest:

Pale Ebenezer thought it wrong to fight
But Roaring Bill (who killed him) thought it right.

The only way in which the dual legitimacy problem could be overcome, so far as one can see, would be for a reformist majority to be elected by popular vote, but of this, at the moment, there seems no likelihood. The traditional reformist party, the People's party, is rejected by the electorate in one election after another, because, being staunchly secular, it is regarded by a majority of the people as the 'Godless' party. In fact the party has only once come to power since 1950, and that was on the wings of a *coup d'etat.*

Inönü, by an act which will always be judged astonishing, introduced a regime, apparently for idealistic reasons, which had the effect of excluding him permanently from power. But his party is still the one preferred by the army, or by a large section of it, and so, inevitably, there is a built-in tendency towards a change of regime. The latest example of this was the near-takeover by the army in 1971.

8 ❋ Economic and Social Problems

TURKEY, economically speaking, is an 'intermediate' country, much poorer than the very rich countries, but much richer than the very poor. There has been a good deal of progress in the last forty years: industrialization, new roads, ports, a tremendous amount of building (much of it of the wrong kind), hydro-electric schemes, new universities, the development of tourism, television, and so forth. But for all that progress has been less than had been hoped for or was thought likely by the 'angry' Young Turks inspired by the speed of Ataturk's modernization of the 1920's and 30's.

Though Turkey has received about 3,000 million dollars worth of foreign economic aid in the last twenty-five years (mainly from the United States), 92% of Turkish villages still have no electric light, 75% no road, and 35% no water. Annual per capita income is £140, well ahead of India (£36), or Egypt (£70), but far behind Greece (£300), and all the countries of Europe. Illiteracy stands officially at 52% of the adult population* – good compared with India (72%), Egypt (73%), or Iran (87%), but surprisingly high seeing that the change of script in 1928 was expected to eradicate illiteracy completely in a few years. The illiteracy figures for two of Turkey's neighbours to the west, Bulgaria and Greece, are 15% and 19% respectively.

Turkey is a potentially rich country. Its mountains are full of minerals. Its climate and topography are so varied that a wonderful profusion of agricultural products can be grown, and, if facilities were available, could be exported. The seas round the long Turkish coasts are crammed with edible fish. But this wealth is so inadequately exploited that Turkey imports fish products. Tourism, in one of the world's most beautiful countries, should be a goldmine; but Turkish tourism manages to lose money. Turkish coffers, as they were in Ottoman times, are perpetually empty.

* Most people think the real illiteracy rate is higher than this official figure, and may be over 60%.

Since 1963 Turkey has had a five-year plan, or rather a fifteen-year 'perspective', which is promising enough on paper. The plan was based on an annual investment of 18·2% of the gross national product, and aimed at sustaining an average growth rate of 7% per year. Three-quarters of the 6,000 million dollars needed to carry out the first five-year plan was to be raised by the Turks themselves, and the remaining quarter was to come from foreign aid. The fifteen-year perspective was intended to push Turkey through the 'take-off' point into a cycle of self-sustaining development. The 7% growth rate, or something not far from it, was in fact reached during the first five-year plan (1963–67) and the first two years of the second, though it was partly nullified by the population increase.

Some vast projects have been embarked on, such as the Eregli steel industry on the Black Sea, and the Keban dam on the Euphrates, which will be bigger than Egypt's Aswan. The new bridge over the Bosphorus, which will link Europe and Asia for the first time in history, was started early in 1970. Many economists feel that this particular project, in the present state of the Turkish economy, is a major folly.

Turkey is handicapped by a shortage of trained economists and a traditional lack of economic experience. In Ottoman times almost the entire commercial and technical life of the empire was left to the Greeks, Armenians, Jews, and other 'inferior' peoples. The role of the Turk was to rule, and often to fight. The removal of the minorities at the end of the empire meant that the Turks had to take over the whole economic life of the country and run it, for the first time, themselves. This is one of the biggest changes any people has undergone. The Turks have not made too bad a job of it. A middle class has painfully grown up.

But economic principles seem not very congenial to the Turkish nature. There is a natural reluctance to save. Turkey is burdened by enormous foreign debts, incurred in the dynamic but planless era of the Menderes government, which she is scrupulously paying off.* There is a more or less constant unbalance of trade. Traditional exports of chrome, dried fruit, tobacco, and hazelnuts

* The 'rescheduling' of her foreign debts in April 1965 greatly helped Turkey. Even so she will have to go on paying off these debts, which amount to over 1,500 million dollars, until AD 2014.

have been falling off. On top of all this, Turkey has been unlucky in not experiencing a big oil strike, which has helped so many other countries out of the red, despite the hopeful prospects which brought dozens of foreign oil companies to Anatolia in the 1950's.

There is far too little revenue for the state, due partly to the extraordinary fact that, in a country where 70% of the population work in agriculture, virtually no agricultural income-tax is levied. Agriculture produces 35% of the gross national product, and 1% of total taxation! The reason for this is purely political. Since democracy, no Turkish government has dared impose a tax and offend the big farmers and landowners on whose support they depend.

Since 1963 Turkey has been an associate member of the European Economic Community, and is due, after a reasonable transition period, to become a full member by 1982. Cassandras are predicting that any such programme is absurd because Turkey can never in this time make herself competitive with the advanced nations of Western Europe.

In the last few years Turkey has been steadily increasing her trade with the east bloc and is taking economic aid from the Soviet Union, in the form of large industrial projects. One of these, a steel mill in the Mediterranean port of Iskenderun, when completed in 1975, will be the biggest steel complex in the Middle East, with an annual capacity of two million tons, and ultimately employing 20,000 men. The Turks are repaying these Soviet credits with exports of hazelnuts, raisins and tobacco.

One of the worst things in Turkey, which everybody who tries to do business there complains of, is the appallingly slow and cumbersome administration. Nobody ever seems able to take responsibility for decisions, and the simplest document has to be signed by innumerable people. Any attempt to do anything quickly comes up against invisible resistance, so that sooner or later, if he doesn't go mad or commit suicide, the entrepreneur resigns himself to the hopeless frustration of the hero of Kafka's 'Castle'.

What this is due to is difficult to say. The natural resignation of the Turk, one of his rooted characteristics, may be to blame. Administrative reform is probably the most urgently needed of all reforms. Sloth is not congenital to the Turk, as is proved by the excellent performance of Turkish workers in Europe. But Turks need galvanizing from above, or they wallow in the resignation and apathy which Islam accentuates.

A particular blight is the telephone. There are first-class technicians and operators, but there is something wrong with the system, which makes all telephone conversations between Turkish cities a 'dialogue des sourds'. There is a well-known story of a tourist arriving in an Ankara hotel who hears somebody shouting and yelling at the top of his voice in the room next-door. He enquires what is going on, and is told that his neighbour is talking to Istanbul. 'Why doesn't he use the telephone?', asks the new arrival.

*   *   *   *   *

In Turkey, as in many countries, real economic progress has been almost nullified by the population increase. This, at nearly 3% net increase per year, is one of the world's highest. The Turkish population has more than doubled in the last twenty-five years (17 to 35 million), and is now rising by over a million a year. At this rate it will be 50 million by 1980. There are various causes for it. The decline in the death-rate is an important factor. A disease such as malaria, which even ten years ago was a killer in parts of Turkey, has been almost completely wiped out.

The basic cause of the population increase, obviously, is the very high birth-rate (about forty-four births per thousand), a result of the early age at which Turkish girls marry (often fourteen or less), the continuance of concealed polygamy, and the terrific emphasis on male virility in Turkey. Turkish men keep on procreating into extreme old age. A case was recently reported from the Gallipoli peninsula of a man who had a son at the age of 105. The mother was 35, and the father had already had 11 children by three previous marriages.

Birth control has been started in Turkey, but it has not got very far. Islam was against it, and Ataturk in his time discouraged it after a series of wars had depleted the population. Opposition to birth control comes from extreme nationalists, whose ardent wish is to see the entire world peopled by Turks, and also from some intellectuals on the curious ground that, as family planning would be practised more by the educated classes than by the masses, it would reduce the proportion of intellectuals in the country.

Promoters of birth control argue that it is now essential, if only to reduce the huge number of illicit abortions. According to the Ministry of Health in Ankara, half a million Turkish women have abortions every year, and ten thousand die in the process. These appalling figures seem to testify to a latent popular demand for a brake on births. They are also a tribute to the enormity of the Turkish birth-rate, which despite so many abortions still provides a population-increase ranking with the world's highest.

This multiplication of the species offsets any satisfactory increase in per capita income and puts terrific pressure on all resources. Many Turkish children still get no primary education. In the schools there are classes of a hundred to a single teacher. Unemployment gets progressively worse. The foreign trade gap yawns ever wider, because exportable products are simply consumed instead of being exported. Turkey, a wheat-growing country, has in recent years been importing vast quantities of wheat. According to a United Nations report, Turkey comes next on the list after India and Pakistan as a country directly faced by starvation.

The Turks have not had to undergo – yet – the famine conditions which keep Asians thin. There is poverty – per capita income of £140 a year is not high – but not misery. The Turk is a big strong fellow, who up to now has usually been in a position to eat his fill. He eats very little meat, fish, eggs, or poultry, but makes up for this by devouring truly vast quantities of bread, cheese, and milk products, and subsists on the wonderful multiplicity of vegetables and fruits which grow in Turkey – a country with a climate so variegated in its different regions that it is said that all the peoples of the world, except tropical Africans and Eskimos, would be perfectly at home in one corner or other of it. But already the inhabitants of eastern Turkey – a remote, mountainous, and relatively unfertile region – have known recurrent hunger in the winter months.

One of the worst long-term problems is the economic imbalance between the western and eastern parts of the country. This is like Italy's north and south, with the difference that southern Italy is at least warm and sunny, even in winter, whereas eastern Turkey, though the scenery is magnificent, is cold and forbidding. There is almost no industry in the eastern cities – Erzurum, Kars, Van, etc. – all of which are bursting under the demographic pressure. Unemployment is endemic. There is a constant internal migration of people from the forlorn east to the sunny, prosperous west – the beautiful Aegean coast with its tobacco, olives, figs and vines. This is like a promised land after the barren massifs and derelict towns of the Persian and Iraqi frontiers, where men live in the winter months by smuggling opium to Iran or cattle to Syria and Iraq.

The backwardness of the east is a serious political problem because this is the part of Turkey where the Kurds live. Almost 60% of the population east of the Euphrates is of Kurdish origin; much of it cannot speak Turkish. The Kurds, with some justice, complain that there is discrimination against the part of the country where they live, or at least that nothing is done for it. There are constant plans to 'develop the east', and a certain amount has been achieved: the Keban dam, the Ataturk University in Erzurum, the new health service based on Mush. But the problem has hardly been touched.

Stagnation in Turkey is partly attributable, perhaps, to the peculiar economic system in force there. Etatism, as we have seen, was one of the six principles of Kemalism; only nobody has ever been able to define what etatism actually is. Ataturk himself said that it did not mean either socialism or liberalism; obviously, it did not mean capitalism either. Ataturk realized that capitalism, as such, was a system which did not work in a semi-oriental country, because entrepreneurs were only willing to invest capital for very high and very quick returns. Etatism was supposed to mean that the state intervened to get desirable industries started, where private enterprise was unable or unwilling to do this.

Ataturk created a number of State Economic Enterprises, such as the so-called Sumerbank (Sumerian Bank) and Etibank (Hittite Bank), called after ancient peoples who in Ataturk's time, according to theories now exploded, were supposed to have been Turks. The Sumerbank controlled light industry – textiles, sugar, cement, and so on – while the Etibank dealt mainly with mining and heavy industry. Further state enterprises were added later, such as the Soil Products Office, the Agricultural Bank, and others.

71

These state enterprises were intended to make a profit, as if they were private business concerns, but the trouble was that almost from the beginning they made enormous losses, and the losses were financed out of the budget. There has been discussion for years about how to make these leaky monsters pay, or whether to return them in part to private industry. Meanwhile Turkish etatism has in practice developed in the form of the 'mixed economy'. This means a regime in which the whole of industry is bisected vertically into a state sector and a private sector. There are state textile factories and private textile factories, state chrome mines and private chrome mines, state sugar plants and private sugar plants, and so forth. The state sector in Turkey is roughly 55% of industry – probably the biggest state sector of any country outside the Communist bloc. This would make it easily adaptable should an extreme leftist regime ever come to power.

The two sectors, far from working harmoniously together to carry out the objectives of the five-year plans, regard each other, as a prominent Turkish economist* put it, as 'rivals to be destroyed'. It has occasionally been suggested (for example by Monsieur Maurice Duverger in *Le Monde*) that Turkish etatism might provide a model for newly independent countries in Asia and Africa which felt that neither capitalism nor communism quite suited their problems. This may be right in theory, but it cannot be said that up to now Turkey has provided a very convincing example of quick economic progress.

Turkish agriculture, which we shall discuss in the next chapter, is mainly in private hands: and, as the peasantry forms the bulk of the population, this weights the economy as a whole in the direction of private enterprise. But there has been a great deal of argument over the years, especially in recent years, as to what the economic regime really is in Turkey, and what Kemalist etatism really means. As it is neither communism nor capitalism, socialism nor liberalism, nor any other recognizable -ism, this very important principle of the Turkish revolution is fair game for doctrinaires of all political persuasions to interpret as suits them best. In fact etatism, like the other five sacred principles, has been blandly adopted by everybody. Still, the leftists are the most

* Professor Osman Okyar.

vocal exponents of it, and I should say, logically nearer to its true meaning.

The Marxists maintain that Turkey, under the Ottoman empire, passed through a roughly feudal stage, as in mediaeval Europe, and has now reached the capitalistic stage, in both industry and agriculture. The obvious dénouement, in extreme leftist eyes, is the communist revolution. Others argue that Turkey's whole economic and social development, especially its system of land tenure, has been quite different to that of Europe: there never was a feudal stage to Turkish society, so there cannot be a capitalistic stage now. For this reason, they say, the Marxist dialectic cannot be applied to Turkey. This may be so: Turkey is in many ways unique. But, as things are at present, some new upheaval may well overtake the pundits while they are still debating what the theoretical nature of the apotheosis should be.

* * * * *

Unemployment and under-employment are perhaps the worst problems in Turkey. All over the country one sees able-bodied men sitting idle in coffee-houses on workdays. There is a widespread paralysis and loss of power. Under-employment is mainly in agriculture. The Turkish peasant, in many parts of the country, only has work for three months out of the twelve. Concealed unemployment is in the towns. Great numbers of peasants, exasperated by the poverty and boredom of the villages, migrate to the big cities, hoping to get jobs, or, like Dick Whittington, to find gold under the streets.

Most find some work or other, but much of it is virtually useless to the community. They buy or sell old clothes, traffic in empty bottles and old newspapers, shine shoes, or sit vacantly in the passages of official buildings. One most coveted job is that of *Odaci** ('room-man'). These room-men are a ubiquitous feature of life in Turkey. For an exiguous wage they carry cups of coffee or tea, and perform minor errands. There are usually one or two outside every office. The room-man, when not rising to his feet to salute some passing notability, sits outside his master's door apparently immersed in a day-dream.

Some measure of the vast pools of unemployment inside Turkey

* Pronounced Odaji.

is the astonishing emigration of Turks in the last few years in search of jobs and better conditions abroad. This is a new phenomenon, because the Turks have historically not been an emigrant people. 600,000 Turks are now working in thirty different countries of the world, mostly in West Germany, or other parts of Western Europe, but as far afield as Canada, and even Australia. Another million are impatiently waiting to go. Many of these Turks abroad are peasants, who have never even seen their local town, let alone a big city. They have gone in one terrific step from an Anatolian village to Vienna, Paris, Brussels, Dusseldorf or Munich.

So large an influx of Muslims has not entered Europe in history. It causes special problems, many arising from the difference of religion: not enough mosques, the fear of eating pork, a different attitude to women, and so on. Turks abroad are highly valued as workers. Many earn good money – sometimes ten times what they would get for the same job in Turkey. But most, sooner or later, go back to their country.

Inside Turkey in recent years there has been a much bigger migration of a different kind: the rush of peasants to the cities. These internal migrations have reached quite phenomenal proportions. The causes are varied: not enough work in the village, the fragmentation of properties which makes land unable to support families, the boredom and primitiveness of life in the village. Apart from this the Turk is by origin a nomad. It means little to him to uplift house and home, pile the family belongings on to a mule or donkey, and set forth hopefully for a better world.

Turkish cities today have a very curious look about them: they are divided into two worlds. There is the world of the regular population, and the separate world of the half-urbanized peasantry. The migrants build their own houses, in tens of thousands, on any land they can find; they don't worry too much who it belongs to. They are not 'shanty-towns' or 'squatters' shacks', but pretty individual houses, each built by a different family in a different style. It is a touching example of collective private enterprise, preferable in a way to the chilling blocks of communal dwellings to be found in socially more advanced countries.

These houses are called in Turkish *Gecekondu* (pronounced 'gedjehkondu'), which means the 'night-built' houses. Theoretically, if a house can be constructed between dusk and dawn, authority must accept it. Prodigious efforts are made to complete the structures in a single night, and this extraordinary feat is often accomplished. Some curious techniques are adopted. People disguise their homes, while under construction, as a ruin, a rubbish-dump, a junk-heap, or even a house in process of demolition. Then comes the dramatic moment when the whole family gathers in the hours of darkness to put the roof on.

But the inhabitants of these districts, because they have no title-deeds, live in perpetual terror that their houses will be demolished. They subsist by widespread bribery of the police and government-officials, who in this way makes a nice addition to their own miserable incomes. No government has done anything serious to check this colossal popular migration, which is as uncontrolled as the ocean. 64% of the population of Ankara, and 45% of Istanbul, now live in the 'night-built' districts. Clearly it is a very grave social problem. These populations are potentially dangerous proletariats, especially as they usually live juxtaposed to the most flagrant wealth. By night the lights of these districts glow with a faint menace like the camp-fires of an investing army.

*   *   *   *   *

It would be tedious to enumerate all the problems which afflict Turkey. Education, of course, is fundamental. Turkish intellectuals suffer from a particularly deep preoccupation about the ignorance of the masses, yet few evince a burning desire to live in villages and impart the blessings of their superior culture. Educated Turks shudder at the thought of a village. There is an absence of missionary zeal about the Turkish élite. Even the extreme leftists, pontificating from comfortable mansions about the urgent need to instruct the peasants, seem reluctant to practise the virtue preached by Lenin, who told the intelligentsia to descend into the recesses of the proletariat and bring it light. Almost every attempt to educate the people has come to nothing, usually for the same reason. For forty years Turkish leaders have suffered from the delusion, common in countries where conservatism is a strong natural force, that the process of enlightening the masses will of itself trigger the cataclysm, in this case the Bolshevik revolution. On the rock of this conviction one scheme after another has foundered. Of these the most hopeful was the Village Institutes, created in 1940 to train peasant children at state expense, and return them to the villages to teach agriculture, hygiene, sanitation, and other techniques of modern civilization. The virtue of the institutes was their practical character. They got the peasant to do new things: carpentry, painting, weaving, arts and crafts. They stirred him out of the sleep of ages, relieved his boredom, made him feel somebody was bothering about him, gave him hope. But soon it was gravely asserted that the experiment was dangerous. To start giving ideas to the peasantry was like putting a spark in a huge barrel of gunpowder. Soon after 1950, the Menderes government, succumbing to intense conservative pressure, passed a law which took the guts out of the Village Institutes. They dwindled into obscurity, and were never revived.

A similar fate overtook the *Halkevleri*, or 'People's Houses', established by Ataturk in the 1930's. These too aimed at a wide educational effect. They taught the people such things as foreign languages, literature, fine arts, drama, and social welfare; they opened libraries and museums, and arranged exhibitions. This project too, after Ataturk's death, incurred the censure of all who trembled at the spectre of revolution. It was suggested that it had been inspired by a similar scheme in the Soviet Union – the *Narodni Dom*. Here was Bolshevism under another guise. The enterprise was quietly knocked on the head.

There were also political reasons for the dissolution of the People's Houses. They had been created at a time when the Republicans had been the only party in the state. When the Democrats came to power in 1950, they suspected the Republicans of using the People's Houses as an instrument of propaganda. Whatever the truth of this charge, Menderes closed the People's Houses and confiscated all their property. The masses were left again to wallow in ignorance and superstition, or to sleep peacefully on the ample bosom of Islam.

Finally, there are the health questions. Of 10,000 Turkish doctors in existence, 3,500 live outside Turkey, while those in the country are largely concentrated in the big cities. There is an acute shortage of nurses – only 5,000 for the country. This is caused by the reluctance of Turkish parents to allow their daughters to enter this profession. There is a widespread belief in traditional Turkish families that for girls to minister to the needs of the male sex in hospitals and clinics is only a shade less immoral than ministering to their needs in less respectable establishments. Though Florence Nightingale is still a great name in Turkey, there is a rooted reluctance to follow her example.

In the remote province of Mush, in eastern Turkey, a scheme of socialized medicine on the British and Scandinavian models was started in 1963, and has since been extended to twenty-three provinces of the east. It is hoped, if all goes well, to have a free, or almost free, health service for the whole of Turkey by 1978, though how this can possibly be financed is difficult to envisage. In this enterprise advice and material help have been given by the World Health Organization.

It is surprising, in one of the most backward parts of Turkey, to find hospitals and clinics staffed with larger numbers of doctors, surgeons, dentists, pharmacists, ophthalmologists, pediatricians, and even psychiatrists, than are to be found in far more prosperous areas. One can only suggest that if a traveller has to fall ill during the course of his wanderings in Turkey, he is strongly advised to fall ill near Mush.

9 ❋ *The Land*

THE LAND PROBLEM in Turkey has become so acute in the last ten years that a confused cry for land reform has gone up, and not only from left-wing circles. It is not easy to get to the bottom of the land situation, because there are almost no records of who owns what, though certain facts are clear. Under the Ottoman empire there was no landed aristocracy as we know it. There were the great local families, almost dynasties, known as the *Derebeys*, such as the Karaosmanoglus of western Anatolia of whom Byron wrote:

> But yet the line of Caraosman
> Unchanged, unchangeable hath stood
> First of the bold Timariot bands
> That won and well can keep their lands.

There has been a great deal of discussion as to whether the Derebeys (literally 'lords of the valley') were feudal potentates or not. Leftists like to think they were, because this opens the way to a Marxist interpretation of Turkish history. The Derebeys have virtually ceased to exist today, but a new class of big landowners, known as *Aghas*, has grown up in various parts of Turkey. Many of them, it seems, have no legal title to their lands, but have simply 'acquired' them, or taken them over from displaced peasants who have moved off into the big cities.

Very few people in Turkey seem to possess any real title to land. In certain areas, especially east and south-east Anatolia, large parts of which are inhabited by Kurdish populations, and where the social system is still partly tribal, there are chieftains who 'own' up to fifty or even a hundred villages, and whose word is law among tens of thousands of peasants. It is rather like the Highlands of Scotland in the sixteenth and seventeenth centuries, with Kurdish equivalents of the Campbells and Macdonalds lording it over their retainers in remote mountain regions. These local barons are extremely important to the politicians at election-time, as they can deliver thousands of votes to whichever political party they condescend to support. There is big competition among the parties to get an influential Agha to change sides at the right moment.

As almost nothing is known about the legal ownership of land, one has to make do with what information there is about land actually held or farmed. In arriving at the following conclusions I have used three main sources: a report by an expert of the Food and Agriculture Organization in 1962; a study by the Central Treaty Organization (CENTO) on rural development in 1963; and the agricultural census carried out by the Turkish State Institute of Statistics, also in 1963. Information from the three sources differs slightly, but is similar enough to show that there is something radically wrong with land distribution in Turkey, and a strong case for reform of some kind or other.

According to the FAO report, about 3% of Turkish farmers are working 35% of all the cultivable land in Turkey. The CENTO survey shows that 0·8% of farmers are working 20% of the land. The 1963 census reveals that about 3·2% of all Turkish farmers occupy 31% of the total cultivable land. These figures, whichever of them may be nearest to the truth, show clearly that there is a highly unequal distribution of land and a considerable number of vast estates.

In one region, that of the rich Cilician Plain in southern Turkey, a land reform study made in 1965 estimated that about 50% of the entire income from agriculture in the region was accruing to 2% of the local farmers. According to this source, there are 156,000 farming families in the Cilician Plain of which 2,800 families had an average of 463 acres each, the remaining 153,200 families an average of 8 acres each.*

These figures may be somewhat exaggerated, but the Cilician Plain is the part of Turkey where 'capitalistic' developments in agriculture have gone farthest. It is an area of very rich cotton and citrus-growers, some of whom are by any standards millionaires. The extremes of wealth and poverty in this part of Turkey make it particularly exposed to the evermore-vocal left-wing propaganda. There are big cotton planters in western Turkey, the

---

* Turkish land measurements are in *dönüms*. 1 *dönüm* equals approximately 1 decare, so that in the following calculations 4 *dönüms* are taken as equalling an English acre.

beautiful Aegean seaboard, though also peasants working small acreages of vines, tobacco, olives, or figs. According to the leftists, there are now large properties in every part of Turkey except the Black Sea coast, which consists mainly of smallish tobacco and hazel-nut estates, and in the north-east near the Russian border, the only part of Turkey where there is high rainfall, successful tea plantations.

At the other end of the scale the vast majority of Turkish peasants are scraping along on tiny plots of land, which are constantly being made smaller by fragmentation. Most are incapable of supporting a family. This is one of the chief causes of the oceanic drift to the cities. Not infrequently peasants, driven desperate by the land shortage, simply seize and occupy the Aghas' lands, and have to be driven off by the local forces of order, sometimes after violent battles in which people are killed. It is also estimated that about a million peasant families have no land at all, and are working more or less as serfs of the big Aghas.

According to the FAO report (which is roughly confirmed by the two others), 75% of all Turkish peasants were cultivating plots of an average size of seven acres – (which means of course that many are smaller than this). Taking a peasant family at an average of six to seven persons, this size of farm, especially on un-irrigated, un-fertilized, or badly eroded soil, which much of Anatolia now is, is far too small. These tiny farms are caused by the irrational working of the inheritance laws. The Sheriat, or Koranic law, under which property at death was divided among innumerable relatives, was abolished by Ataturk in 1926. But the Swiss code which replaced it seems not to function very differently. It still divides property up among descendants, leading, though slightly more slowly than the Sheriat, to the same result.

A further absurdity is that many of these holdings are not even in one piece, but are divided into several separate parcels, often miles apart. It has been calculated that 70% of all peasant holdings in Turkey are in the form of four or more separate plots, and that 16% of them are made up of between eleven and thirteen plots. These plots may be separated from each other by as much as thirty or even fifty miles. Imagination boggles at how, in these circumstances, Turkish peasants get any rational farming done at all.

The intense pressure on the land comes not only from the small size of the farms, but from the advancing soil erosion. This has reached the proportions of a national disaster. Turkey is rapidly going the same way as the North African granaries of the Roman Empire – becoming a desert. Much of Anatolia, being in the same climatic area as Iran and central Asia, has low rainfall. The peasants in these areas, from time immemorial, practise dry farming. This means that the land lies fallow every second year. The theory is that in this way it gathers moisture and accumulates nutrients. There is no scientific rotation of crops. There has been continuous growing of corn on the Anatolian plateau for centuries, exhausting the soil.

The result is that Turkish wheat yields are easily the lowest in Europe. The national average varies between 900 kilograms per hectare in central Anatolia, where rainfall is low, to 1,200 in damp areas such as the Black Sea coast. The same figure in most countries of Western Europe is well over 2,000. In the last two years there have been successful experiments with high-yielding Mexican wheat, which has $2\frac{1}{2}$ times the yield of Turkish wheat, but this is only suitable for the coastal regions and will not grow on the plateau.

Another reason for the impoverishment of the soil is that Turkish peasants still use almost no fertilizers despite devoted efforts by UN and American experts to get them to do so. In most parts of Turkey the peasants burn the dung of farm animals as fuel. This is done because of another Turkish national catastrophe which has been going on for years, if not centuries: deforestation. Apart from the Black Sea area, where there are lush deciduous forests, there are hardly any trees left in Turkey. The peasant has no fuel. He has to burn something, poor fellow, and the nearest thing to hand is dried manure. It makes a cheerful blaze. It has been calculated that 67 million tons of fresh manure (equivalent to $3\frac{1}{2}$ million tons of commercial fertilizers), are burnt by the Turkish peasantry every year.

Deforestation is due partly, but not entirely, to the depredations of the Turks. René Grousset quotes Strabo in support of the thesis that central Anatolia was already a steppe before the Turks got there in the eleventh century AD, and claims that the Turks were attracted to it from central Asia because it *was* almost a desert.

Other historians have recorded that at the battle of Ankara, in 1402, the Tartar conqueror Tamerlane hid his elephants in the 'forest'. The site of the battle is near Ankara airport, and anybody can see that today treeless plains and hills surround the historic spot. There seems no question that over the centuries there has been a massive deforestation of Anatolia; and there is equally no question that it is still going on today.

The penalties for chopping down trees in Turkey are extremely strict, and forest offences are in theory punishable by death. But the forestry service is hopelessly understaffed, underpaid, and overworked, and has virtually no authority to apply the laws. The peasants chop down the forests, as a UN expert put it, 'as freely as the air they breathe'. Lofty sentiments, emphasizing the importance of trees to nations, are often to be seen inscribed in gigantic letters on bare hillsides in Turkey: they read more like a lament for the past than an exhortation for the future.

Demographic pressure on the land has led to great areas of pasture being converted to the growing of wheat and other crops for food. In the last ten years 2½ million acres of grassland have been ploughed up *per year*. This enormous reduction in the amount of available pasture has coincided with an equally vast increase in the number of animals grazing it. All forms of livestock except camels have increased in the last twenty years: sheep by 11 million, goats by 9 million, cattle by 5 million, horses by 200,000, donkeys by 500,000, water-buffaloes by 400,000. Only camels have gone down by 50,000 (camels are frowned on in westernizing Turkey as being oriental animals). There are now about 15 million more animals grazing than there is pasture for them to eat. In parts of Anatolia today one frequently sees great flocks of sheep apparently subsisting on nothing.

One reason for the big increase in livestock is the lucrative smuggling of sheep and cattle from Turkey down into the Middle East. The animals are driven across the land frontier into Syria, where they fetch much higher prices than in Turkey. This is usually done under cover of darkness. A friend of mine in a foreign oil company, who was camping once near the Syrian border, told me that he was kept awake at nights by the thundering of hooves past his tent as great armies of sheep and cattle were driven down into the Aleppo plain.

Of all these animals the most devastating and ubiquitous is the goat. The goat population has risen in recent years to so enormous a figure that some people claim that half the goats in the world live in Turkey. This is an exaggeration; but it is probably true that there are more goats in Turkey (an estimated 25 million) than in any other single country, and nearly twice as many as in the rest of Europe. Roughly a quarter of these animals are mohair goats, whose creamy glistening fleeces are a familiar sight in the Ankara region. (Mohair is still an important Turkish export.) The rest are a national menace. Their voracity stops at nothing. They devour the vegetation, destroy the forest, and aggravate the soil erosion by scampering about all over the plateau. Turkish foresters calculate that more than a million cubic metres of timber are lost every year through the depredations of goats. In southern Turkey they are especially thick on the ground, and one often sees unending streams of the creatures, usually tended by a dreamy boy with a stick. No government, for fear of offending the peasants, has dared tackle this problem. The peasant loves his goats, the politician his votes.

*   *   *   *   *

No land reform has yet been seriously attempted in Turkey. Ataturk was said to have intended one, but was preoccupied with other matters. The leftists today tend to regard Ataturk as a member of the bourgeois class, and himself a large landowner, who never had any intention of carrying out social reforms. In 1945 President Inönü passed a land reform bill which remained abortive. Since then nothing much has been done, mainly because no ruling party has dared offend the big landowners who 'deliver the vote' in their particular regions.

It is clear that the land problem in Turkey involves, even more than the splitting-up of big estates, the amalgamation of small ones. It must be remembered that there is a serious natural shortage of agricultural land in Turkey. The country is so mountainous that only about 16% of its whole area is suitable for cultivation. The natural shortage causes many conflicts in Turkey. According to official figures, no less than two million lawsuits a year arise out of land disputes. At times whole villages fight pitched battles over some piece of land, in which lethal weapons are used.

People are killed, or grievously injured, fighting for a plot of ground no bigger than a cricket-pitch.

The land problem is further vexed by the fact that Turkish farmers, however rich they may be, pay almost no tax at all. Ataturk exempted agriculture from taxation to encourage its expansion. That was all very well in the 1920's; but it is a grave scandal today. It not only involves a loss of revenue so enormous that it endangers the financing of the five-year plans, but is a grotesque social injustice which plays straight into the hands of Communist propaganda.

In 1962 Professor Nicholas Kaldor, the well-known British economist, visited Turkey at the invitation of the Turkish government to advise on the question of an agricultural income-tax. He estimated that Turkish agriculture, though it produced 42·5% of the net national product, contributed 0·8% to direct taxation! In his report Kaldor suggested that a progressive tax levied on an 'upper crust' of 16% of the richest Turkish farmers would produce the phenomenal sum of £40 million (sterling) a year. Kaldor's advice was considered impracticable for political reasons. His report was hastily shelved, and was never published.

In 1963 a modest measure of agricultural income-tax was enacted, which was officially expected to bring in £6 million a year. In fact it brought in about £1,700,000, due mainly to massive tax evasion and incompetent collection. In Turkey there is a long and very effective tradition of tax evasion, aggravated by a lack of book-keepers and cumbrous and indolent methods of collection. The result is that some of the richest men in Turkey contribute virtually nothing to the exchequer.

Despite these injustices, one of the striking things in Turkey, even today, after years of leftist propaganda, is the relative absence of class feeling. Ataturk made a declaration on this subject, as he did on most others. He described the Turkish people as 'a fused mass, without distinction or class'. The doctrine known as Populism, which was one of the six principles of Kemalism, amounted roughly to the belief that Turkish society was genuinely free from any opposition between the classes. This belief is still strong. One must remember that Socialist and Communist ideas, with which all of us are so painfully familiar over the last hundred years, are only now beginning to penetrate Turkey. We shall see in the next chapter how between 1926 and 1961 Turkey was almost completely insulated from all leftist thought and doctrine.

During my stay in Turkey I was constantly made aware that the virus of Socialism, call it envy, call it a sense of injustice, had hardly yet penetrated the Turkish mind. Innumerable very poor people, usually clothed in rags, used to call at my door to traffic in old clothes, old bottles, or old newspapers. I often had interesting conversations with these vagrants. There was a real feeling of equality between us, and on their side, so it seemed, a total indifference to my much greater material well-being. If anything, they appeared to despise it. Nobody had yet told them how miserable they really were. That was to come.

Since 1960 class feeling has much increased. Some of the most brilliant and caustic pens in the Turkish press have for years now been preaching the class war. Even the 'fused mass' of the Turkish people is getting the message at last. The Turks are like southsea islanders, never yet exposed to disease, who, if once they catch the germ, might well fall victims to a raging epidemic. Islam may protect them; but only a little, and probably not for long. We must look now at leftism, still a relatively new phenomenon in this country, and try to see how far it could take Turkey, and where it might lead.

10 ❊ Could Turkey go Communist

THE GREAT OUTBURST of aggressive leftism, which is such a phenomenon of the last few years in Turkey, is in part merely a readjustment of the political scene to the fact that for thirty-five years, up to the military revolution of 1960, the Left was almost totally banned in Turkey. In 1925 Ataturk dissolved the Turkish Communist party and arrested or exiled its leading members. Leftism of any serious kind became a punishable offence under two articles of the law borrowed from the penal code of Fascist Italy.

These clauses (Articles 141 and 142), which are still in force today, threatened persons intending 'the overthrow of the established economic and social order', or those who propagated such an aim. The vagueness and severity of the law were sufficient to deter anybody who wanted to form a left-wing party or express socialist views. After 1950, when anti-Communism in Turkey reached its zenith, the maximum penalty for this offence was increased from Mussolini's ten years imprisonment to one of death. This made Turkish leftists complain, not without justice, that the law in their country was literally 'more Fascist than the Fascists'.

Between Ataturk's death in 1938 and the fall of the Menderes government in 1960 Turkey became a sort of McCarthyist mausoleum. Some macabre jokes are told about this period. The phrase 'Russian salad' was erased from Turkish menus and replaced by 'American salad'. A university professor, whose bookshelf had been found to contain the French encyclopaedia *Larousse*, lost his job because it was supposed that 'Larousse' implied a connection with Russia. Clearly the man was a Communist spy. An over-enthusiastic American Trades Unionist working in Turkey was arrested on a charge of subversion. When the police came to fetch him, he protested: 'But I'm no Communist; I'm an *anti*-Communist!' 'We don't care *what* kind of Communist you are . . .', came the gruff reply, as they led him gesticulating away.

Could Turkey go Communist?

One of the chief consequences of the army's seizure of power in 1960 was to open the gates to leftism – the floodgates, one might say. In 1961 the Turkish Labour party was formed, the first serious left-wing political organization tolerated for thirty-five years. In the same year the leftist weekly *Yön* ('The Direction') started publication with an uncompromising manifesto in its first number declaring bluntly that 'economic development under a system of private enterprise is slow, painful, costly and... incompatible with social justice'. The manifesto was signed by 160 intellectuals and officers in the armed forces, including significantly several members of the 1960 junta. The 1961 constitution, drafted under the aegis of the military government, contained a reference to 'Social justice' which had not figured in any previous Turkish constitution. After that, Turkey underwent a veritable invasion of left-wing thought and ideas.

The works of Marx, Lenin, and Mao, and other Communist classics, became available in the Turkish bookshops, something unthinkable in the '50's. Several of the important newspapers 'went left'. The most brilliant daily columnists are declared socialists. Many, in scarcely veiled fashion, preach revolution. They are ferociously nationalist and anti-American, postulating an 'independent Turkey' withdrawn from NATO and (by implication) having close ties with Russia. The significance of this is that it could not have happened were it not tolerated by at least an important section of the army. The danger is that Turkish minds are undergoing their first prolonged exposure to Marxist dogma at a time when the rising pressure of social and economic problems is spreading increasing hopelessness about the democratic regime.

In recent years, there has been a rising tide of anarchy which many people assume to be engineered by the Left. Turkey, said to be immune to the Bolshevist virus, suddenly felt in danger. Some saw, if not Russia, the hand of China behind the series of strikes, marches, and noisy disorders which afflicted the country. Much of the trouble arose from right-wing reaction to the growing leftism. Right-wing students in the universities and colleges clashed violently with left-wing students. The youth, ferociously divided and bristling with lethal weapons, fought battles with each other, sometimes under the eyes of the police. In one year eighteen students were killed in these violent affrays.

Peasants, in a series of spontaneous revolts, seized the land; squatters in the big cities invaded apartment blocks. Right-wing forces raised the cry that a Communist takeover was imminent. There were reports that the Turkish Labour party was a secret Communist party, directly controlled from Moscow. All this coincided with warmer relations between Turkey and the Soviet Union than had existed for fifty years, and the sending of thousands of Russian technicians to help in economic projects, whom the anti-Communists claim to be subversive agents.

The names of a few influential Turkish leftists are worthy of mention. Çetin* Altan, writing in various papers, rolled out a daily column for more years than anybody can remember. His was the most caustic and resourceful pen in the Turkish press. Day after day, year after year, his articles poured forth in an unending stream, challenging taboos, unearthing scandals, lampooning absurdities, exposing injustices, and propagating ideals. He made many enemies in the process. There are at least seventy pending lawsuits against Altan, and it has been calculated that if he were sentenced for all of them he would go to prison for 250 years.

Yaşar* Kemal is a writer whose novels are already well-known in the West (*Memed, my Hawk, The Wind from the Plain,* etc.). This man is vastly creative, pouring forth books like rivers, few of them less than five hundred pages long. He is a large genial man, like a friendly bear, a sort of Turkish Balzac. He has a strong, original style which ordinary Turks understand, full of pungent sentences and poetic imagery. He himself comes from a peasant background in eastern Turkey. He had the extraordinary experience, at the age of four, of seeing his father killed in front of his eyes while at prayer in the mosque, in a blood feud. Though his books are novels, full of vivid and memorable characters, there is a strong social theme running through them.

Dogan Avcioglu*, our third representative leftist, has a more directly political impact. He was for many years editor of the Socialist weekly *Yön*, more recently editor of *Devrim* ('revolution')† He has good contacts with the army. He had to lie low for a time in 1963, after a suspected connection with the second Aydemir

* Pronounced Chetin.
* Pronounced Yashar.
* Pronounced Avjioglu.
† Now banned.

putsch. Avcioglu made his name in 1969 with the publication of a massive and highly influential book, *Turkey's Regime*. This work, 526 pages of close print, is the most detailed and voluminous analysis of Turkey's economic and social condition which has yet been published. The book sold 32,000 copies in little over a year, a staggering figure in Turkey. In its detailed exposition and apocalyptic tone it is rather like a Turkish version of Marx's *Das Kapital*. Avcioglu is a Marxist of a kind, but a *sui generis* Marxist. He believes in revolution, not by the proletariat, but by the army.

This variation of classical Marxist theory is necessary because, from the viewpoint of the Left, there is no satisfactory proletariat in Turkey. The peasantry is, for the time being at least, conservative and Muslim. Leftism has still barely penetrated the Turkish villages. Even Turkish workers are only now beginning to become class conscious. The Trades Unions, except for their extreme left-wing, are still committed to 'bourgeois democracy'. As there is no satisfactory proletariat, the Marxists pin their hopes on another class: the 'national bourgeoisie'. This means bureaucrats, intellectuals, writers, and the middle-rank officers of the armed forces.

One result of the new toleration of the Left after 1960 was the rehabilitation of the best-known and most gifted of Turkish Communists: the poet Nazim Hikmet. Nazim Hikmet should be more famous than he is, because he is a very fine poet indeed. Ataturk was an admirer and used to say regretfully: 'A pity our greatest poet is a Communist!' Nazim Hikmet spent twelve years of his life in a Turkish prison (not under Ataturk, but under Inönü). When finally released in 1951 he escaped to Russia, and lived there till he died in 1963. He was denounced as a 'traitor' for having done so, but it was hardly surprising, considering the treatment he got in his own country.

One of Nazim Hikmet's most famous poems compares the peasants to sheep led docilely to the slaughter:

> You are like a sheep, brother.
> When the coated shepherd lifts his stick
> You are back among the flock in no time,
> And almost proudly you run to the slaughter-house.

The Turks

> You're the strangest creature on earth:
> Stranger than the fish that swims in the ocean
>   but does not know the ocean.
> And the cruelty and oppression of the world are
>   due to you.
> If we are hungry and weary, and red with our
>   own blood,
> If still we are trodden underfoot, like
>   grapes in a winepress,
> I can hardly bring myself to say that the
>   fault is largely yours,
> But the fault *is* largely yours, brother.

For many years officially known in Turkey as the 'great national traitor', whose works were read secretly and passed from hand to hand, Nazim Hikmet has today been renamed the 'great national poet'. His poems are lavishly used in Communist broadcasts beamed to Turkey from eastern Europe. With their strong direct appeal to the classical sentiments of revolt against injustice and tyranny, they probably have a greater effect on the average Turk than all the writings of Marx, Engels, and Lenin put together.

Since March 1971 there has been something like a swing-back to the attitude of the 1938–60 period. The growing clamour of the leftists has caused a right-wing reaction in high places. Under the Erim government there were numerous arrests and trials of 'communists'. All prime ministers now run the country in close collaboration with the army high command, and it seems likely that the generals, more than ever, fear the danger of a Communist takeover.

This led the leftists themselves to denounce the recent government as a fascist 'junta' similar to that of the colonels in Greece. But so far there has been no military takeover on the Greek model. The democratic regime continues, at least in form. Moreover if the generals are right-wing, there is no particular reason to think that a majority of the colonels and captains are the same. The army, as usual, is silent and enigmatic.

* * * * *

It has generally been assumed that Communism had no chance

in Turkey because it came from Russia, and the Russian was the deadly enemy of the Turk. True, there is endemic distrust of Russia in Turkey, due to Muscovy's historic southward thrust to Constantinople and the Straits. But it would be unwise to bank on this assumption, for two reasons. Communism today emanates from many different centres, not least China, a country about which Turkey has no historic inhibitions, and whose problems are in many ways remarkably similar to those of Turkey. There is evidence of growing Chinese influence in Turkey. Secondly, Turkish-Russian hostility is not an immutable law. The two countries have had friendly relations in the past, and the much-discussed rapprochement between Ankara and Moscow in the last nine years has coincided exactly with the rise of leftism inside Turkey.

It is sometimes forgotten that Ataturk and Lenin, in 1920 and 1921, made what virtually amounted to a revolutionary common front against the West. The Bolsheviks contributed gold, arms, and moral support to the Turkish nationalist movement. The Russians had their doubts as to whether Kemal was a Communist, though he went some way, when he needed Soviet help, to make them believe it. Some of the messages exchanged at that time between Turkish and Bolshevik leaders make curious reading today. 'Now that the Turkish and Russian peoples have broken the age-long chains which bound them,' wrote Ataturk to Lenin in 1922, 'their new-won freedom has exposed them to attack by the great capitalist and imperialist powers.' He went on to talk of 'the similar circumstances and ideals of our two peoples'. Ataturk, as it happens, was not a Communist (though he might well have been). Once he had established his own power in Turkey, he suppressed the Communist party, and it has remained banned to this day (it still exists in exile, centred on Moscow and Paris).

But there is a fascinating and little-known period of Turkish history, roughly between 1917 and 1919, when Turkey might well have gone Communist. In that anarchic flux at the end of the Ottoman empire, when Ataturk had not yet emerged, the Bolsheviks in Moscow had great hopes of Turkey. In 1917 Turkish peasants welcomed the Russian revolution, and local peasant soviets were set up in many places. Turkish and Russian troops fraternized on the Turkish eastern frontier. There were popular demonstrations against capitalism in Turkey (even though few Turks at that time had the faintest idea what the word meant).

There were pro-Communist movements among Turkish students, some of whom wanted Lenin to be awarded the Nobel Peace prize. A number of Turkish intellectuals became Communists. The Turkish Communist party, which in fact is one of the oldest in the Middle East, was the first to become a member of the Comintern. On 1st May 1919, a procession of workers several miles long marched through the streets of Constantinople. *Izvestia* gloated: 'The Straits, which centuries of Czarist imperialism failed to annex, have fallen like a ripe plum into the hands of the Russian working class!' (via the Turkish working class, of course).

In this confused period, at least four different Communist parties were operating in Turkey. One of these was the mysterious 'Green Army'. This was a secret organization, with a Communistic philosophy, strongly anti-western and pro-Muslim, which had become a legend among the Anatolian peasants. Green was the holy colour of Islam. It was supposed by devout or credulous Turks that angels and martyrs would descend from Heaven, clothed in green, and would help them in battle. Many Turks held the mystical belief that a Green Army of thousands of warriors on horseback, with swords drawn, would appear suddenly from some ancient Turkish homeland in Central Asia and destroy the Greek armies which at that time were advancing through Anatolia. Some supposed this army would be led by Enver Pasha, the brilliant young soldier who had ruled Turkey in the last stages of the Ottoman empire, and who at that moment was flirting with the Soviets in a struggle with Mustafa Kemal, and indeed was his chief rival for power inside Turkey.

The Green Army was an example of that curious romantic mixture of Communism, Islam, anti-Westernism, and Pan-Turkism, which is so potent in Turkey, and which seems to show, among other things, that religion is no more a serious barrier to Communism than it was in Russia itself. Communism, despite its atheism, has never scrupled to use fanatical religious movements to serve its ends. During the trial of 167 suspected Communists in Istanbul in 1953, a number of the accused were found to have connections with religious fanatics. The dangerous *Nur* movement, which propagates the restoration of the Caliphate, the Koranic law, and the veil in Turkey, has been discovered with Communist tracts and left-wing revolutionary propaganda in its possession. The *Nur* movement is also connected with Kurdish nationalism, a time-honoured instrument of Soviet subversion in the Middle East.

In 1920 Ataturk, alarmed at the spread of Communist ideas in Turkey, created a puppet Communist party of his own. He explained the purpose of this in an interesting letter to General Ali Fuad (Cebesoy), at that time commanding the Turkish armies against the Greeks in western Anatolia: 'We can see from the way public opinion reacts to propaganda put out by the party how far the principles of Socialism and Communism can be applied, digested, and accepted in this country. . . . The utmost attention must be given to ensuring that the army remains well-disciplined and under the control of its commanding officers. *Any Communist ideas must be limited to the senior commanders.*' (My emphasis.) Ataturk seems to have been more realistic about the possibility of Communism in the Turkish army than most Turks are today.

In 1920 the four Communist parties or movements were: the semi-secret Green Army; the real Turkish Communist party, which was underground; a legal movement known as the People's Participation party; and Ataturk's puppet party, which was of course open and official. (Some say there was a secret fifth party led by Enver.) This was the period immediately after the Treaty of Sèvres, when Turkey, defeated and dismembered, was fighting for her very existence. Many Turks at this time looked openly to revolutionary Russia for their salvation.

In September 1920 a huge Turkish delegation went to the Communist-inspired 'First Congress of Eastern Peoples' in Baku. The Congress was attended by high-ranking Communists such as Zinoviev, Radek, and the Hungarian Bela Kun. Hovering on the fringes at Baku was Enver, who hoped for Moscow's support in his power-struggle with Mustafa Kemal. But the Russians, when they saw that the Turkish armies were defeating the Greeks in Anatolia, dropped Enver (if they had ever intended to support him) and threw their weight behind Kemal. The latter then out-witted them all. Having disposed of the danger of Enver, and driven out the Greeks, he turned on the Communists and routed them also. Thus Ataturk can be said to have saved his country, not only from defeat and foreign occupation, but possibly from Communism too.

One of the most sinister episodes of this half-lit period was the murder of Mustafa Subhi, founder of the Turkish Communist party, together with fourteen members of the party executive, in a motor-boat in the Black Sea in January 1921. They were on their way to the Soviet Union by sea, after a visit to Turkey. On somebody's orders, a second boat full of armed men went after the first, murdered all fifteen Turkish Communists, and dumped their bodies in the sea. The only survivor of this massacre is said to have been the Russian wife of Mustafa Subhi, a handsome Jewess, who was taken as booty by Yahya Kaptan, the ruffian who, on somebody's orders, did the deed, and who was himself murdered in mysterious circumstances a year later.

Who was behind the killings? Some say it was Enver, but it is more often assumed to have been Mustafa Kemal himself. He distrusted the Turkish Communists, because he felt they were a challenge to his own power. We may never know the truth, because this sanguinary event was hushed up by both Russians and Turks. When the Soviet Commissar for Foreign Affairs enquired of the Turkish Ambassador in Moscow about the fate of the 'Turkish comrades', the envoy replied blandly that 'they might have met with an accident at sea'. The Commissar apparently did not press his enquiries. The incident was quietly buried. Two months later, in March 1921, the Turco-Soviet Treaty of Friendship and Brotherhood was signed. Both sides were anxious not to disturb the excellent relations which subsisted between Ankara and Moscow.*

* * * * *

The point of this historical digression is to show that Turkey is not, as has sometimes been thought, in some mysterious way impervious to Communism. It is true that, for various historical reasons, Marxist doctrine never really entered the country in any important form. Ziya Gökalp, the influential Turkish thinker who preceded Ataturk, pronounced against Marxism and the doctrine of the class war. Ataturk himself, as we have seen, was no Com-

* The Russians did protest, rather feebly, some time later.

munist. The doctrine of the Ataturk period was Kemalism: but what was Kemalism? The famous Six Principles were all vague enough to be argued either way by ingenious debaters.

The one serious attempt to provide a theoretical basis to Kemalism was made by the group of prominent intellectuals who published the periodical *Kadro* between 1932 and 1934. The three leading spirits in the group were: Şevket Sureyya Aydemir, a former Pan-Turanian who had also been a Communist; Yakup Kadri Karaosmanoglu, Turkey's best-known writer of the Ataturk generation; and Burhan Belge,* a brilliant publicist and polemical writer, who was right-hand man to Menderes after 1950, and came to grief, along with his master, in 1960.

Kadro's ideology was a curious mixture of Left and Right. It was typical of Turkey in that it eschewed all known doctrines of both camps. It managed to combine Communism and Fascism, Socialism and Liberalism. It was eclectic. But the paper had enormous influence in Turkey. It ceased publication in 1934, at Ataturk's wish, for reasons which are not quite clear. We shall see in a moment that this question of formulating Kemalism in terms of right or left is an important one. Let us now come back to the present day.

The first point to notice is that the extreme Left has no chance whatever, in the foreseeable future, of coming to power by normal democratic means. The Turkish Labour† party is tiny in political terms and hopelessly split. The various left groups outside parliament, though highly vocal, are not yet organized in any dangerous form. The Trades Unions are mostly committed to a vague moderate socialism. The Republican People's party declared, seven years ago, that it was 'left of centre' but nobody believes it is a left-wing party because it is paralysed by an internal struggle between socialist and conservative wings.

It is unnecessary to enumerate the various personalities and groups into which the Turkish Left is already divided so soon after its rebirth. Suffice to say that they are all, or appear to be, at loggerheads with each other. Despite this, the power of the extreme Left in Turkey is very considerable, partly because of the

---

* Burhan Belge had other claims to fame than having been a husband of Zsa-zsa Gabor, the one fact about him invariably mentioned by the foreign press.

† The TLP was banned in July 1971.

noise it makes and the brilliant writers it employs, but more because the various brands of extreme leftists, however much they may quarrel with each other, are together on fundamentals. They all agree that the democratic regime is no good, and has to go.

The real question, of course, is how far the growing din and volume of revolutionary leftism has influenced the army. The army may be genuinely reluctant to seize power in the form of an open coup, but it takes very seriously its role as the social conscience of Turkey. Though it is generally accepted that there are conflicting political currents in the army, there is evidence that the dominant ideology among the politically conscious middle and lower-rank officers may be Left rather than Right. How far left is the big question.

This is where the matter of doctrine has some importance. Whatever the army officers may or may not be, the army is Kemalist. Any new revolution, if it comes, will be made in the name of Ataturk. If the leftists can convince the radical officers that Kemalism equals Socialism, even Marxism, they have won the day. This of course is what they are busy doing. Of the six Kemalist principles the two most important, Etatism and Secularism, are more easily adaptable by Leftist than Rightist philosophies. Etatism can easily be identified with state ownership of production, distribution and exchange, which is the basis of Communism; while secularism can be interpreted as a fierce anti-clericalism or even atheism, both of which chime only too well with the concepts of the extreme Left.

*   *   *   *   *

Turkey in some ways resembles pre-revolutionary Russia or China: a country overwhelmed by unsolved problems, full of frustrated people champing for reforms, but with a political regime which appears unable to get them done. The colossal population increase, the paralysing unemployment, the absurd injustices of the land and tax systems, the underpaid creaking bureaucracy, the unchecked drift of peasants to the cities, the almost complete failure of the parliamentary regime to get on with the job, all this is bound to make Communism, as a system, seem increasingly attractive to many impatient Turks.

The last two years since 1970 have seen the rise of the Turkish

Peoples Liberation Army, small, well-knit, extreme left-wing, violent, anarchic. It is inspired by the ideals of Ho Chi-Minh and Guevara. The TPLA is responsible for much of the present unrest and violence. It is supported by Dev Genç, the extremist student body, and much of its activity originates from the Middle East Technical University in Ankara, where many left-wing student leaders at one time studied. Its philosophy is part idealistic, part purely destructive.

The extreme Left, though they pay lipservice to the great Ataturk, almost openly regard his reforms as 'bourgeois' and superficial. For them Westernization v. Islam is a false issue. Westernized intellectuals and religious reactionaries, in their eyes, are *both* conservative forces. Turkey is a pre-revolutionary country and the 'real' revolution is still to come.

These are the 'Neo-Kemalists'. Dogan Avcioglu outlines the thesis towards the end of his massive book: 'In the dynamic conditions of modern Turkey the task of the Neo-Kemalists is to push Ataturk's revolution further, to carry it deeper, and to apply it to the foundation of things. . . . It is a task of the utmost difficulty, in which stubborn obstacles will need to be overcome.' His final chapter has a suitably apocalyptic title: 'The road to power'.

11 ❊ *Right-wing Currents*

THE LEFT is fairly comprehensible in Turkey because at least it is founded on Marxism; the Right is a much more shadowy and conglomerate affair. It is associated with the religion, because Islam is a powerful conservative force in Turkey. There are also Pan-Turkist and racist currents, traditionalists, extreme nationalists, and all the heterogeneous elements in the country – big business, rich landowners, feudal lords, and parts of the army (mainly the upper reaches) – which fear a Communist takeover. Many of these right-wing elements borrow strength from the great powerhouse of Islam.

The labels 'right' and 'left' hardly make sense in a country like Turkey, where it is usually difficult to say what parties stand for. Often they are mere groups gathered round a sort of tribal leader, with no comprehensible programme. The extreme right-wing National Order party,* founded in January 1970 as a breakaway from the ruling Justice party, seemed to stand secretly for the restoration of the Caliphate and Koranic Law (to do so openly is illegal), and for a complete return of Turkey to the Islamic world; at the same time the party violently attacked capitalism. It peddled a brand of Islamic socialism which is a potent mixture in Turkey because it promises the people two things they most want: religion and material progress.

Equally the Nationalist Action party, led by Colonel Turkesh, has Pan-Turkist and racist leanings, yet at the same time is radical-reformist. Most Turkish parties have elements of right and left in them, and there is hopeless confusion about principles. Politicians sometimes resign from one party and pass blandly to another at the very opposite end of the political spectrum. The Republican People's party, though it calls itself 'left of centre', is in fact torn between conservative and socialist wings, and it is difficult to say which is stronger. The one wholly leftist organization is the Turkish Labour party, which, like the Bolsheviks in Russia before 1917, regards all the other parties as conservative.

* Banned in May 1971.

The right-wing parties are something of a lunatic fringe, but are dangerous because they make play with two strong (though in the past contradictory) forces in Turkey: religion and nationalism. Both Nationalist Action party and National Order party constantly have photographs taken of their leaders praying in mosques during election campaigns, and the photos are given the widest publicity. Both parties are violently opposed to birth control, on grounds that it would 'hamper the development of the great Turkish nation'.

The best-known figure on the right is Colonel (retd.) Alparslan Turkesh, one of the most prominent of the thirty-eight officers who seized power in May 1960, and leading personality of the 'fourteen' who wanted to stay and carry out 'radical reform'. Turkesh, aged fifty-five, and leader of the Nationalist Action party, claims to stand by the democratic regime, but has been remarkably unsuccessful in democratic politics. His party won only a single seat in the 1969 elections. He may still be a man to watch, however, if only because of the unknown number of officers in the forces who think like him.

Turkesh is an ambitious and to many people a slightly sinister figure, whose alleged Pan-Turanist and racist tendencies make what minorities there are left in Turkey feel queasy from time to time. The Left call him mockingly the 'Bashbug' (Commander-in-Chief of the old central Asian Turks), and the 'mighty colonel'. His party has a trained corps of 10,000 young commandos, the 'Grey Wolves', which is unpleasantly evocative of the Hitler Youth Movement. They march about singing nationalist songs, raiding night-clubs and what they call 'nests of immorality', and generally making a nuisance of themselves. Their nationalism is pushed to absurd lengths. The Ankara headquarters of the Nationalist Action party has a swimming-pool shaped, most uncomfortably, in the form of the island of Cyprus.

In the previous chapter I gave the impression that any new upheaval in Turkey would necessarily be leftist; but could there be a right-wing pre-emptive coup, as in Greece? How many friends has Colonel Turkesh in the armed forces? It is logical to assume that, if the composition of the officer corps reflects that of the educated classes as a whole, there must be extreme right- as well as left-wing officers. Others, perhaps, are merely 'reformist', without being consciously right or left. Kemalism, though the left-wing interpretation of it has been to the fore in recent years, is still vague enough to form the basis of a right-wing radical movement. A right-left split in the army would of course be extremely dangerous, as it could lead to civil war.

What is virtually certain is that the religious reaction, in the sense of a government committed to the restoration of the Caliphate, Koranic law, and so forth, and the undoing of Ataturk's work, has no chance of coming to power. An army takeover is bound to declare itself 'Kemalist', and though Kemalism, as we have seen, has come to mean many things to many men, it still does not quite mean all things to all men. An entirely reactionary regime cannot come to power, because the whole of the officer corps, judiciary, intellectuals, writers, youth, and other so-called 'sound forces' of Kemalism, are against it. This can be ruled out. On the other hand a right-wing takeover by extreme nationalists or anti-Communists is not impossible.

One has to realize the vast importance of nationalism in modern Turkey. Ataturk made it one of the key-principles of the Republic. In the 1924 Constitution it came second after Republicanism itself. In the 1961 Constitution it is again enshrined in Article 2. But in Turkey nationalism is not a perquisite of right-wing parties only. The Left is as nationalistic as the Right. This it has in common with many countries of the world (for example North Vietnam), where extreme leftist nationalist regimes have come to power.

What one can say, almost for sure, is that the ferocious nationalism of the extreme Left would make it impossible for Turkey, if it went left, to become a satellite of the Soviet Union on the model of the countries of eastern Europe. This does not mean that an extreme left-wing regime in Ankara would not collaborate closely with the Russians (such as in the matter of the Straits), if it suited Turkey's interests.

*　　*　　*　　*　　*

The third so-called 'right-wing' doctrine is Pan-Turkism. This needs to be mentioned because it is an important element in the Turkish make-up. Pan-Turkism is based on the sense of consanguinity which many Turks of Turkey feel with the great belt of Turkish peoples living in the Soviet Union and China (about 40 million in all). From time to time there have been attempts to unite all these peoples into a single vast state, on the lines of Pan-Slavism, Pan-Arabism, or Pan-Germanism. Enver tried to do it after the First World War, and in fact it was the cause he died for. Ataturk dropped the idea, mainly because its realization would have presupposed the break-up of the Soviet empire, which was hardly compatible with being on good terms with the Russians. There was a revival of Pan-Turkism in Turkey in 1942, when German advances into Soviet territory seemed likely to lead to a Russian defeat. Colonel Turkesh (at the age of twenty-five) was an active Pan-Turkist at this time.

Pan-Turkism should be distinguished from Pan-Turanianism. The latter aims at the unification, not only of all Turks, but all peoples of 'Turanian' origin: this would include Hungarians, Finns, Esthonians, Bulgars, Yakuts, Tungus, Mongols, etc. That seems a hardly practicable aim; but Pan-Turkism, because of the geographical proximity of Turkey to the Turkish republics of central Asia, and the fact that together they would make a more or less compact block, is a slightly more feasible prospect.

I describe Pan-Turkism as a 'so-called' right-wing doctrine because there seems no evidence that it does not also exist, at least in the form of extreme nationalism, on the Left. It is generally called 'right-wing' because it is confused with racism. Turkish racism is, however, an even greater absurdity than other forms of racism. The Nazis at least had their blonde blue-eyed Aryan to work on. There is no such Turkish or 'Turanian' type. The Turks of modern Turkey, as we have seen, are a far more mixed race than the Germans, or even the British. They probably have as much Greek or Armenian in them as Turk. It would perhaps be possible to isolate a pure Turkish type in central Asia, but not in Anatolia.

Ataturk renounced Pan-Turkism because he was against territorial expansion and wanted good relations with Russia. But this does not mean Pan-Turkism is not latent in Turkey and could not re-emerge, as it did in 1942. The Turks, having governed one of the world's largest empires, were reduced after the First World War to the status of a relatively small republic. There is evidence that Pan-Turkist aspirations still exist, perhaps as an emotional substitute for the loss of empire. At a Congress of the Nationalist Action party not long ago, one of the delegates was frantically applauded by his audience when he declared excitedly: 'Let us create a mighty state of 100 million Turks!'

I remember a conversation I once had at a cocktail party with a Turkish officer in the 1960 Junta (not Colonel Turkesh), who made a very similar statement. I had asked him what Turkey aimed at. The officer (who had had a few drinks) replied: 'Our first aim is to create a nation of 50 million Turks. Our second is to join hands with all the other Turks in the world.' Incidentally, this officer described himself as a 'leftist'. His wife, a sophisticated westernized lady, told me how she had recently met a group of Turks from central Asia. She was enthusiastic about this 'thrilling experience'. 'They have the same mentality as we,' she said.

So long as the strongly pro-Western element in the Turks is uppermost, such feelings are rarely expressed; but occasionally the cat slips out of the Pan-Turkist bag. I often feel that if the Turks are rejected from Europe, or for any reason become fundamentally embittered with the West, Pan-Turkism might revive in Turkey. I now want to say something about the philosophic background to these ideas, which is interesting and comparatively little known in the West.

*　　*　　*　　*　　*

Pan-Turkism is associated with the name of Ziya Gökalp (pronounced 'Gerkalp'), who lived from 1876 to 1924. Gökalp is the leading Turkish thinker of the twentieth century. He reminds one slightly of Nietzsche, in his strong language and downright opinions; and more than any other writer he pored over the problems of the Turks. His writings were immensely influential in Turkey, especially in that fluid period towards the end of the empire, when there was more freedom of thought than there has been since the rigid orthodoxy imposed by Kemalism.

Gökalp came from Diyarbakir, the fine old Roman city in south-east Turkey. This is a mainly Kurdish area. But Gökalp always denied he was a Kurd, and claimed that, even if he was, the question was irrelevant, because he *felt* a Turk. Whatever his real ethnic origin, he became the leading prophet of Turkish nationalism. Many of his ideas, but not all, were later incorporated in

Ataturk's reforms. In some things Ataturk did not follow Gökalp, mainly in matters connected with the religion. Gökalp would have kept the Caliphate, whereas Ataturk abolished it. Unlike Ataturk, he had a religious background, and if he had lived would probably have tried to sponsor some kind of reform of Islam.

Gökalp was convinced that the Turks had to be completely in either the western or the eastern civilization. 'There can be no nation with two civilizations,' he wrote. Like Ataturk, he wanted his people to be fully in the western. He admitted that Islam was a problem ('it is religion that separates us from Europe'), but maintained that religion and civilization were two different things. It was a confusion of thought to talk about the 'Christian' and the 'Islamic' *civilizations*. He argued that the Turks and the Byzantines, though of different religions, had *together* belonged to what he called the 'eastern civilization'. This meant that peoples of different religions could belong to the same civilization; thus there was no reason why the Turks, while remaining Muslims, should not belong to the West.

Gökalp maintained that Islam, far from being a source of backwardness, was 'the most modern religion', and in no way conflicted with modern science. In order to prove the progressiveness of Islam, he advanced the curious notion that Protestantism in Europe was a move away from Christianity towards the principles of Islam – a form of 'Islamicized Christianity', as he expressed it. Industrial progress in the Protestant countries had been made possible by breaking free from the authority of Rome. This was similar to Islam, because Islam too was a religion without central authority. Thus the western countries had made progress by becoming like Islam. I am not competent to pronounce on this theory; I merely give it as an example of Gökalp's thinking. It seems not to explain, however, why no Muslim country has yet reached the level of a modern industrial state.

Before Gökalp's time Pan-Turkist ideas had already been launched by foreign Turcologists such as the Frenchman Léon Cahun and the Hungarian Arminius Vambéry, whose researches had shown that the Turks belonged to a great and ancient nation with a cultural tradition going back centuries before Islam. In 1897, some celebrated verses by the Turkish poet Mehmet Emin had started with the words:

'I am a Turk, my religion and race are noble'
and had continued:

'We are Turks; with this blood and this name we live'.

To understand the great impact of these lines one must realize that for centuries, under the Ottoman empire, the word 'Turk' had been an object of scorn and contempt to the Ottoman upper classes, for whom it had meant a 'yokel', a 'bumpkin', or a 'clod'. In those times anybody of importance called himself, not a 'Turk', but an 'Ottoman'. 'Turk' meant an ignorant peasant. The Turks under the empire had lost all pride in their race; they were so used to being called stupid by the Ottoman genteel classes (most of whom lived in Istanbul and never went near a village), that they had come to believe it themselves. They had entirely forgotten their pre-Ottoman past, until they were suddenly reminded of it by Mehmet Emin's poem, and later, as we shall see, by the writings of Gökalp.

More stupendous still in restoring Turkish self-confidence (to anticipate), was a remark by Ataturk in the 1920's:

'He's a lucky fellow who can say "I am a Turk".'

The impact of this one tremendous dictum by Mustafa Kemal has lasted to the present day in Turkey, and is renewed in every generation of Turks which hears it. It shows the extent to which, under the empire, people had been taught to suppose that it was nothing but a misfortune to be a Turk.

Gökalp thrilled the Turkish intelligentsia of the day with his concept of a vast Turkish nation stretching from the Danube to the China Sea. He claimed kinship with such peoples as the Huns, Mongols, Tartars, even Scythians, Hittites and Sumerians. (In this he was followed by Ataturk.) He praised the good qualities of the ancient Turkish civilization: its courage, tolerance, uprightness, and lack of imperialistic ambition, where there had been complete equality between men and women, and (according to Gökalp) monogamy had been practised. He envisaged a state unifying not only all the Turkish peoples, but the Hungarians, Finns, and Bulgars. This was the Pan-Turanian ideal. In 1911 Gökalp*

* There is a first-class English translation of selections from Gökalp's works: *Turkish nationalism and western civilisation*, translated and edited by Professor Niyazi Berkes. Columbia Press 1959.

published his most famous poem, 'Turan', the last couplet of which read:

The country of the Turks is not Turkey, nor yet Turkestan
Their country is a broad and everlasting land, Turan.

Under these influences Turkish minds were turned back to the origins of their race, to such forgotten realms as the *Gökturk* empire, which between the sixth and eighth centuries AD had stretched from the Caspian Sea to the Great Wall of China. It may not have been a very attractive region, consisting as it did mainly of inaccessible deserts and mountains; but in the eyes of romantic Pan-Turkists it was *their* country, *their* homeland. For them the Caspian and Aral Seas, or Lake Baikal in Siberia, were Turkish inland lakes; they dreamt continuously of such places as Bokhara, Samarkand, and Tashkent – Turkish cities – or of men like Tamerlane – a Turkish conqueror.

It is interesting to note that when the officers of the 1960 junta were asked, in press interviews, which historical figures they most admired, most of them (including the revolutionary leader General Gursel) replied 'Tamerlane'. Many Turks today are proud to claim relationship with the Huns and Mongols, and names such as Attila and Jenghiz are common in modern Turkey. When, in 1959, President Bayar had an audience of the Pope, several Turkish newspapers wrote with the utmost seriousness that this was the first meeting between a Pope and a Turkish President since Attila had met Leo the Great in AD 452. Attila, to us a monster, was in their eyes a Turkish head of state.

Strange semi-mystical concepts filled the minds of the Pan-Turkists, such as the 'mountains of Ergenekon', supposed to be somewhere in the Altai range in north-east Asia, where in some legendary period the ancestors of the Turks had taken refuge from the assaults of the Chinese and had lived for four hundred years in a sort of Turkish Shangri-La. Another curious Turkish ideal is *Kizilema*, the 'red apple', a sort of prophecy of a Turkish promised land somewhere in the West. It was variously associated with the orb of Justinian, the dome of St. Peters in Rome, or some European goal of Ottoman conquest, Rome, Vienna or Granada, never achieved. Along with these vague ideas went a feeling of community with all the Turkish and Turanian peoples in the world – a great

brachycephalic solidarity, and a mystical nostalgia for the bound-
less spaces of the Russian and Siberian steppe, where Turks and
Russians had lived side by side, and which created between these
two peoples, so hostile to each other in recent history, the common
bond of the steppes – agoraphilia, the love of great spaces. These
romantic departments of the Turkish soul were stirred by exciting
currents of Pan-Turanianism which swept Turkey in the last
years of the Sultans. In 1914 Ziya Gökalp started a new poem,
this time with a more aggressive tone:

> The land of the enemy shall be devastated,
> Turkey shall be enlarged and become Turan.

(One should remember that Turkey and Russia were on opposite
sides in the First World War.)

These ideas were adopted enthusiastically at the time by many
well-known Turks, such as the authoress Halide Edip, and Omer
Seyfettin, another distinguished writer, but they are soft-pedalled
today, and outwardly regarded as a little absurd. They were later
abandoned even by Gökalp himself, and were rejected completely
by Ataturk. But Gökalp's original idea was that Turkey would take
the lead in the unification of all the Turks of Asia, in the same way
as Prussia did in the unified German state.

Though Ataturk gave up Pan-Turkism in the political sense, he
followed Gökalp in giving the Turks pride in their 'Turkishness'
and making them conscious of their pre-Islamic past. One aspect
of this was the extraordinary reform of the Turkish language,
begun in Ataturk's time, in which thousands of Arabic and Persian
words were ejected and replaced by pure Turkish words. Ataturk
also sponsored the Sun Language theory, which said that all
languages in the world were derived from Turkish, and propound-
ed the idea that the Sumerians, Hittites, and Etruscans, and even
the Irish and Basques, were Turks. These theories encouraged
many Turks to feel they were the race from which all the peoples
of the earth had sprung.

In this context, it is interesting to see what young Turks are
taught in the way of history. The following passages are taken
from one of the history-books of Ataturk's time, which, I am told,
is still widely used today. According to this book, there was
originally a great sea in central Asia called the 'Turkish Sea',

which later dried up and became a desert, forcing the Turks to become nomads. An eastern branch of the Turks, rather before this catastrophe, had migrated to China and founded the Chinese civilization in about 7000 B.C. Ideogram inscriptions show them to have been an agricultural people who worshipped the sky, earth, water, sun, and stars. The book goes on:

> The civilization established by the Turks in China, by its civilized learnings, its high morals, its pure and simple religion, kept its reputation up to recent times, as one of the world's most important civilizations.

Another column of Turks, it seems, entered India and founded civilization there. In India, according to the book, there was no native civilization, but merely 'dark-skinned peoples resembling flocks of monkeys'. The Turks who penetrated to the far south of the subcontinent came later to be called Dravidians.

Other groups of Turks forged north-west into Europe (the Celts), southwards into Syria, Palestine, Egypt, and along the North African coast into Spain. Turks who settled in the Aegean and eastern Mediterranean founded the Cretan civilization. The book continues:

> 'Until recently it was believed that an independent Greek civilization had extended over the whole of the Mediterranean basin. In the then limited state of historical knowledge, this civilization was confined to the Greeks. ... Later, when a broader view was taken of the origin and spread of civilizations, this primitive view was dropped. It was realized that the whole system of religious belief, tradition, science and art came from previous civilizations, in particular that of the Hittites.
>
> The Phrygian and Lydian civilizations, which people had thought were connected with the Greek civilization, were in fact a continuation of the civilizations of western Anatolia, in particular the Hittite.'

The theory at this time was, of course, that the Hittites had been Turks.

Western Anatolia was also the source of the Roman civilization, the book goes on, because it is certain that the Etruscans, who founded the Roman civilization, came to Italy from Anatolia. As for Europe:

> 'The Turks who followed the route past the Black Sea and Caspian penetrated deep into Europe and reached the Atlantic Ocean. Some of the first to arrive crossed the sea and occupied Great Britain and Ireland. . . . Almost nobody today disputes that a number of artistic periods in Europe were initiated by these migrations. . . . The migrants, who were far above the nations of Europe in ideas, art, and knowledge, rescued the Europeans from their cave-life and set them on the road to intellectual development.'

This account of things, which is still taught in Turkish schools today, is accompanied by a large map of the world in which the whole of central Asia, from the Caspian Sea to Mongolia – the original Turkish homeland – is coloured in red. From this central mass snakelike arrows wriggle outwards all over the globe to mark the Turkish migrations. I mention this, not in order to make fun of it – I am not enough of an ethnologist or historian to know whether there is any truth in these assertions – but simply to show what a different view of the past is obtained by educational methods in different countries.

Once, when I first arrived in Turkey, I spent some time attending classes in the University of Ankara to improve my knowledge of the language. One of these was a history class. History as set forth above was being taught by one of the most serious professors, with the help of the map showing the snakelike migrations. At the end of one of these lessons I asked some of the students whether they believed this version of history. Several replied without hesitation 'Yes'; others smiled, looked sheepish, or said that the book was 'out of date'. From this I concluded that, although this history is still taught as an encouragement to the national pride of the Turks which Ataturk considered so necessary, not all the younger generation take it seriously.

One of the greatest literary benefits to the Turks, in Turkish eyes, was performed by H. G. Wells in his *Outline of History*. In this book Wells was supposed to have shown the services rendered by the Turks to civilization, and by so doing to have done much to reconcile them with the West. On Ataturk's orders, the book was translated at break-neck speed into Turkish, and copies were distributed all over the country. One can still see it today, a massive volume in the Arabic script, full of illustrations. Wells, along with Lamartine, Pierre Loti, Disraeli, and others, took an honoured place in the pantheon of 'friends of the Turks', in contrast to Gladstone, Lloyd George, Byron, Lawrence, Peter the Hermit, and other anti-Turkish villains.

12 ✽ *Turkey, Russia and the West*

TURKEY lies at a vastly important geographical fulcrum where many forces and ideologies converge. Europe and Asia, Christianity and Islam, Communism and Arabism and not-yet-dormant Hellenism, all meet each other in or around Turkey. It is the point where the Soviet southward thrust impinges on the Middle East. Turkey holds the Straits and the Anatolian peninsula: the first a unique waterway, the second a land-mass of great strategic value. It is occasionally suggested that, with the development of ICBM's and other long-range weapons, the Straits and Anatolia have lost their significance, but such arguments seem hardly valid. With Soviet naval presence in the Mediterranean and beyond now one of the chief aims of Moscow's policy, the Straits are as important as ever, while Anatolia is still the physical barrier to Russian expansion southwards. These features might lose their relevance in a nuclear holocaust, but short of such a cataclysm they remain crucial.

In 1949, when Turkey applied for membership of NATO, there was opposition from other members. It was argued that by no stretch of the imagination could Turkey be regarded as a North Atlantic power, and to include her would cause a dangerous extension of the alliance eastwards. In fact it has always been something of a mystery how NATO, in the event of a sudden Soviet aggression in eastern Anatolia, could fulfil its obligations to Turkey. This is one of the main considerations which have led the Turks, in recent years, to seek a rapprochement with Russia. For the same reason the Turks have always preferred the old NATO policy of 'massive retaliation' to the new one of 'flexible response'. In Turkish eyes the advantages of NATO membership are certainly more marginal today than they were.

It is worth envisaging for a moment the international repercussions of some upheaval in Turkey, which installed, say, a Soviet-friendly regime in Ankara and took Turkey out of the alliance. Not only would the West be deprived of the large NATO infrastructure which for years has been built up in the country, but such an event would be a major victory for the Soviets in a positive sense. It would relieve them of all serious anxiety about passage through the Straits, outflank Iran, intensify pressure on Israel, and create what would almost amount to a continuous chain of Soviet-aligned states down through the Middle East into Africa. The linch-pin of the area, seen from the western viewpoint, would be removed. The loss of Turkey, the only stable rock amid the shifting sands of the Arab-African world, would be sure to send a profound psychological shock through the capitals of the West.

I am not suggesting that this is imminent, merely underlining the geopolitical importance of Turkey, which many people forget or take for granted. Detachment of Turkey from the West is a persistent goal of Soviet policy. Among other things, the problem of the Straits is not finally solved for Moscow. The Montreux Convention (of 1936) gives Turkey complete discretion in wartime, or even in a situation where Turkey judges there is 'imminent danger of war', to close the Straits to foreign warships. This means that in the event of war between Russia and the West, a belligerent Turkey could cut the Soviet Mediterranean fleet off from its Black Sea bases. Put bluntly, a neutralist or pro-Soviet Turkey would presumably not do this, but a Turkey allied to the West would certainly come under pressure to do so. It is in the light of this consideration that we should look at one of the most important developments of the last years, the Turco-Soviet rapprochement.

Relations with Russia have always been vital for Turkey. The Turks have a frontier of 366 miles with the Soviet Union and another 124 miles with Communist Bulgaria. The long exposed Turkish Black Sea coast directly faces Russia. Turkey has to be perennially cautious in dealing with her vast northern neighbour. Her position is especially delicate when she has some treaty relationship with the West. It is worth remembering that in October 1939, when Turkey concluded an alliance with Britain and France at the start of the Second World War, the Turks insisted on the inclusion of a special protocol, of a highly unusual kind in international treaties, providing that under no circumstances could the alliance with the two powers involve Turkey in war with the Soviet Union. This illustrates the extreme delicacy of Turkey's position.

The Turks

Moscow's aggressive attitude towards Turkey in 1946, demanding territorial concessions in eastern Anatolia and Soviet bases on the Straits, drove the Turks to look for support in the West, and in 1952 to become members of NATO. Throughout the 1950's, the period *par excellence* of the cold war, tension between Ankara and Moscow was acute. The first break in this situation came in 1959, when Menderes, unable to obtain the economic aid he needed from the United States, started to look northwards. Menderes had arranged a visit to Moscow for July 1960, but was overthrown by the army coup two months before. Later, inevitably, the CIA was credited with having engineered his downfall because he was getting too friendly with the Russians. If so, it was a singular error of judgement by the Americans, because the successors of Menderes went much further than he did. Whereas Menderes's projected trip had the appearance of a crude attempt to blackmail the West into giving Turkey more money, subsequent Turkish governments made clear that the changed relationship with the Soviets was something desirable for its own sake.

The Turco-Soviet rapprochement proper began in 1963 under Inönü and the Republicans, but has been continued, and in some ways pushed further, by the right-wing Justice party. One can assume from this that the rapprochement has the approval of the army. The rapprochement is officially explained in Ankara as merely a rational consequence of the softening of the cold war, in the sense that as the Americans and other NATO allies are talking amicably with the Russians there is no earthly reason why the Turks should not do so too. Why should Turkey be *plus royaliste que le roi*? This is true, of course, but it is not the whole story.

In fact the Turks have gone further in friendly relations with the Soviets than can be explained in this way. There is something like co-operation between the two countries. They have taken a similar pro-Arab line on the Middle East. On Cyprus they are together in opposing *Enosis*. Recent visits by Turkish and Russian leaders to each other's countries, give an impression of increasing understanding and confidence between the two old enemies. In addition Turkey is taking about 366 million dollars worth of Soviet credits (the only member of NATO to do so), in the form of large-scale industrial projects, such as the big steel mill at Iskenderun.

When the rapprochement started in 1963, it was seen as a tactic by Turkey to gain support from her northern neighbour in the Cyprus conflict, which at that time seemed to be going seriously against her. It is arguable, however, that the true nature of the operation was rather the reverse: that the Cyprus issue was used by the Turks as a means to obtain a more independent position within the western alliance, thereby facilitating the approach to Russia which was anyway needed in Turkey's interests. Seen in the whole context of Turco-Russian relations in the last fifty years, the latter interpretation may be nearer the truth. The rapprochement is a normalization, rather than an aberration, of Turkish policy.

If one examines Turkish-Russian relations since 1920 one can see that these have been friendly, or reasonably co-operative for at least as long as they have been hostile. The extreme tension between the two countries between 1946 and 1960, sandwiched between relatively friendly periods before and since, was the result of Stalin's unwise pressure in 1946 which drove Turkey into the American camp. One of the first acts of the Soviet Government after the death of Stalin was to reassure the Turks that territorial claims on their country were finally renounced. The Turks, after what they had gone through in 1946, were at first wary about believing these assurances; but the diplomatic skill and apparent sincerity of the Russians (for their own ends) seem gradually to be overcoming Turkish suspicions.

* * * * *

An important fact about Turco-Soviet relations, which is often forgotten or soft-pedalled, is the extent to which Mustafa Kemal's nationalist movement in 1919 was directly helped by the Russian revolution. It is not merely that Lenin assisted the Turkish War of Independence with Russian money, arms, and other forms of support; it is rather that Kemal's whole successful struggle, culminating in the Treaty of Lausanne of 1923, might have been impossible if the Bolshevik revolution had not occurred. The friendship of revolutionary Russia was vital for Ataturk, who was fighting against desperate odds in the west, by securing his eastern front and ensuring he would not be taken in the rear by a Russian attack from the Caucasus. The Turkish-Russian Treaty of

Friendship, signed by Ataturk and Lenin in March 1921, was for Turkey a Reinsurance Treaty.

It is highly improbable that Czarist Russia, if it had not been overthrown in 1917, would have sided with the Turkish nationalists. It is much more likely, in the light of Moscow's historic designs on Constantinople and the Straits, that it would have supported the Treaty of Sèvres, which drastically dismembered Turkey in 1920.* Sèvres, if it had been implemented, would virtually have ended Turkey's independent existence, whereas the Treaty of Lausanne, the fruit of Kemal's victories, gave his country roughly its present frontiers. The vital difference for Turkey between the two treaties is expressed in the Turkish saying: 'Sèvres, death; Lausanne, life'.

The Bolsheviks, for their part, were deceived into thinking that Mustafa Kemal was a Communist, and he skilfully led them up the garden path in this respect. The result was that the immense territory to the north and east of Turkey was friendly, relieving Kemal on this score and allowing him to concentrate on the war in the West. Though Turkey's debt to the Russian Revolution is not often stressed today (partly for electoral reasons, since it is always assumed that the ordinary Turk is violently anti-Russian), it creates a bond of sympathy between the Russians and the heirs of the Kemalist tradition inside Turkey. It is curious to reflect, in the light of the extreme anti-Communism which for forty years has been such a feature of Turkey's internal politics, that the Bolshevik revolution was one of the events which most enabled Ataturk to succeed.

The Turks, with the accumulated experience of Ottoman times behind them, are highly skilled at foreign relations. They have been remarkably successful in complex and difficult balancing-acts between the powers. The best example of this was in the Second World War, when Turkey, under President Inönü, managed not only to remain neutral during almost the whole of a global conflagration so near to her borders, but maintained simultaneous treaties of alliance or friendship with Allies, Axis, and Russia. This was an amazing piece of acrobatics. In face of strong British and American pressure to enter the war, the Turks argued that for

* What the Western Powers would have done in such a case is an interesting question.

Turkey the Soviet danger was as great, if not greater than, the German – and in fact was perennial. If Turkey had been even partially occupied by the Nazi armies, a Soviet 'liberation' on the post-war model in eastern Europe might well have been her fate. This argument was understood by the Allies, though Churchill and Roosevelt were disappointed by the Turkish stand.

Inönü was again at the helm in 1963 and 1964, the years in which the origin of the Turco-Soviet rapprochement coincided with one of the most serious outbreaks of trouble in Cyprus. The sequence of events is an interesting one. Shortly after the Cuba crisis in November 1962, when the Russians climbed down by removing their rockets from the island, American Jupiter missiles were withdrawn from Turkey. It was officially explained by Washington that the Jupiters were out-of-date, and were in any case no longer needed on Turkish soil because Turkey would in future be defended by Polaris submarines based in the Mediterranean. It was rumoured at the time, and has since been virtually confirmed (not least by Mr. Inönü himself), that this mutual withdrawal of weapons by the Soviet Union and the United States was a piece of horse-trading between the two nuclear super-powers. The Ankara government seems not to have been consulted on this decision by its American allies.

In May 1963, for the first time in thirty years, a large Turkish parliamentary delegation set forth on a visit to the Soviet Union, the initial step in what turned out to be the striking change of relationship between the two countries of the last nine years. This was the turning-point. From now on Turkey became cooler with America and warmer with Russia. At the end of 1963 violence flared up in Cyprus, and continued intermittently through much of 1964. We shall see now how Turkey's change of policy was eased by the development of the Cyprus conflict.

*   *   *   *   *

The essence of the Cyprus problem was, and is, that Turkey is adamantly opposed to *Enosis*, on grounds that union of the island with Greece would upset the strategic balance in the eastern Mediterranean established by the Treaty of Lausanne. Cyprus is only forty miles from the Turkish coast, and the long thin promontory of the island which stretches to the north-east is often romantically described as 'the dagger which points at Turkey's heart'. Cyprus of course belonged for more than three hundred years to the Ottoman empire, and most Turks even today regard the island simply as Turkish property. The traditional Turkish interest is expressed in the Senator's speech from *Othello*:

> When we consider
> Th'importancy of Cyprus to the Turk
> And let ourselves again but understand
> That, as it more concerns the Turk than Rhodes,
> So may he with more facile question bear it,
> For that it stands not in such warlike brace,
> But altogether lacks th'abilities
> That Rhodes is dress'd in; if we make thought of this,
> We must not think the Turk is so unskilful
> To leave that latest which concerns him first,
> Neglecting an attempt of ease and gain
> To wake and wage a danger profitless.

The gist of this rather sloppily-written Shakespearean passage is that Cyprus is much more important to the Turks than Rhodes. The canny senator warns the Duke of Venice not to be misled by an Ottoman feint in the direction of the latter island.

When I was working as a correspondent in Ankara, I once showed these verses to Dr. Galo Plaza, of Ecuador, one of the long succession of cheerful but cynical United Nations mediators who tried to solve the baffling little Cyprus conundrum. I remember him throwing his hands in the air in mock horror: 'For Heaven's sake don't show this to the Turks. Things are difficult enough, without Shakespeare!'

The early stages of the Cyprus conflict, in the mid-1950's, were mainly a struggle between the Greek Cypriots and the British colonial power, with the Turks at that time hardly interested in the island. There is strong evidence that the British government of the day deliberately encouraged an indifferent Turkey to take a more active interest, as a useful counter-weight in the struggle against the Greeks. One of the most violent expressions of this artificially contrived Turkish indignation was on the night of 6th–7th September 1955, when a terrifying Turkish mob destroyed quantities of Greek property in Istanbul. It should be noted that at the Yassiada trials in 1960 evidence was given by defence witnesses that the Turkish government had been put up to staging a Cyprus demonstration by the then British Foreign Secretary Mr. Harold Macmillan, but that the demonstration, mis-managed by Menderes, had degenerated into an uncontrollable riot. Though there has never been any confirmation of this story, it has a Palmerstonian touch about it which carries conviction.

Even at the most frenzied periods there were moments of comic relief in the Cyprus affair. When I arrived in Turkey in 1958, mass meetings were being addressed all over Turkey by the Turkish Cypriot leader Dr. Fazil* Küchük, at which the popular Turkish slogan was 'Partition or Death'. Two years later, when a Cyprus agreement excluding both partition and *enosis* as possible solutions to the problem was accepted by the Turkish government, one Turkish politician not ungifted with a sense of humour suggested that all the Turks who had been yelling 'Partition or Death' at mass meetings should commit suicide – a remark which was hardly well received by the people concerned.

* * * * *

There is no need here to go into the details and successive stages of the Cyprus problem (which is still unsolved today); I only want to show its function in relation to the Turco-Soviet rapprochement. The main issue in 1964 was whether Turkey, under the London and Zurich agreements of 1960, had a legal right to intervene in Cyprus, in a military sense, to prevent *enosis*. The agreements appeared to give her that right, but were open to differing interpretations. A Turkish invasion of Cyprus would have meant war between Turkey and Greece, two NATO allies, and this of course the United States and other members of the alliance were anxious to avoid. At one very critical moment in June 1964, when a Turkish invasion seemed imminent, President Johnson wrote a letter to the Turkish Prime Minister Mr. Inönü, apparently couched in rather blunt Texan language, informing him that if Turkey invaded Cyprus, and as the result of an ensuing conflagration was involved in war with Russia, Turkey's NATO allies would have to consider whether in such circumstances they would be under any obligation to help her.

* Pronounced Fuzzle.

It is a matter of opinion, of course, whether the Turks at this time were seriously contemplating an armed move against Cyprus. It is my personal opinion, having observed the crisis at close quarters, and knowing Mr. Inönü's natural caution, that they were *not*. But the 'Johnson letter' has never been forgotten in Turkey. It was held by most Turks to be not only an affront, by its use of language, but as symbolic of the fact that the United States had abandoned Turkey on a matter of cardinal importance. There were violent demonstrations against the United States. From this time dates the rise of the strong anti-Americanism which is today obliging the Americans to keep what they engagingly describe as a 'low profile' in Turkey. The Johnson letter has been erected into a milestone of almost equal importance to the Soviet notes of 1946 demanding bases on the Straits – only in the reverse sense; driving them, not into, but out of, American arms. Turkish-American relations are today dated 'B.L.' and 'A.L.' ('before letter' and 'after letter'). The letter and its aftermath were skilfully used by the Turkish government as a justification for Turkey's gradual move to a position within the western alliance more independent of the United States and more friendly to Russia.

Turkey is not neutralist, and shows no immediate signs of becoming so. But her new relationship with the Soviet Union, and the large credits she is receiving from the Russians, mean that she is almost combining the advantages of non-alignment with membership of the western alliance. It has been described as 'Turkish Gaullism', and has certain features in common with de Gaulle's policy of independence of the United States and *entente* with Moscow. But it is not really a parallel, if only because Turkey's geographical position is completely different to that of France, and because Turkey possesses the Straits. The Straits are still the 'key to Russia's front door', and possession of the key to somebody's front door inevitably makes ones relations with that somebody a very special one. The facts of geography seem to condemn Turkey to be either the intimate friend or intimate enemy of her vast northern neighbour – but in either case intimate.

The Russians, of course, have important stakes to play for in their policy towards Turkey, and their first objective is probably still the Straits. Soviet pressure on Turkey in 1946 was based on arguments that the Turks had failed to apply the Montreux Convention, and had let Axis vessels pass through the Straits, thereby endangering Soviet security. These charges were staunchly refuted by the Turks, with moral backing from London and Washington. The Soviet moves drove Turkey into the western camp. Since then the Russians have changed their tune, but presumably not their aims. Under the present regime they may have almost completely free passage of the Straits, but so long as Turkey is in NATO Russia cannot be absolutely sure of the Straits. The Russians want Turkey out of NATO, which for them would virtually amount to a revision of the Montreux Convention by other means.

One aspect of the Straits which has perennially annoyed the Russians is that the narrowness of the Dardanelles, and more especially the Bosphorus (which is only five hundred yards wide in places), allows the Turks and their allies the closest check on Soviet warships passing from the Black Sea into the Mediterranean and back. There are people with powerful binoculars all over the banks of the Straits. It is obvious that Turkey, so long as she is a member of the western alliance, can pass on most useful information to her allies. On the other hand, the friendlier relations between Ankara and Moscow are, the more delicate Turkey's position between her western allies and her northern neighbour becomes.

An indirect success for Moscow is Turkey's pro-Arab stance on the Middle East, though the Turks have other reasons for this than a desire to please the Russians. The Turks, in general, regard the Arabs as a disorderly lot who were never better governed than they were from Constantinople. Turkey has no enthusiasm whatever for Arab nationalism or Arab unity – rather a permanent interest in keeping the Arabs divided. But in the last few years there has been a marked shift by the Turkish government towards the Arabs, partly for electoral reasons, to please the Muslim voters inside Turkey, but also because Turkey needs Arab support in the United Nations on the Cyprus issue.

In general, while relations with Moscow have improved, those with Washington have worsened. There has been a drastic reduction, not only in American economic aid to Turkey, but also in American military presence. Virtually all the American bases and installations are now being handed over to the Turks, or are coming under joint administration. But the Americans are keeping their hands on Injirlik, near Adana in south Turkey, which the Pentagon apparently still regards as vastly important, and in fact is the only American airbase for a long way east of Spain. Injirlik is the base which gives the Turks the greatest anxiety about being dragged into nuclear war, and there is a rising clamour for it also to be handed over, which the Americans have up to now firmly resisted.

The strident anti-Americanism of the last years has caused a big change in the relationship between the two countries. Visits of the 6th fleet to Turkey, which only a few years ago were still hailed with rejoicing, are now the occasion for riots and demonstrations. As part of the 'low profile' policy, the 6th fleet no longer calls at the big Turkish ports, such as Istanbul and Izmir, but at lesser harbours around the coasts. Such modest havens as Bodrum, Marmaris, Antalya, Alanya, and Mersin, have recently been astonished by the arrival of warships of the world's most powerful navy.

Turkey's strategic importance to the western alliance is still great, though perhaps not quite what it was. Some years ago, at the height of the cold war, an impressive map was published in *Le Monde* showing how nuclear weapons based in Anatolia could penetrate further into the Soviet Union than from any other NATO country, and could reach Soviet industrial complexes beyond the Urals. These advantages have since been rendered obsolete by the development of weapons whereby the great nuclear powers can obliterate each other comfortably from their own territories, making advanced bases like Turkey hardly required. Turkey is still useful as a listening-post to keep NATO informed about what goes on in the mysterious inner spaces of the Soviet Union, though the radar installations, early-warning systems, and tracking-stations with which Anatolia is stuffed have to some extent, it seems, been replaced by the work of communications satellites.

Turkey is unlikely to leave NATO or demolish her other links with the West so long as the democratic regime lasts in its present form. Both main political parties support the alliance, though Mr. Inönü has expressed periodic doubts about how NATO could effectively defend Turkey, and fears that his country might be dragged by the Americans into nuclear war. The only political group which definitely advocated withdrawal from NATO was the Turkish Labour party, but this party, besides being irremediably split, is at present negligible in political terms. As things stand, only a major upheaval seems likely to take Turkey out of the alliance.

13 ❋ *What are the Turks like?*

WHAT SORT of people are the Turks? It is time we came to this question, because we don't know the Turks too well. We had a few months of what might be called intimate enmity with them at Gallipoli in 1915, when we came to respect them as good soldiers, and in a way to like them. But we hardly knew them. We are probably more familiar with Arabs, Africans, Indians, even Chinese, because we have dealt with all these peoples over long periods in the empire.

Many Englishmen are somewhat vague even about the geographical whereabouts of Turkey. A London doctor I went to see before one of my visits to Ankara said cheerfully: 'So you're off to Turkey! Going through the Canal or round the Cape?' – as though the place were somewhere east of Suez.

We cannot know the Turks in the same way as the other nations mentioned, because they have never been colonized or governed, but have usually governed others. That they have always been masters in their own house is certainly one of the factors which have formed their character. I am not of course talking about the Turks of central Asia, who now live in the Soviet Union and China; their mentality, because they have been a governed people, is different to that of the Ottoman Turks, who for six centuries ruled a vast empire. Despite this, their origin in the deserts of Asia influences the character of the Turks, as does a thousand years of Islam, and six centuries of being half-in, half-out of, Europe.

This makes the Turk an unusually interesting being. You can't lump the Turks with any other group of peoples. They live in the Middle East, but they are utterly different to the Arabs. Most people would say they are not (yet) Europeans; but they are not Asiatics either. As being neither Asiatic nor European, or both perhaps, one can bracket the Turks most easily with their old enemies, but new friends, the Russians, with whom they have a good deal more in common than one might suppose.

We have seen what an enormous impression Ataturk made on his own people with the one sentence: 'He's a lucky man who can say "I am a Turk".' With that celebrated dictum Ataturk boosted the morale of the Turk. But another of Ataturk's lapidary phrases about his people had an impact almost as great. This was 'Biz bize benzeriz'* which means 'We resemble ourselves'. This curious apothegm, hardly less famous inside Turkey than the earlier one, came at the end of a speech in which Ataturk was comparing the political regime in Turkey with regimes in other countries. He concluded:

'So what does it matter if our regime does not resemble democracy, does not resemble socialism, does not resemble anything? Gentlemen, we should be proud of not resembling anything; because we resemble ourselves, gentlemen!'

Part of the charm of this remark came from the fact that it is an alliteration in Turkish, and alliterations are always attractive, as well as being easy to remember. The phrase has been exposed to a good deal of mockery in the outside world. People have savagely lampooned it as a truism, because of course all nations resemble themselves. What annoyed them about the dictum was that it implied that, though all nations were unique, the Turks were more unique than others. Yet, after living eight years among the Turks, I have often found myself thinking that Ataturk was right.

This may come partly from the fact that the Turks have migrated in relatively recent history, not only from one part of the world to another, but from one civilization to another. They are one of the few peoples, for example, who have three times changed the script they write in (Runic, Sogdian, Arabic, and now Roman). They have in them elements of Islam, Taoism, Shamanism, and Zorostrianism, and fragments of the Chinese and Byzantine cultures, as well as the modern European and western civilization, all mixed up together, while absorbing, during their habitation of Anatolia, many of the cults and practices of the innumerable peoples who lived there before them. At the same time, through all this extraneous matter, they have preserved intact the customs and traditions of the age-old Turkish race. The Turkish soul, as souls go, is an unusually complex one. I say this by way of

* Pronounced Bizz beezeh benzérriz.

introduction. I shall try now to give a fair portrait of the Turks as I see them.

*   *   *   *   *

The Turk is unusually full of contradictions. Not only has he East and West in him, Europe and Asia, but an intense pride combined with an acute inferiority complex, a deep xenophobia with an overwhelming hospitality to strangers, a profound need for flattery with an absolute disregard for what anybody thinks about him. Few peoples, capable of such holocausts, are at the same time so genuinely kind, helpful, magnanimous, and sincere, as the Turks are. This, I think, is what strikes people most strongly when they arrive for the first time in Turkey.

The Turk is lazy and apathetic; yet ask any factory boss in Europe who employs Turks, and he will tell you they are the hardest workers he has. Turks respect the authority of the state like few other peoples; yet have a passion for individual freedom. They pine for an autocrat to lead them; yet insist on democracy. They are dour and taciturn, emotional and eloquent. They are an unusually serious people; but their most popular mythical hero, Nasreddin Hodja, was so thorough-going a humourist that even his tomb is a joke. The gate to the tomb is tightly secured with a huge padlock, but, as there are no railings attached to it, anybody who wants to can walk in.

Those who fought the Turks at Gallipoli admired them, as veterans of the campaign will testify. It is curious that the extermination or deportation of the Armenians, carried out as deliberate policy by the Young Turk government in 1915, the event which in recent times gave the Turks such a savage name in the outside world, coincided exactly with the campaign which made many westerners appreciate their best qualities. This is perhaps typical of the contrasts in the Turkish nature.

It is true that the Turk, when goaded beyond a certain point, has something in him to which the familiar adjective 'terrible' applies. They themselves admit it. 'If a Turk ever gets really angry with you', a Turkish friend once said to me, 'you run for your sweet life!' As Aubrey Herbert put it:

> The Turk was unbusinesslike, placid, and lazy or long-suffering. But when he turned in his rage he poured out death

in a bucket, and guilty and innocent suffered from his blind
anger.

But it is equally true that under normal conditions the Turk is
the kindest, most helpful, most sincerely friendly man on earth.
It is as if his nature compensated its capacity for one extreme by
its habitual propensity to the other. During my time in Turkey I
came to appreciate the great understanding, courtesy, and humanity of the Turk, as well as his tact, and his avoidance of hurting
people's feelings. In all my eight years in the country no Turk
ever made a deliberately wounding personal remark to me, and
they always showed the greatest human understanding.

The Turks have an interesting relationship to money. Turkey
is a poor country: Turks know as well as anybody else the importance of money. But they have a disdain for it which is rare.
When I first arrived in Ankara I took a taxi from one part of the
capital to another, but found that I had not enough money on me
to pay the fare. The driver (who had never seen me in his life)
immediately relieved me of all anxiety. 'It is of no importance', he
said with a wave of the hand. 'You can pay me some other time.'
He did not even ask for my name and address. I gave them to him,
of course, and about a week later, certainly not earlier, he called on
me and collected the fare.

It is the same in shops. Go shopping in any quarter where you
have never been before, and find you have forgotten your money:
the shopkeeper will give you anything you want without payment,
apparently with complete confidence that you will not do him
down. Trust is of enormous importance to Turks. Any hint that
you do not trust a Turk causes deep chagrin. Furthermore the
Turks consider it quite beneath their dignity to appear preoccupied with money. This applies even in matters which in our
countries would be regarded simply as a business arrangement. I
shall give an example.

When I was a foreign correspondent in Turkey, I used to have
a Turkish journalist to help me. This was normal practice. The
Turkish journalist, working on his own newspaper, would keep
me informed about events I might otherwise have missed. It was
a regular job, sometimes involving quite hard work. Though the
Turkish correspondents who helped me in this way usually

became good friends, the actual work was regarded by me as a business arrangement. But whenever I engaged a man for the job my Turkish friends were reluctant in the extreme to discuss the question of payment. They gave the impression that the work should be done out of 'arkadaşlik' (comradeship or friendship), despite the fact that Turkish journalists are badly off, and what I had to offer, though modest, was a considerable addition to their income.

When, after a great show of reluctance, they condescended to accept payment, I had always to convey the money in a very particular manner. There was no question of taking banknotes out of one's pocket and handing them over. That would be far too crude, even if nobody else was present. I always put the money into a closed envelope. When payment-day arrived, I would visit my friend in his office. We would discuss the news, drink Turkish coffee or tea, talk about every subject under the sun. Finally, when I was about to leave, I would take the envelope out of my pocket and hand it to him hurriedly, while he, not even glancing at it, would put it straight into a drawer and shut the drawer with a bang, as if I had handed him something useful but quite unmentionable, such as a packet of contraceptives. It was at such moments that I particularly loved the Turks.

Among the Turks the most shameful of all crimes is theft. In fact, except in the big cities, it is almost unknown. I have been taken round Turkish prisons, large crowded prisons, where there was not a single thief. When a thief goes to prison, he is spat on and ostracized by the other prisoners, whereas murderers are the élite of the prison. Astonishingly enough, thieves are usually excluded from general amnesties from which even murderers profit. Many people might feel this to be a case of mistaken priorities; I, for one, would rather be robbed than killed. But contempt for stealing lies deep in the Turkish moeurs.

Their peculiar attitude to money does not make the Turk very gifted for business. The Turk was a nobleman, above anything so sordid as commerce. This was the way things grew up in Ottoman times, though presumably in earlier periods of their history, when the Turks had a pastoral existence on or near the great caravan routes which traversed Asia, they must have been familiar with trading. Toynbee has pointed out that Turkish minorities in Russia made excellent merchants, because they were obliged to engage in such pursuits. This shows that the nature of the Turk is not incompatible with commerce.

By 1923 almost all the minorities had left Turkey or been deported. The Turks had to take over the whole commercial and technical running of the country, which formerly had been done by the subject races. This is perhaps the greatest revolution the Turks have lived through, greater even than the Kemalist reforms, because they had to acquire aptitudes previously not needed. It was the first time the Turks had to bother about making money. The process of adaptation was difficult.

The Turks are aware of their own shortcomings in matters of commerce. I was talking once to a Turkish shipowner on a sea-front near Istanbul. He had a fleet of small freighters which plied along the Black Sea coast. He said: 'You British, Americans, and Greeks, will always outdo us in commerce. This is how we *Turks* do business' – and he took three large strides *backwards* along the quay. It was a bizarre but expressive gesture.

Lack of experience in commerce may come partly from the fact that the Turks are not traditionally a sea-going, but a land-based, people. A friend of mine, who lived for a time in a Turkish village by the coast, told me that the villagers took no interest whatever in the sea, and had no dealings with it, even for fishing. For them the sea, as my friend put it, was simply 'the place where the land ends'. Turkey's best seamen and fishermen are mostly Lazes, a Caucasian people who settled in the Black Sea region at some period in the past.

Today there are outstanding Turkish businessmen, industrialists, and technicians, even millionaires. Yet salesmanship seems not to go very easily with the Turkish nature. When I first arrived in Turkey one could enter a shop or store where one's presence was utterly ignored by the shopkeeper. His attitude was positively chilling, as if the last thing he wanted you to do was to *buy* anything. When finally one ventured to enquire whether a certain object was in stock, the salesman would scarcely deign to reply, but would merely indicate, by a well-known Turkish gesture, that the answer was No.

That gesture, an upward movement of the head, with half-closed eyes, and sometimes also the faintest click of the tongue, is the one which accompanies the famous Turkish negative 'YOK'.

This is the one word which all visitors to Turkey learn, however short their stay. 'Yok' is the negative to end all negatives; indeed could safely be defined as the quintessence of all negation.

Often the word itself is not pronounced, and the gesture alone suffices to convey the meaning. This gesture is one of the most irritating I know. It signifies not merely negation, but complete unconcern on the part of the person who uses it. That upward nod and weary closing of the eyes says not only 'This does not exist', but seems to add: '. . . and it is a matter of the utmost indifference to me whether it exists or not'.

An important Turkish characteristic is something which might be called indifference, apathy, or neglect. There is a certain Turkish amnesia, as if the Turk were given to some inner contemplation, and not quite intent on practical matters. (This makes the Turks rather incompetent waiters.) A Turk will sit for hours, telling the beads of a Muslim rosary, or listening to that interminable music which seems to induce in him a condition of terrestrial Nirvana. Basically, it seems to me, the Turk is a romantic dreamer, though of what he is dreaming it is hard to say. He also loves to indulge in sadness and gloomy forebodings. Turks tend to be natural Cassandras, prophesying doom. Most Turkish songs are sad songs.

The traditional Turkish scorn for money is perhaps linked with his national pride. One must never forget that the Turks are a people with a great imperial past. In a public park in Ankara there is a tremendous monument to Ataturk, adorned with superhuman figures, and inscribed with the words 'Be proud, work hard, be confident' (in that order). This was the great man's injunction to his people. A Turk's first duty is to be proud. The Turks have followed this advice. Among the many complex characteristics of the Turks, national pride is in daily evidence.

One day, in the town in western Turkey where I wrote this book, I went out for a walk and met a Turkish boy of about ten years old. He had never seen me before, and our conversation went as follows:

'Hi, Uncle, are you American?'
('Uncle' is the usual way for a child to address a grown man.)
'No, English.'

'You ought to have been a Turk.'
'And why, pray?'
'Because it is better to be a Turk.'
'How interesting!'
'If you like, we can make you a Turk.'
'Thanks, I prefer to stay as I am.'
'But Turks are best' (a statement of obvious fact).
'That is a matter of opinion.'
'Turks are best', the boy repeated with complete certainty.
'Why are you so sure?'
Silence. I repeat the question – twice.
More silence. Finally, with immense pride, out it comes:
'Because Ataturk threw the Greeks into the sea.'

(The winning of the War of Independence is of course a source of pride to all Turks, and this, for children at least, is the normal way of expressing it.)

As a Parthian shot I told him:

'We British threw the Germans into the sea – twice'; which, if not strictly true, gave him something to think about. I walked away, humming to myself the Bo'sun's song from *Pinafore*:

> But in spite of all temptations
> To belong to other nations
> He remains an Englishman.

Another example. One of my first visits in Turkey was to the tailor. I badly needed an evening suit. My measurements were taken, and a few days later I went for a fitting. The tailor had made an excellent start; but I ventured to point out, as tactfully as I dared, that I should be glad if the coat could be a shade shorter than he had made it. The tailor's reaction was unexpected. Drawing himself up to his full height (and he was a very tall man), he gave me to understand conclusively that there could be no question of making any changes in his creation. Turkish tailors were the best, if not the only, tailors in the world. The suit as he had cut it was exactly right. To suggest anything different was an insult to Turkish tailoring.

In the end, as we could not agree, I went to another tailor, and the first tailor was perfectly prepared to lose the material he had embarked on, as well as a promising customer. He didn't dream of asking for money. The second tailor, who has since made me a number of excellent suits, though a shade more accommodating, was almost equally proud. But I would like to end this episode by saying that Turkish tailors have something to be proud about. I have not met better tailors anywhere.

One sometimes hears astonishing outbursts of chauvinism in Turkey. My driver on a trip in south Turkey treated me to a lengthy tirade about the magnificence of the Ottoman empire, which according to him had engulfed, not only the entire Balkans and Middle East, but the whole of Italy and most of France and Germany as well (he modestly stopped at the English channel). He was convinced of the truth of this history and brushed all counter-argument aside. When we passed Anamur castle, on the south coast opposite Cyprus, he went into rhapsodies about this wonderful 'Turkish castle', ignoring a large notice which said that it was built in the third century AD, eight hundred years before the first Turks arrived in Anatolia. (In fact it is probably Armenian.)

My wife and I were once taken round the house of a rich cotton magnate in Adana, Turkey's fourth-largest city. In one of the many rooms of his sumptuous mansion was a picture of horsemen galloping into a city. My wife, who is Viennese, asked what the picture was. 'It is a picture of the Turks galloping into Vienna', replied our host blandly. After a moment of speechlessness, my wife said indignantly: 'But the Turks never galloped into Vienna. They failed to capture it.' 'On the contrary', replied our host, and proceeded to enlarge on other mythical Turkish conquests. Whether he really believed this, or it was only something he ardently wanted to believe, we never found out. In the minds of many Turks historical truth is often supplanted by a fervent imagination.

Though the Turks, over the centuries, have adopted many of the modes and appearances of Europe, they have still in them a strong element of the East, even the Far East. They have kept many of the oriental virtues: the extreme courtesy and hospitality, the not-too-precise sense of time, the bringing of gifts and making of visits, the appreciation of certain real values, the awareness and acceptance of death, the distrust of the too direct, too blunt, approach, a realization of the futility of both hurry and worry. As in the Far East, I have found that it rarely pays to get angry with a Turk, and certainly never to lose one's temper; you are merely despised, while achieving nothing.

The Turks still use to some extent, I think, the smile which conceals rather than expresses, as eastern peoples do. In talks with Turks of all kinds below the level of the 'westernized fringe', I have often been reminded in some indefinable way of similar talks I had years ago in China or Vietnam. The Turks seem to me to have kept in their character and tradition many of the best sides of the East, though their long intermixture with more western peoples, in Anatolia and eastern Europe, and the influence of Islam, may have helped to reinforce that virility which is prized among the Turks almost more than any single quality.

The Turks are still, essentially, a male society. Women have admittedly made great strides under the Republic, and there are outstanding women in many walks of life. Turkish women long ago entered professions, such as that of judges for example, until recently closed to women in Britain. There are numbers of Turkish women in parliament, as well as professors, writers, and journalists. Women have made a great impact on the arts. There are fine actresses, ballet dancers, opera singers, and musicians. The best pianist and violinist while I was in Turkey were both girls. Yet despite this there is far less equality between the sexes than the existence of a few outstandingly modern and westernized ladies might suggest.

A man's most important relationships are still with other men: with his male relatives or friends. It is striking, even in cities, how rarely one sees a man walking with a woman, even his own wife. Of course in Ottoman times a man was never supposed to recognize his wife when he passed her in the street, and today one will often see simple Turks walking a pace or two ahead of their wives, as if they had no connection with them. When couples meet, it is usually the men who embrace (they kiss) and fall into conversation, while the women stand rather lamely aside. The essential bond is between the men.

Certain things are not done in public, and can profoundly shock simple people. There was a case in Ankara, while I was there, of a night-watchman who actually shot a man he saw kissing a girl in the street, and at his trial made it clear that such a thing was deeply shocking to him. A friend of mine was reported to the police by a taxi-driver in Istanbul because he kissed his wife on the forehead in a taxi (though the driver may not have known it was his wife). Taxis in Turkey usually have inside lights on, to discourage 'immoral' behaviour.

It is easy to change laws; it takes longer to change a mentality. The harem has long been abolished as an institution in Turkey; but the concept behind the harem, which is roughly that men and women are two separate worlds, persists, and is only gradually being broken down. Even at sophisticated parties in the big cities, there is a tendency for the women to huddle together in part of the room. It goes against the grain for a woman to sit among the men. On the boulevards there are now Paris-type cafés, where men and women sit together, but the popular coffee-houses are packed with men only, dense oceans of maleness. When I once took my wife into one of these coffee-houses, she was almost stared into walking out again. I might as well have brought a rhinoceros.

The Turks are aware of the more liberal attitude of western countries in these matters. At a time when Turkish workers were badly needed in Germany, a series of articles appeared in the Turkish popular press depicting in appetising terms the freedom the first emigrants were enjoying in relations with the opposite sex, as compared to Turkey, with lubricious descriptions of nightlife in German cities. A special supplement carried the headline 'In Paris love is different'. The article below gave intimate descriptions of the sexual freedom permitted in the French capital, providing such fascinating statistics as that 80% of all Parisian husbands are unfaithful to their wives, or that 50,000 illegitimate children are born in France every year. The implication was that Turks went to Europe as much for sex as for money.

The consequences of this segregation of the sexes and the predominantly male society in Turkey gives Turkish men a rather special relationship to women in which love in the purely physical sense probably plays a more important part than in western countries, where it includes a more equal companionship between men and women. The idea of *Arkadaşlik* (comradeship or friendship), which is one of the strongest things in Turkey, is mainly between man and man. Male Turks all do military service, and are still, in a sense, a nation of soldiers. It is common to see men walking hand-in-hand in the street – something one also sees in many eastern countries. This is the natural bond of affinity. One gets the impression that *arkadaşlik* is more important than love. A natural consequence is the almost exaggerated concept of loyalty which is so striking a feature of the Turks.

This type of loyalty is somewhat primitive, perhaps, in the sense that it rules out dispassionate judgement. On the other hand, it means that when a Turk is a friend, he is an unusually faithful friend. In fact for Turks you are generally either a friend or an enemy: you cannot be merely objective. If you try to be, especially at critical moments, you are regarded as slippery or hypocritical, as the British (and later the Americans) were when they tried not to take sides in the various Cyprus crises.

I experienced this rather bitterly as a foreign correspondent during the period following the 1960 military revolution and the trials of the Menderes regime. In articles where I was obliged to comment, I tried to be impartial, to give equal weight to the arguments of the ousted leaders as well as those of the revolutionaries who had overthrown them. This was a hopeless failure, and probably I should have done better not to try. The Turks simply did not understand it. 'Why does our friend stab us in the back?', wrote one paper.

The concept of honour (*namus*) is very important. The words for 'dishonourable' (*namussuz*) and 'shameful' (*ayip*) are both very much in use. In the villages men kill to avenge an insult. Among the peasantry murders frequently arise from the most trivial imaginable causes. An argument starts, which gradually gets more and more heated. Finally one will say something which the other regards as a reflection on his honour. As most peasants carry arms, one will often kill the other. An official in the Ministry of Justice, who for years was prosecutor in a country district in Anatolia, told me that about 90% of all the murders he had to deal with in his job arose from disputes over trifles.

As I write this I have in front of me a newspaper cutting about two brothers in eastern Turkey who started eating a watermelon. When they had finished it, one started chaffing the other that he had eaten the bigger share. The argument got more and more heated, until suddenly one brother drew a large knife, attacked the other with appalling ferocity, and chopped him to pieces. It is important to add that crimes of this sort are never committed under the influence of drink. Public drunkenness is almost unknown among the Turks.

It is generally assumed that men have strictly 'dishonourable' intentions towards women. I remember being astonished the first time I was invited to a wedding-party. It was in the city of Izmir. There was dancing, and I was surprised to see that most of the girls danced with each other. There were only two or three couples where men were dancing with girls, and in each case I was told either that the couple was married, or that the girl was dancing with her brother or with some other close relative. It would have been out of the question, they said, for the girl to dance with any man outside this intimate circle. No other man could be trusted to be *samimi* (literally 'sincere', but here roughly translatable as 'having honest intentions'). This of course no longer applies in sophisticated circles, but is the rule among the people as a whole.

The extent to which not only girls, but older women, are coddled, shadowed, and protected by their menfolk in Turkey is extraordinary. Usually a Turkish husband will not allow his wife to walk a few hundred yards without being accompanied, even by day. When she goes to a certain place, he will wait outside so that she can call for help if she is molested. Women in general tend to huddle together in flocks, like sheep in danger from wolves. Clearly there is some reason for this, but the system seems to me to be self-defeating: the women have reason to be apprehensive, but the men are more than normally frustrated. There is little doubt that many Turks go to western Europe because of the greater freedom there is there in these matters.

The importance of the family is enormous in Turkey, and the system is patriarchal. Respect for parents is crucial. A middle-aged man will almost never drink, smoke, sit cross-legged, or even address his own children, in the presence of his father. Ismet Inönü has related that even when he had reached the rank of corps commander in the Turkish army he did not venture to smoke when his father was present. The grandfather, or great-grandfather while he lives, remains the undisputed monarch of a Turkish family.

The Turks are deeply aware that there is hostility to them in many parts of the world. 'We are a nation of many enemies', said an officer in the 1960 Junta, echoing what Ataturk had said forty years before. Almost like the Jews, the Turks are conscious of their differentness to the other peoples around them: Arabs, Slavs, Greeks, Persians. In recent history, when Turkey was an exceptionally solid member of the western camp, the Turks felt they could ignore this. But what they regard as the failure of their western allies to support them over the vital question of Cyprus has convinced them of the need for a change. They feel that Europe, and the West in general, is unfairly bound to the Greeks, for sentimental reasons which are no longer valid.

There is in the Turks, despite their kindness, gentlemanliness, and overwhelming hospitality, a certain deep xenophobia which may come from the fact that, at times in their history, every man's hand has been against them. They retire into an inner fortress of themselves. One should never push the Turks too far. They have an ultimate capacity to defy all comers, to take on the whole world. There is a Turkish saying: 'I am a Turk, and your enemy, even if I were the last man on earth.' 'Come the three corners of the world in arms, and we shall shock them' is a line which every Turk would understand.

This partly explains their attitude to the minorities who still live in Turkey, though here the question of the religion also comes into it. I have seen little anti-semitism, *as such*, among the Turks. (It is to be found in the extreme right-wing Nationalist Action party.) The Jewish community in Istanbul is disliked, because, like the Armenians and Greeks, it is a minority which cannot completely be assimilated or relied on. These three peoples are looked upon as the 'clever races', and their relative craftiness is expressed in the Turkish saying:

> One Greek can cheat two Jews.
> One Armenian can cheat two Greeks,

which shows the Armenians as the most, and the Jews as the least, cunning of the three. Traditionally, Turkey has had a good record for toleration of the Jews.

One of the striking features of the Ottoman empire (until the period of the Armenian massacres) was the wide practical toleration accorded to all minorities. This toleration has, on the whole, continued, except when bitterness over Cyprus, or some other external cause, has driven the Turks into violence or injustice. The notorious Capital Levy of 1942 was one example, the anti-Greek riots in Istanbul in 1955 another. In the past, the dislike of minorities was based on religion, though there is evidence that it goes deeper than this. A case in point are the *Dönmes*. These are Jews who converted some centuries ago to Islam. They pass as Turks, and are Muslims; and the few hundred *Dönme* families are well known. Yet one senses that the *Dönmes* are never quite fully accepted or completely trusted by the real Turks, as if they were still regarded as secret Jews.

* * * * *

The Turks have many excellent qualities: dignity, nobility, honesty, sincerity, kindness, hospitality, great physical courage and endurance. Even their relative silence has often been appreciated, compared to neighbouring peoples who weary one with their clamour. Despite this taciturnity, they are a naturally eloquent race. They usually have quantities of poetry at the tip of their tongue. They have a strong romantic, even emotional, strain in them. Their minds seem full of heroic legends of long ago. On important occasions the most stolid-looking people will make speeches in a vein of extravagant nationalism which to us seems quite out of place. Almost every Turkish speech is in the style of a peroration.

The Turks like to suppose that they are a Mediterranean people, yet this is not really quite their nature. The typical Turk is not volatile or explosive, nor a mercurial extrovert. He is more of a bottled-up volcano, which after a long period of inactivity makes one tremendous eruption, rather than a series of more innocuous minor puffs. An example of this are the occasional violent scenes in the Turkish parliament: a wonderful sight to see.

At one moment, in that vast chamber, the deputies are relaxed and smiling, placid as a calm sea on a summer's day; the next, at some provocative word, it is as if a hurricane had swept the waters. Men leap simultaneously from a hundred seats; fists whirl; briefcases, books, shoes, chairs, glasses, anything which can be called a missile, hurtles through the air. There is an indescribable tumult, a veritable maelstrom of men. Usually it lasts for a matter of minutes. Then, as suddenly as it began, it ceases. The shrieking tempest drops, the waves subside. Perfect calm is restored. Men who a few moments ago were punching each others' noses sit peacefully side by side. In mature dignified silence the legislative process goes forward.

14 ❀ The Life of the People

THE PEASANTRY is roughly 70% of the population and lives in 35,000 villages scattered throughout Turkey. These villages are still in many ways a world apart, with traditions and a social structure so different to the towns that sociologists speak of a 'cultural dualism' that really makes two Turkeys instead of one. In many villages brides are bought and sold for money, polygamy continues in veiled forms, and the use of magic is widespread. Turkish cities have developed from an 'Anatolian' tradition running back to Byzantium and Rome and beyond, whereas much in village life can be traced to the pre-Islamic customs of the Turks in central Asia. This dualism is slightly blurred today, because of the vast influx of peasants to the cities. Yet the gulf is profound.

It is more than a gulf: it is an opposition. In no country I have visited do the educated classes speak of the 'ignorance' and 'backwardness' of their own peasants so much as in Turkey. Turkish intellectuals are absolutely at sea in villages. For them they are like a foreign country, and the peasants a foreign people.

This dualism at the heart of Turkey was vividly expressed in a famous book, *Yaban*, published in 1930 by Yakup Kadri Karaosmanoglu, a scion of the great family of Derebeys which once more or less governed Aegean Turkey, and one of the finest writers of the Ataturk generation. Karaosmanoglu was marooned for months in an Anatolian village at the time of the War of Independence, and the book is the *cri de coeur* of an intellectual stranded in a society which to him is utterly strange. ('Yaban' means 'the foreigner' or 'the outsider').

For the hero of the book (the author), the peasants might have been Martians. He found more in common with the animals than the human beings. He was on good terms with the village donkey, the goats, the sheep, even the geese. The villagers were completely alien to him. A typical comment from the book: 'I know how birds make love; I know how cats make love; but I cannot conceive how these peasants do it.' He finds it difficult to believe that the villagers are his own nation and speak his own language.

Twenty years later another book achieved even greater notoriety: *Our village*, by Mahmut Makal. This is one of the rare works penned by an authentic peasant. It is a factual, earthy, humorous account of the squalor, poverty, and ignorance of the author's village in central Anatolia. The book shocked everybody to the core, and the author was imprisoned as a 'Communist'. *Our village* particularly disturbed educated Turks in the big cities, who in the twenty years since *Yaban* had been only too delighted to forget the peasants, of whose life they knew about as much as a first-class passenger in a transatlantic liner knows about what is going on at the bottom of the ocean.

Westernized intellectuals fear this foreign world of the peasants. They see the villages as hopelessly unprogressive, sunk in magic and superstition. If this is so, it is largely the fault of the intellectuals themselves, who for centuries have regarded the peasant as a clod, fit for nothing but messing about with manure or making useful cannon-fodder in the Yemen. Ataturk reversed this trend, helping agriculture and recognizing the peasant as the 'master of Turkey'.

In the last twenty years, under the influence of better roads, democracy, and such things as the 'transistor revolution', there has been a considerable awakening of the Turkish peasant, and a notable change in his state of oriental resignation, as the rush to the cities seems to prove. For my part I have always found the Turkish peasant a most sterling fellow: sober, kind, honest, overwhelmingly hospitable, and remarkably interested in, and sometimes well-informed about, the outside world. For all that, the life of the villages is a special life, and more needs to be said about it.

* * * * *

Of all Ataturk's reforms the most astonishing and far-reaching was the adoption of the Swiss civil code. Civil law deals with marriage, divorce, property, inheritance, and the whole daily lives of ordinary people. The new law abolished polygamy, and gave equal rights to women in what up to then had been a world dominated by men. A sign of how revolutionary this was is that no Muslim country except Turkey has done it. Others have adapted the Koranic law to make it conform with modern life, but none of them has replaced it, as Ataturk did, with a code of law taken from Europe.

It is interesting to recall the idealism with which Ataturk and his collaborators embarked on this remarkable enterprise, in 1926. The Minister of Justice of the day, Mahmut Esat Bozkurt, setting forth the reasons for importing a European code of law, argued that communities governed by religious law, such as Turkey and other Muslim countries, were primitive communities. If Turkey was to be civilized, it was not enough to adapt parts of the European civilization to Turkish ways; the Turks had to change *their* ways to fit the European civilization. This was the essence of Kemalism. Sociologists argued that a foreign code of law, unsuited to all Turkish customs and traditions, would be rejected by the people, as the human body extrudes an alien organ. But the Minister expressed complete confidence that the new law would be accepted, concluding with the stirring words: 'The day this code becomes law, Turkey will have shut the door on the old civilization, and opened it on the new.'

'Law', it has been said, 'is the distilled essence of the civilization of a people.' The Swiss civil code, at the time of its adoption by Turkey, was the finest and most modern civil code in the world; that was why Ataturk chose it. It was to be an instrument to civilize Turkey. As a Turkish lawyer, a strong Kemalist, said to me once with portentous gravity: 'The civil code draws our people upwards to civilization' – a strange and interesting concept. Nevertheless the Swiss code in Turkey has remained something of an unattained Nirvana.

The Turks took the code as it stood, but one important change was made immediately. This was in the minimum age of marriage. The Swiss ages were twenty for men and eighteen for girls – too high for Turkey, where girls often marry at fourteen or less. The Swiss ages were reduced to eighteen for men and seventeen for girls, but this was not enough. Pressure for a further reduction became so terrific that even Ataturk did not resist it. Down went the ages again, to seventeen and fifteen respectively, but in practice lower. Judges were given discretion to allow younger marriages if parents produced 'serious' reasons, which of course they frequently did. In the villages today, whatever the law may say, girls are often married at thirteen, and are betrothed even younger, in accordance with the Turkish peasant dictum: 'The girl's in the cradle, the trousseau's in the box.'

There were no more big changes in the Swiss code, but a very odd situation exists today in Turkey. It is useless for anybody to pretend that the law is observed: it simply isn't. The most flagrant example is marriage. The new law abolished polygamy in name, but in fact it is allowed to continue.

What happens is this. In the villages, few peasants bother to have a civil marriage, as the law prescribes; but they all have religious marriages. A civil marriage *only* is not respectable in a village. In the eyes of the peasants it is 'living in sin'. The only respectable form of marriage in a Turkish village is a union blessed by the Imam; but this is not a legal marriage. As relatively few peasants have a civil marriage, much of the peasantry is thus technically unmarried, and their children illegitimate. A Turkish newspaper estimated in 1965 that 6 million Turkish children below the age of ten were, legally speaking, bastards.

This may worry the state, but it doesn't worry the peasants. Socially, they are perfectly respectable through the religious marriage, and legally they suffer no disadvantages whatever for lack of a civil marriage, nor do the children. The way this happens is as follows. Every few years an act is passed by the Turkish parliament to enable the vast section of the community which is in a state of illegality to rectify its position. These acts do not automatically legitimize the Imam marriages or the offspring of them. They are more in the nature of an amnesty for the huge army of law-breakers.

The result of this is that polygamy in the villages has only nominally been abolished. A peasant can make several Imam marriages, while in the eyes of the state remaining single. There is no punishable offence in concurrent Imam marriages, only in concurrent civil marriages. This curious state of affairs explains, amongst other things, why there is such a low divorce-rate in Turkish villages, something most observers have noted. Clearly, if a man can have more than one wife with impunity, and without the obligation of a legal marriage, one of the main reasons for divorce is obviated.

Optimists claim that civil marriages are on the increase, and

Imam marriages decreasing. I have heard it argued that Turkish men accept the principle of a single wife, because the ancient Turks were said to have been monogamous in central Asia, and polygamy is an odious practice imported by Islam. The optimists maintain that rural Turkey is gradually being civilized by the example of urban Turkey. 'Monogamy is seeping downwards from the towns to the villages', one intellectual informed me with unconscious humour, almost as if it were some ghastly disease.

Personally I have seen no evidence that this is so. Others claim that, under the influence of democracy, village customs are spreading to the towns. Rather than monogamy seeping downwards, polygamy may be seeping upwards. It is extremely difficult to know the truth of this matter. What seems extraordinary to me is that the Swiss code, in its most fundamental provisions, has remained a dead letter from its inception. This has harmed the struggle for female equality, allowing Turkey to remain a world where man is supreme.

*   *   *   *   *

In many parts of Anatolia men pay cash for their wives, as if they were buying a buffalo or an ox. This is the ancient Turkish custom of Bride Price. The custom is pre-Islamic. It seems to be rooted in the idea that the main object of women, besides bearing sons, is to work in the house and the fields. The peasants indignantly deny that their daughters are bought and sold. Theoretically, the bride price is a *quid pro quo* for a trousseau and/or furniture provided by the girl's father, but this is hardly valid because the value of such endowments rarely equals a fraction of the bride price.

The old custom is gradually dying out, but still continues in many parts of Turkey, especially eastern, central and southern Anatolia, less in the Aegean and Black Sea areas. Bride price can vary from a mere £50 in poor villages to £1000 or more in the east. A Kurdish sheikh recently sold his daughter by the kilo. This was considered rather a joke.

The bride price system puts a considerable strain on the young in Turkish villages. In matters of sex, a Turkish village is about as liberal as a Calvinist hamlet. Pre-marital relations are an unpardonable offence against village morals, hardly expiable even by death. A girl's 'honour' is something which greatly enhances her cash value – the money her father feels fully entitled to pocket in compensation for the disaster of having a daughter. With such ferocious sanctions, youthful escapades are usually taboo.

Village marriages are still almost invariably arranged between the parents, as the result of negotiations between the two families, and the girl's father expects an advance payment of the bride price at an early meeting. As for the young men, if they cannot afford the bride price, which often for years they cannot, there is only the risky alternative of abducting or kidnapping a girl.

An abduction of this kind, though quite frequent, causes considerable drama in a village. A young man, sometimes helped by a male friend, simply seizes the girl from her home, in a delightfully primitive way, and carries her off to the mountains, the forest, or the nearest town. From the legal viewpoint, much depends on whether it is a forcible abduction or a genuine elopement – or, put more bluntly, whether it is rape or requited love. If the girl can be proved unwilling, the man goes to prison for up to ten years; if she is willing, he will normally get away with it.

An abduction is of course a serious pecuniary loss for the girl's father, since if her honour is lost he will only get a fraction of the bride price. From the young man's point of view, of course, the main point of the abduction is to avoid paying the bride price. In most cases the girl's father breathes fire and slaughter for a time, but is mollified if the erring couple present him with a grandson (though not a grand-*daughter*).

So much for love, sex and marriage in the Turkish villages. Now for a more terrible subject. The blood feud still hangs over rural Turkey like the wrath of God. Feud is prevalent in many parts of Anatolia, especially in the Kurdish east and on the Black Sea Coast. Some authorities reckon that there are running feuds in most Turkish villages, and that at least a third of them have experienced a feud killing at one time or another. No government has made any serious attempt to stamp out feud. It is punishable by death under the penal code, but appears to be condoned by the Koran, by whose law the peasantry claims to live.

The scene of the drama is not always a village. Once, when I was in Istanbul, a young boy leapt to his feet suddenly in a crowded café and emptied six chambers of a revolver into the heart of the middle-aged man sitting next to him. Some years before, the man had murdered his father. In May 1965, in the eastern town of Siirt, a sixteen-year-old boy shot dead the three principal citizens of the town in the open street, for the same reason. In October that year, in a village in north-west Turkey, an elderly man and his two sons entered a house and cut the throats of a woman of seventy-four, her twenty-five-year-old grand-daughter, and her two great grand-daughters of four and one and a half. The entire family was wiped out. This was the latest act in a feud which had lasted for fifteen years. Quite recently a feud ended in eastern Turkey after sixty years, with fifty killings on the two sides.

These feuds cause turmoil in the villages. A horrible atmosphere of fear and hatred arises. Whole families go about armed to the teeth, in fear of sudden death. For years death may not come; then one day, in a field, on a jobsite, perhaps even in a mosque, at a moment when the victim least expects it, he will be struck down. The killer, smoking gun or reeking blade in hand, may make no attempt to escape, or may flee to the protection of some powerful neighbour, at whose mercy he will henceforth live. Meanwhile the family applaud the deed. Relatives of the killer, overjoyed that vengeance is accomplished, kiss the fingers that pulled the trigger. The endless cycle goes on.

In theory these feuds can last for ever, and often do so for generations; then, sometimes, they are allowed to die out. A way of settling them can be for the family which last killed to give a girl in marriage to redeem the blood debt. 'To mix the blood wipes out the blood', it is said. In this way at least a truce can be arranged, which allows both families to live in peace. If it fails (if there is no son of the marriage), the situation may become worse, because feud is brought into the bosom of the family. The girl's husband may harbour a secret hatred for his in-laws. If hatred explodes, shots will ring out again, and this time over the breakfast-table. It is quick, primitive justice. There is only one good thing to be said for the blood-feud system: so awful is the cycle of revenge, that nobody lightly embarks on premeditated murder.

Some parts of Turkey are still notorious for violence, especially the Black Sea area, known as 'Turkey's Texas', where it is said that some seven hundred people a year are murdered, in blood feuds or otherwise. One sometimes wonders, on reading these appalling facts, whether for the Turanian peoples the act of killing is quite the irremediable sin it is for us. According to Barthold, there is a Shamanistic belief that in the after-life a murderer will have his victim as a *servant*, and that a man's prospects in the next world will be advanced in direct proportion to the number of lives he has annihilated in this. Is it possible that an echo of this extraordinary belief still remains in a corner of the soul of the Turanian peoples (though they have long abandoned Shamanism), which could explain why human life seems relatively unimportant to them?

An interesting aspect of feud in Turkey is that fathers often get their young sons to do the deed for them. If a grown man kills, he may be hanged, or go to prison for life; but a boy goes to a reformatory and learns a trade. I was once taken round one of these reformatories, near Ankara. There were two hundred and fifty boys between the ages of eleven and fifteen. They looked serious, intelligent, hardworking peasant children. Most were being taught crafts of one kind or another: weaving, carpentry, shoe-making, and the like. Half the boys had already killed their man, almost all of them in feud. One of the boys made me an excellent pair of boots, which I still have. Sometimes I feel queasy when I think of the other job those hands did that made my boots.

*   *   *   *   *

All over Turkey there are magical practices which would have rejoiced the heart of Sir James Frazer, and filled a further volume of the *Golden Bough*. The rain prayer is common in many parts of Anatolia. Rain-making practices include hanging a scorpion from a tree, burning a snake alive, or writing a prayer on the head of a dog, which is then thrown into the water. Drought is often regarded as a collective punishment for sins. In Ottoman times, apparently, the Christian minorities were considered particularly effective supplicants for rain, on the curious grounds that the bad breath of the Infidels would so sicken the rain-making angels that they would do anything to get rid of them, rather as one gives money to a pestiferous beggar.

Many magical practices are connected with childbirth or marital relations. The vital thing for every Turk is to have a son. Daughters are a disaster, and Turkish peasants, asked how many children they have, will omit daughters from the count.* A barren woman is regarded as sub-human. More recently, however, the vertiginous population increase has favoured devices for contraception. For this, ground-up mule's hoof is often used, based on the fact that mules are sterile. In one part of western Turkey a home-made contraceptive is brewed from a mixture of opium, tar, garlic, coffee, onions, mules-hoof, and burnt eggshells, boiled together in water. Macbeth's witches might have envied this. One can only hope it is as effective as it must be unpleasant.

When a baby is born, the first forty days of its life are a period of special danger, since it is exposed to the bad influence of witches, djinns, and devils. Newborn babies are often 'salted' – that is, rubbed all over with salt to make them strong, and are almost always tightly swaddled, to protect them. In some places a tortoise is put under their pillows at night; great virtue is attributed to tortoises among the Turks.

The most widespread of all superstitions, though this is not confined to the peasantry, is the evil eye. In Turkey it is called Nazar, the 'look'. One must never praise other people's property, and above all not young children, without adding the saving word 'Mashallah'. The forty days period of infants is felt to be so dangerous that parents will sometimes make their babies look as ugly or dirty as possible, or put their clothes on back-to-front, to deceive the evil eye. Children all over Turkey, and domestic animals, wear the blue bead as a protection against the eye. Particularly dangerous is said to be the look of blue-eyed, blonde-haired persons. The protective power of the blue bead is based on the principle of sympathetic magic that parts of a whole, even when separated, remain in contact. The danger from the blue eyes goes into the blue bead, like lightning into a conductor.

Great faith is placed in *muskas*, or magical charms, in which Shamanistic or Koranic texts are written by accomplished magicians on pieces of paper, usually in the Arabic script, and are then swallowed, or sewn into the clothing. Most buses and taxis in Turkey have blue beads or tortoise-shells hung up in the drivers' cabs. Turkish buses and lorries usually have the words

* Unwanted peasant girls are often sent away to the city, where they are used more or less as slaves by middle-class families.

'Trust in Allah' written in large letters on the front above the bonnet; and at 70 m.p.h. on a hairpin bend this is about the best thing one can do.

Once when I was motoring in western Anatolia, a smartly-dressed man by the roadside thumbed a lift. I took him on board. After an unfreezing period, he started telling me his troubles. He was proprietor of a restaurant in Izmir, the western seaport, and was on his way to the city of Konya, to see a magician. He had for some time been on very bad terms with his wife. Lately he had taken to beating her regularly.

The man was convinced that some enemy had cast an evil spell on his marriage, and was in search of a counter-spell which would put things right. He would sew the counter-spell into the bed-clothes, and live happily ever after. I was about to laugh, but realized that he was in deadly earnest. When we arrived in Konya, I deposited my friend at the address he wanted, and the last I saw of him was ringing the magician's front-door bell. It was an interesting example of a man some way up the social scale indulging in magic.

In fact, the peasants are not the most reactionary or fanatical class in Turkey. The worst reactionaries and fanatics live in the provincial towns of Anatolia. It is here that you most often see the black *charshaf*, symbol of the reaction, and occasionally the veil itself. If Turkish peasants are addicted to magic, that is mainly because from time immemorial nothing has been done for the peasants. Where doctors are non-existent, magicians are at a premium. They may sometimes be equally effective.

*   *   *   *   *

In the popular life magic and religion are mixed with a rich, romantic folklore of songs, drama, legends, poetry and humour. In former times Anatolia was full of minstrels, who wandered from place to place improvising words to the music of the *Saz* (many-stringed lute), the favourite instrument of the Anatolians. They were called *Ashiks* or *Ozans*. There are still some left today. Their poetry is almost always sad, and often has a religious or mystical tinge.

The greatest of them was Yunus Emre,* who lived in the

* Pronounced Emreh.

thirteenth century. By contrast to the cumbersome and complicated court poetry of the Ottoman period, which was so larded with Arabic and Persian words that it was incomprehensible to ordinary people, his poems are beautifully simple and direct,

> Say, is there anywhere on this Earth
> A wanderer like me?
> So plagued by fears, so full of tears,
> A wanderer like me?
>
> Down, down to Damascus
> And up to the Caspian Sea
> I roamed around, yet never found
> A wanderer like me.

Yunus Emre had a vast influence; he is honoured annually, and pilgrimages are made to his tomb. Another folk poet was Pir Sultan Abdal, an Alevi, whose powerful pen stirred a great revolt in Anatolia in the sixteenth century, for which he was hanged by the Pasha of Sivas.

Some of these wandering poets were religious mystics, and it is interesting that they seem to have had a good deal to do with the spreading of Islam in Turkey by making it seem more attractive to the Turks. They were not approved of by the orthodox Muslims, who were against art and music, but, as we know, Turkish Islam was always unorthodox, and several of the Turkish sects and orders, such as the Alevi and Mevlevi, used forms of worship based on music and dancing.

In these ways Turkey was linked less with Arabia, the home of orthodox Islam, than with Persia, and it is from Persia that the greatest influences have come in Turkish art, music, and mysticism. The best-known example is the ritual developed by the Mevlevi order, founded by the great Turkish poet and mystic Mevlana Jelaluddin el-Rumi, who lived in Konya in the thirteenth century, and whose name is deeply revered in that city.

It seems that Rumi started whirling one day in the street, and kept rotating and rotating as if he would never stop. This was taken up by his followers as a religious rite – the dance of the Whirling Dervishes. The 'adepts' believe that by spinning round and round continuously in the same direction they can achieve union with God. It is an exceptionally beautiful spectacle, which can be seen every December in Konya, ostensibly as a show put on for tourists.

In recent years the Whirling Dervishes have become one of Turkey's biggest tourist attractions,* despite the fact that the show is in midwinter, because Konya is the only place left in the world where one can see it. The Dervishes even travel abroad. There is also a group of British Dervishes in London.

A little suspected side to the Turks is their humour. One of the great Turkish legendary heroes was a humourist – Nasreddin Hodja. There are innumerable stories about this mythical sage and jester. He is supposed to have lived at Akşehir, in south-west Anatolia, in the fourteenth century. The stories attributed to him show the importance of humour in the affairs of life, and the practical wisdom of getting out of awkward or perilous situations with some remark which makes everybody laugh.

In many of the stories Nasreddin acts as a sort of court jester to the Tartar conqueror Tamerlane. A typical one is where the great emperor weeps for two hours because he has caught sight of his face in a mirror and is appalled by its ugliness. Tamerlane eventually stops weeping, but the Hodja goes on. When Tamerlane asks why, he replies: 'If Your Majesty weeps for two hours after only catching a glimpse of your face in a mirror, there is every reason for me, who see you all the time, to weep much longer.' This was pretty near the knuckle. Most of the Hodja's replies to Tamerlane are a good deal more diplomatic.

These Hodja stories do not always come off in translation, as much of the humour lies in the language. A celebrated one is that of the cooking pot – a little homily on wishful thinking and the acquisitive instinct. The Hodja one day borrows a saucepan from his neighbour. When he gives it back he puts another smaller pot inside. 'What's this?' asks the neighbour. 'Oh, I forgot to tell you,' says Hodja casually, 'your saucepan had a baby.' The neighbour, though somewhat taken aback, says nothing and keeps the smaller pot. Soon afterwards the Hodja borrows the big saucepan again, and the neighbour lends it with alacrity. A week or more goes by and the saucepan does not come back. Finally the man goes and asks for it. 'I'm sorry', says the Hodja, 'I have bad news. Your

* See Appendix.

saucepan has died.' 'But you can't expect me to believe that' says the neighbour. 'Why not?' replies the Hodja with unanswerable logic, 'you were quick enough to believe that it had given birth'.

Another famous story is about a donkey. One of Nasreddin's neighbours, whom the old man particularly dislikes, calls to borrow the Hodja's donkey. 'No,' says Nasreddin, 'the donkey is out.' At that moment the donkey, which is in the stable behind the house, lets out a deafening roar. 'But, Hodja,' protests the neighbour, 'how can you tell so blatant a lie. The donkey is there all the time.' 'You impudent rascal,' shouts the Hodja furiously. 'What the devil do you mean by believing my donkey and not believing me? I don't want a man like you for my neighbour.'

A slightly more subtle story, on the theme that anything goes when dealing with somebody you dislike, is about the neighbour who comes to borrow the Hodja's rope. 'I'm sorry,' says Nasreddin, 'I can't lend you my rope, my wife's spreading flour on it.' 'How do you mean, spreading flour on it?,' asks the astonished neighbour, 'you must be joking.' 'I'm perfectly serious,' replies Hodja, 'if I don't want to lend somebody my rope, flour can very easily be spread on it.' This piece of gratuitous impudence by the Hodja has passed into the language. 'To spread flour on a rope' is idiomatic in Turkish for not doing something you don't want to do.

Some stories have an almost shaggy-dog quality. Hodja goes into a shop to buy trousers, but changes his mind and asks the salesman to give him a coat instead. He takes the coat and walks out of the shop. The shopkeeper shouts: 'But Hodja, you've forgotten to pay for the coat.' 'That's funny,' says Hodja, 'didn't I leave you the trousers instead?' 'Yes, of course, Hodja, but you never paid for the trousers.' 'Don't think you can pull a fast one on me,' replies the Hodja, 'I never took the trousers, did I?' So saying, he walks out of the shop, leaving the shopkeeper so confused that he gets away without paying.

A story I personally like is that of the young man who has lost all his money and comes in despair to the Hodja. 'What will become of me,' he moans, 'I have no money and no friends.' 'Don't worry,' says Nasreddin, 'you'll soon be alright.' The young man brightens up. 'You mean I'll get rich again, and get back my friends?' 'No,' replies the Hodja, 'but you'll get used to being poor and friendless.'

Another personal favourite is a remark of the Hodja about the omnipotence of God. 'God must be almighty', he said on one occasion, 'or something would once in my life have turned out as I wanted it.' With this comment, we can leave Nasreddin Hodja. He is an attractive figure. He turns up in Persia, and other eastern countries. But the Turks claim him as theirs and theirs only, and nobody has seriously disputed the claim.

The other traditional source of popular humour, now alas almost extinct, were the Karagöz shadow-plays, which for centuries delighted the people and were an unfailing relief from the stuffy Ottoman bureaucracy. Karagöz was a sort of cross between Punch-and-Judy, Laurel and Hardy, and the chansonniers of Montmarte. The two main characters were Karagöz, the 'common man', and Hadjivat, the pompous Ottoman intellectual, who gets on Karagöz's nerves with his pretentious speech. Many of the scenes end with Karagöz kicking Hadjivat off the screen. There is a lot of good knockabout fun. But Karagöz is more subtle than he seems, and will sometimes assume ignorance for purposes of Socratic irony.

There were many other characters, including women. They were all coloured puppets, operated against a transparent screen of linen cloth, lit in old days by an oil lamp, which was especially good at casting just the right quality of shadow. Extreme skill was required of the puppet-master, who had not only to imitate the voices of many different characters, but to have a capacious memory to carry all the different plots and dialogues in his head. Unfortunately there are very few of these puppet-masters left. The shadow-plays are extremely ancient, and are believed to have come to Turkey from the Far East. They were immensely popular among all classes under the Sultans, when people in city and village would crowd round the lighted screen and be doubled up with laughter for hours on end.

In later Ottoman times the shadow-plays developed a strong strain of political satire, some of it of a most daring kind, mocking not only officialdom and the police, but also corruption in high places. A French traveller in Turkey at the end of the nineteenth century records being taken to a show in which Karagöz poked fun at the Sultan's son-in-law, who was Chief Admiral of the Turkish fleet, and a well-known nincompoop. A young man starting his career asks Karagöz for advice, and gets the reply: 'As you are completely ignorant, I advise you to become a Chief Admiral.'

In another show it was suggested that a close relative of the Sultan was a homosexual. After this, political satire was banned, and the plays never afterwards quite recovered their old quality. Since then, press, radio and the cinema have almost driven them out.

Turkish humorous periodicals, what I have seen of them, seem not of a very high quality, though I used to get a lot of fun out of reading the Turkish press.* There are fine cartoonists and excellent satirical writers. Invective is often ferocious. There is biting mockery, especially by the leftists, about the democratic regime. Here is a typical example, from the left-wing columnist Çetin Altan:

> A horse, an ox and a donkey lived up in the hills. One day the Devil whispered to them 'Why not go to town and see what the humans are like'. So they did. A few years later they met to compare notes.
>
> The horse said 'It was an evil day which took me to town. The humans caught me, saddled me up, and forced me to carry heavy loads and pull heavy carts. I barely escaped with my life'.
>
> The ox said much the same.
>
> The donkey laughed: 'I had a good time', it said. 'When I got to town, I saw a big crowd. People were shouting, so I shouted too. In fact a general election was going on, and the people elected me. . . . Whenever they shouted, I shouted too. Everybody applauded me. The louder I shouted, the higher I rose, till I reached the highest posts.'
>
> 'Well?', said the horse and the ox.
>
> 'Well, I became a politician, and ruled the country', said the donkey.
>
> 'But didn't they spot that you were a donkey?'.
>
> 'They did in the end, but by that time four years had gone by'. (Four years is the period between elections in Turkey.)

With this sort of thing being written about the democratic regime, it is rather difficult for it to gain universal respect.

---

* I never saw anything to approach the sublime achievement of the Nigerian newspaper which once described a deceased bishop, in an obituary, as 'a lifelong martyr to gonorrhoea'.

Amasra: the town on its peninsula

Amasya: the river and houses backing on to it

Istanbul Yali

Istanbul: Arnavutköy, houses on the waterfront

Of the humorous writers, the most gifted and prolific is Aziz Nesin, who in thirty years of writing has produced about seventy books and more than two thousand stories. Nesin writes very simply but with devastating wit, ridiculing almost every aspect of officialdom. He was especially good under the Menderes government, when he spent five years in prison.

One of his many good stories is that of an Anatolian village which gets an order, through the local government representative, to kill thirty wild boars and deliver their tails to the government, as part of an official campaign to prevent damage by boars to farm crops. The peasants are baffled, because there are no wild boars near their village, or, for that matter, anywhere in the surrounding country. One of them dares to tell this to the government representative, who explodes with fury. He quotes from the official circular: 'The wild boar is the great enemy of maize-growers. All boars must be destroyed, and maize production increased.'

'But,' stammers the peasant, 'we don't grow maize here; we never have done.'

'Very well,' bellows the official. 'Don't just sit on your backside in the coffee-house doing nothing, but go out and *plant* maize. The boars will come and eat it, you will kill the boars, and the government's orders will be carried out.'

Another of his characteristic stories of Turkish life is 'Where the cat came from'. A man sees a cat run out of a house, and starts wondering what made it do so. The scene then switches to a cabinet minister arriving in his office in the morning in a bad temper. He summons the Undersecretary, and, on some pretext or other, gives him a piece of his mind. The Undersecretary is furious, and vents his fury on the Director-General. And so it goes on down the line. The Director-General takes it out of the assistant Director-General, the assistant Director-General out of the Inspector; the Inspector curses the Messenger, the Messenger the Porter, the Porter the Tram Conductor. The Tram Conductor goes home in a towering rage and gives hell to his wife, who vents her feelings by booting the cat out of the kitchen. That explained where the cat came from.

This sort of story is very popular with simple people in Turkey, because everybody can understand it. It sums up exactly what goes on in so many government offices, and in everyday life.

15 ✳ *The Country*

TURKEY is at last moving into the orbit of the travel agencies, though Turkish tourism is only in a stage of preparation. The Turks were reluctant to embark on it too quickly, feeling that the arrival of large numbers of travellers before adequate roads and hotels were in place would do their country more harm than good. In fact a great deal has been done to improve Turkish roads in the last twenty years (mainly with American aid), and today one can penetrate on a fair network to every part of the country. Hotels, though sometimes uncouth in the remoter places, are good on the coastal fringes, and are almost always redeemed by the friendliness of those who run them.

Turkey is now in that pleasant stage of a rough-and-ready paradise for tourists, but with very few tourists about. On most of the south coast, the 'Turkish Riviera', there is one picture-book sandy beach after another, with a blue sea quietly breaking, and hardly a soul to be seen. You may find a few fishermen mending their nets, or perhaps a camel sitting on the sands, staring sardonically at the waves. In a few years time, no doubt, this wonderful shore will sink invisible beneath a horde of humans – but not yet. For the time being the tourist has it more or less to himself.

There is another delightful feature of Turkey. It is a large and mountainous country, and parts of it are still rarely visited or difficult of access. Journeys in remote places have more about them of adventure and exploration than of mere tourism and travel. If you stick to Istanbul and the coastal fringes, you can enjoy the pleasures of the French Riviera or the Costa Brava. But if you penetrate, at the cost of some discomfort, or even danger, into the inmost recesses of Anatolia, you can still feel, if not exactly Marco Polo or Sven Hedin, at least a latterday incarnation of those eighteenth and nineteenth century worthies who travelled through Ottoman Turkey with apparently limitless time at their disposal, and equally limitless space in which to record their observations and impressions.

154

Another fascination of Turkey arises from its geographical position. It lies at a meeting-point between three completely different climatic zones: the Euro-Siberian, Mediterranean, and Irano-Turanian. This gives it a variety of topography and vegetation much greater than most countries of the same size, ranging from deserts and high mountains to Mediterranean coastal regions and European forests and pastures. It is a paradise for naturalists and botanists. There are said to be 8000–9000 different species of wild flowers in Turkey. It is also a great country for hunting, especially the wild boar and the brown bear. There are lynxes in the forests of the Black Sea, hyaena on the central plateau, and gazelles in the deserts of the south-east. There are still said to be panther in the mountains of the Aegean.

One of the most notorious, but also most beautiful, of the Turkish flowers is the opium poppy, which is grown on a big scale by peasants in the western provinces. From here, until a few years ago came the bulk of the opium and heroin consumed by drug addicts in Europe and the United States. The American government put considerable pressure on the Turks to reduce cultivation of the opium crop, and the planting of opium has now been banned. Oddly enough the Turks, though they grow some of the best opium in the world, hardly smoke it at all themselves.

Of the three zones the Irano-Turanian, comprising central and eastern Turkey, is the largest. This is very dry in summer and cold in winter. The Euro-Siberian zone is mainly the Black Sea coast and the Istanbul region. Near the Black Sea you have deciduous forests, with European trees such as ash, beech and oak, plus the birds and animals which go with them – a beautiful and luxuriant coast, where you find a cool breeze at the hottest season. A pleasant trip in summer is to take one of the steamers which ply from Istanbul along this coast, stopping at several ports on the way there and back. At the eastern end you get a glimpse of Russia and the snowy Caucasus, and the round trip takes about a week.

The meeting of the three zones, and the amazing climatic and topographical diversity of Turkey which results from it, means that you really have Western Europe, the Mediterranean, the Middle East, and central Asia, all in the same country. To drive, say, from Ankara to the Black Sea is like going from Samarkand to Gloucestershire in an afternoon. Ankara is girdled by plains which are roughly in the same topographical bracket as the Gobi desert, while on the coast you have lush forests, blackbirds singing, and the quiet drip of trees after the rain.

You get the same impression in a reverse sense driving by car from Istanbul to Ankara. Theoretically, one goes from Europe to Asia when one crosses the Bosphorus, but not in practice. The Anatolian side of the Straits looks the same as the other, and the coastal regions are European in character. But somewhere along the route between the two cities you pass insensibly into Asia. It is an interesting pastime to try to spot where the transition comes. Personally, I place it at the village of Gumuşova (the 'Silver Plain'), about a third of the way along the road; but the two continents overlap, and the boundary is a subtle one.

When I was in Ankara there was always a good deal of amiable snobbery among foreign residents about the inaccessible places they had been to, and the 'journeys into the interior' they had managed to achieve. What difficult roads had they travelled on? How Spartan had they been in enduring the rigours of the less sophisticated hotels? Those who have stayed at the Banana Palace, for many years the only available hotel in Anamur, Turkey's southernmost town, are today almost in the category of an élite.

Most diplomats feel called on, sooner or later, to disengage from the social whirl of the capital and plunge into the Anatolian steppe. The call of the wild seems, for them, to be irresistible. When I was there one ambassador's wife even announced her intention of going to *live* in an Anatolian village, and it needed all the eloquence of her husband, plus the pressure of duties at home, to dissuade her from such an exploit.

To the modern Turk this passion of foreigners for visiting the rough corners of his country seems incomprehensible and, one suspects, undesirable. While ambassadors and their wives are pining for a life among the peasants, the one idea of every educated Turk is to put as many miles between himself and a village as is humanly possible. Turks gravitate by nature to Istanbul. When one tells them about a journey one has made to Hakkari, Erzurum or Diyarbakir, they stare at you in bewilderment, almost horror, as if you had crossed the Gobi or penetrated the jungles of the Congo.

* * * * *

The jewel in Turkey's possession is of course Istanbul, and many people get so bogged down in this wonderful city that they never see the rest of Turkey. Anatolia seems like a shadowy hinterland, though Aegean Turkey and the south coast are now becoming well-known. It is extraordinary how many famous places of the classical world are to be found on these coasts: Ephesus, Miletus, Pergamum, Sardis, Halicarnassus, Troy, and Antioch, to take a few names at random, are all in Turkey. At Sardis, Croesus lived, the richest man of his time; at Halicarnassus Herodotus was born. In the hills above Ephesus the Virgin Mary is supposed by many people to have spent her later years, and to have died. At Perga, on the south coast, St. Paul preached in 46–47 AD, at the start of his campaign to evangelize Asia Minor. Paul, whose birthplace Tarsus is near the modern Turkish town of Adana, struck inland to Iconium (Konya) and possibly Ancyra (Ankara), and, as we know, visited and lived at Ephesus.

Ankara, in 51 A.D., was capital of the Galatians, the people to whom Paul addressed one of his most ferocious epistles, containing that heartfelt and doubtless well-merited outburst: 'O foolish Galatians!' The Galatians were a Celtic people who, for reasons best known to themselves, had migrated from Europe (against the prevailing stream) eastwards into Asia Minor. Ankara was their capital for several hundred years. St. Jerome records that in the fourth century AD the population of central Anatolia spoke almost pure Celtic, a language not unlike modern Welsh, which they wrote in the Greek script. There are Celtic place-names to be found still in the country round Ankara, a souvenir of the Galatian occupancy, and from time to time one can spot an unmistakably Gallic type among the Turks. The Celts were a hopeless lot of barbarians who revelled unashamedly in war and slaughter, and sometimes acted as mercenaries for other warlike peoples. They never succeeded in founding an empire, even a transitory one, but are credited with two surprisingly useful inventions which have survived to the present day: wine-barrels and trousers.

We are wandering in the steps of St. Paul in all these regions, as H. V. Morton has so delightfully told us,* but we should not forget that Paul himself was wandering in the steps of a good many

* Not to mention Malcolm Muggeridge and Dr. Alec Vidler.

other people. The early history of Anatolia is of such complexity that it is difficult even for professional historians to unravel. Perhaps the most interesting archaeology in the last hundred years has been done in Turkey, culminating in the extraordinary Neolithic excavations of the British archaeologist James Mellaart, which have enabled the Turks, in their touristic brochures, to proclaim something few other countries can equal: 'eight thousand years of art'.

In these years the archaeologists, as they did earlier in Crete, have been digging up the background to the western civilization. We tend to think that our civilization 'began with Greece', and of course in a sense it did. But where did Greece begin? What was behind Greece? Archaeologists of many nations, working in Anatolia in the last fifty or a hundred years, have been tracing the link which connects the classical Greeks with their forerunners the Mycenaeans, Dorians, Lydians, Phrygians, and Hittites, and seeing how the cultures of these earlier and lesser-known peoples led gradually to the extraordinary florescence of Greece in the fifth and fourth centuries BC.

A great deal has been discovered, for example, about the Hittites, who were previously regarded as an obscure Biblical tribe, but are now known to have been a tremendous people, the equals and rivals of the Egypt of the Pharaohs. The Hittites, probably an Aryan people coming from the North or West, arrived in Anatolia about 2000 BC. They established, first a kingdom, then a mighty empire, based on their capital Hattusas, the site of which is four hours drive east of modern Ankara. The ruins of this capital give a vivid impression of grandeur, solidity, and power. Many finds from the Hittite excavations are housed in the Ankara museum – a museum well worth a visit. There you see the lions, bulls, stags, sphinxes and jewellery, the reliefs of gods, kings, warriors and priests, which are the characteristic art of this great people.

The Hittites seem to have found central Anatolia an agreeable homeland, as the Ottoman Turks did later. Some writers have compared these two peoples who, at epochs separated by three thousand years, founded large empires from the same general region. Both were good soldiers and administrators; both had a remarkable conception of law and the state; both were strong, fierce, resolute, durable peoples. Suppiluliumas, most brilliant of the Hittite kings, can be compared to the greatest Ottoman sultans. His name is one you find yourself murmuring, once you have learnt how to pronounce it, as you drive through the vast shimmering plains east of Ankara, the typical 'Hittite country'. But he's a bit of a tongue-twister. Some Hittitologists refer to him irreverently as 'Old Soopy-Loopy'.

The Hittite empire collapsed about 1180 BC, and was followed by a violent inrush of lesser peoples. After a period of confusion the Phrygians, who seem to have migrated from the direction of Europe, became the dominant power in Asia Minor. Their peculiar rock monuments, and the tombs of their kings, can be seen today in the country west of Ankara. After this came the Lydians, based near the coast at Sardis, whose territory at one time stretched eastwards as far as the River Halys, the modern Kizilirmak. The last king of Lydia, Croesus, was defeated by the Persians under Cyrus, and Persia was the first power, in the sixth century BC, to master Asia Minor from end to end, though the Greeks infiltrated on the coasts. Next, like a great sword-thrust from the west, came Alexander of Macedon, who crushed the Persians at the Battle of Issus (333 BC) and occupied the whole of Anatolia in the reverse direction, carrying the Hellenic culture with him. Following the confusion caused by his early death at the age of thirty-three, during which city-states such as Pergamum flared up briefly and brilliantly and were extinguished, there emerged gradually from the west the massive power of Rome. Anatolia was then incorporated in the Roman empire.

After this there came a long and exhausting struggle between Rome and Persia, in which many east Anatolian cities and fortresses changed hands. Satraps were replaced by proconsuls, proconsuls by satraps. By the sixth century AD Roman rule in Asia Minor had given way to that of Byzantium, centred on the east-Roman capital Constantinople – a more ramshackle empire than the Roman, both Greek and Christian. Then a totally unexpected force erupted with extraordinary abruptness from the deserts of the south: the Arabs, carrying the religion of Mahomet. Anatolia became the battleground for a new struggle: Christianity versus Islam. The Arabs were twice repulsed, in 672 and 718 AD, from the walls of Constantinople. In most parts of Anatolia the Byzantines held out, until, in the eleventh century, a new and formidable enemy appeared from the east: the Turks. They came in waves out of central Asia. At the battle of Malazgirt, in 1071 A.D., the Seljuk Turks defeated the Byzantine armies, captured the Byzantine emperor, and opened the whole of Anatolia to Turkish occupation. Twenty-six years later the Crusades began.

Crusaders and Byzantines fought for possession of the peninsula against Arabs and Turks, but for the Christians it was finally a losing battle. The Seljuk Turks founded their own highly cultured and artistic kingdom in central Anatolia at Konya (the old Inconium), but themselves succumbed in time to the terrible Mongols. When the Mongol tide had ebbed, about the fourteenth century AD, a new tribe of Turks, the Ottomans, who had settled in north-west Anatolia with their capital at Brusa, suddenly started to expand rapidly northwards. They crossed the Straits, marched into Europe, captured Constantinople from the Byzantines (1453 A.D.), and in course of time established one of the largest and most durable empires the world has seen. It lasted for six hundred years, and only finally collapsed, along with four other empires, in the holocaust of the First World War. In 1918 the Turks were driven out of most of Europe and the Middle East; but, thanks to the genius of Ataturk, they hung on to Constantinople, Thrace, the Straits, and the whole of the Anatolian mainland, which together form modern Turkey. Such, briefly and roughly, is the history of Anatolia in the last four thousand years.

Wherever one travels in modern Turkey this history is always with one. It stimulates ones interest, but is a stiff challenge to one's knowledge. It helps, of course, if you can distinguish a Hittite from a Phrygian temple, a Greek from a Roman amphitheatre, a Seljuk from an Ottoman minaret, or an Armenian from a Crusader castle. The mixture of civilizations is extraordinary. Anatolia is a land squeezed between East and West, between Persia and Greece. At places like Side* and Perga, on the south coast, Greek ruins lie in wonderful profusion on the shore. You can clamber about among them, thinking of Socrates and Plato. But push inland a little, and see your first Seljuk caravanserai (there are many in Anatolia), and immediately you sense the influence of Persia, and the very different philosophy of 'Omar Khayyam':

* Pronounced 'Seedeh'.

The grape that can with Logic absolute
The Two-and-seventy jarring Sects confute:
The sovereign Alchemist* that in a trice
Life's leaden metal into Gold transmute.

Under this influence you can relax, get a little intoxicated on excellent Turkish wine (Anatolia has made good wine since the time of the Hittites), perhaps watch a bear dance a jig to the music of pipe and drum, go to sleep, wake up with a hangover, regret it, and go back to Plato. All this, in a sense, the Turks took over.

The Turks are in a curious position as regards tourism. They have only inhabited their country for some nine hundred years, whereas the total known history of Anatolia, taking it from the arrival of the Hittites, is at least four thousand years. This makes the Turks rather like custodians in a museum: they have more than three thousand years' worth of other people's monuments to look after, many of them Christian. Nobody with an eye on the past can help feeling it a little strange, for example, to see notices in Izmir pointing 'to the House of the Virgin Mary' (at Ephesus), or that a Muslim people should have as one of their main tourist attractions the supposed last residence of the Mother of Christ. The Pope's visit to Ephesus, in 1967, and the indulgence declared by the Vatican for Catholics who go there, has caused a vast influx of Catholic pilgrims to Turkey. It is an interesting reversal of history that the successor to the Popes who launched so many crusades against the Turks should now be helping them with their tourism.

This profusion of civilizations other than their own may embarrass the Turks, and be partly the reason why up to now they have been reluctant to embark on a full scale touristic effort. But I should hasten to add that what the Turks themselves have contributed to their country is, in the opinion of many experts, fully up to the aesthetic level of those who went before them. There may be no Turkish monument quite like the Temple of Apollo at Didyma, or the celebrated theatre at Miletus; but the sublime beauty of Istanbul, apart from the sea, comes mainly from its skyline of mosques and minarets, and these were contributed by the Turks.

Ottoman mosques are particularly splendid, as those of Istanbul,

* In the first edition of the *Rubaiyat* Fitzgerald has 'the subtle Alchemist'.

Bursa, and Adrianople, amongst others, prove. And in central and eastern Anatolia, especially in such places as Konya, Kayseri, Sivas, and Erzurum, are some of the finest examples of Seljuk Turkish art: mosques, medresehs,* libraries, gateways, palaces, forts, bridges, and caravanserais. One need not go to Bokhara or Samarkand to know that the Turks are an artistic people. Furthermore they have on the whole treated with respect the relics of past cultures with which their country is so lavishly sprinkled.

*　　*　　*　　*　　*

A part of Turkey I personally like is the steppe country between Ankara and Konya, and the huge salt lake at the centre of it, which is said to be saltier than the Dead Sea. Not long ago this area was still an almost impassable desert, to be crossed only by camels (or later by Jeeps); but now there is a fine motor-road which takes one from Ankara to Konya in a bare three hours.

When I was working in Turkey, and got tired of journalism, I always found it a relief to head southwards into the great pallid plains of central Anatolia. This is the hub, the umbilical centre, of Turkey – a dusty, sultry fulcrum. The salt lake itself is a strange inert ocean, constantly evaporating and refilling, in which mirage-islands float like sleeping whales. There is almost no sign of life, except for a few primitive villages which look unchanged since the Hittites.

Two important roads lead southwards from Ankara across the plateau, one of which passes to the west of the Salt Lake, the other to the East. The first runs to Konya, then on down through the Taurus gorges, past the place where Frederick Barbarossa was drowned in 1190 leading the Third Crusade, to Silifke (Seleucia) on the coast. From here one can drive westwards along the southern riviera, of which more later.

The road east of the lake breaches the Taurus by the classical pass of the Cilician Gates, emerging from that gloomy but celebrated defile into a different world from the plateau: orange-groves, cotton-fields, palm-trees, and a feeling of the south, and of the sea. This is the Cilician Plain, the most fertile part of Turkey. The plain centres on Adana, the noisy, teeming, colourful capital of the south, and Turkey's fourth largest city. Here one sees

* Old Muslim colleges.

swarthy faces and Semitic noses, and can hear Arabic spoken in the street. There are also extremes of poverty and wealth: squalid slums on the one hand, the luxurious villas of cotton- and citrus-millionaires on the other. There are said to be more Cadillacs per head in Adana than in any town in the *world*, and I can well believe it. A good town for revolutions!

Konya, of course, is a most interesting old city. It was the Roman Iconium, but its associations today are with Islam, especially the unorthodox, mystical Islam of the Mevlevi. There are many fine mosques, and a beautiful museum, with a sun-drenched courtyard full of roses, and flying pigeons, and inside the museum the tombs of the sheikhs and chelebis, illuminated Korans, most precious carpets, and many strange musical instruments. As one wanders about in one's stockinged feet (shoes are removed to protect the carpets), the mysterious music of the rebab (the single-stringed violin used in the Mevlevi rite) is heard in the background.

Konya has a reputation for conservatism, and of all the Anatolian cities it is the one most associated with Islam and the old Turkey, and of course, through the Seljuks, with Persia. Konya and Ankara, facing one another across the Anatolian steppe, are symbolic, in their way, of the two different poles in Turkey: the old centre of Islamic mysticism and culture, and the new straightforward capital of the modern secular state. For this reason and because of the Mevlevi, Konya is inevitably a seat of tradition, and, in the eyes of the fiercer Kemalists, a nest of reaction.

From Adana the coast road to the west runs along a dizzy corniche to the charming town of Anamur, Turkey's southmost point, right opposite Cyprus. In clear weather the island can easily be seen. In Anamur there are interesting Roman remains, and a magnificent Armenian castle right on the shore, its walls literally washed by the waves. This is banana country, the only part of Turkey where the fruit grows; the reason is that, sheltered by the stupendous southern bluffs of the Taurus, it never freezes.

This is a splendid coast, with numberless beaches and secluded coves. At the western end is the beautiful old town of Antalya, situated on a large blue bay fringed by mountains. Here again the relics are mainly Roman. Further east is Alanya, a great castle on a rock, used as a winter-palace by the Seljuk kings. Between Alanya and Antalya, at Aspendos, there is a classical theatre in such perfect condition that G. E. Bean, in his *Turkey's Southern Shore*, calls it 'the best-preserved ancient theatre of any kind anywhere in the world'. In the hills behind Antalya are the ruins of Termessos, four thousand feet up, a wonderful site for an ancient city, and one of the best things to see in Turkey. Also near Antalya, children may be surprised to learn, is the tomb of Santa Claus, whose real name was St. Nicholas of Myra.

* * * * *

If now we go back to Adana and strike in the opposite direction over the Amanus Mountains, we come to a completely different part of Turkey: the south-east. There are still traces of Roman rule here, in the old cities of Urfa and Diyarbakir. This was Rome's frontier country, in long wars with the Persians, Parthians, and others. The whole area is quite different in character to the west and south coasts. There is no more sign of the Greeks, but one becomes aware of mysterious peoples like the Assyrians, Mitannians, Hurrians, and Urartians. All the cities of the region have a quite amazingly complex history. There are interesting religious survivals, such as isolated pockets of Jews, and Christian communities which broke away from the main body of the religion centuries ago, and have lived entirely surrounded by Muslims, who massacred them from time to time, and some of whose customs the Christians adopted.

An example are the Jacobites. These Jacobites have nothing whatever to do with the House of Stuart, but are a Monophysite sect which went off on its own after the Council of Chalcedon (451 AD), because it refused to accept the dogma of the dual nature of Christ. Its followers believed that the divine and human in Our Lord were fused in a single nature. One can have a very interesting discussion on this question with Jacobite monks in south-east Turkey, if one can find a language to do it in (they only speak Arabic, Turkish, and Syriac). The Jacobites have a beautiful old monastery, Deir Zafiran, about four miles outside the town of Mardin, with a wonderful situation on a rocky hill overlooking the Syrian plain.

The monastery used to be the seat of the Jacobite patriarchate, but the patriarch now resides in Damascus. I stayed a night in it in 1965. The monks are delighted to see anybody, especially someone of their own religion. They are rather out of touch with the modern world, and have an excessively strict regime. They eat no meat, eggs, butter, milk, or cheese, and subsist entirely on bread, rice, and fruit. They touch the ground with their foreheads 200 times a day, and recite all the 150 psalms. One gay young monk told me he could accomplish the latter dreadful chore in exactly one hour – an average of 2½ psalms a minute!

The whole of this area resounded in past times with the unedifying squabbles of jarring Christian sects (in particular Jacobites and Nestorians), which are related with masterly irony by Gibbon. The historian was not very kind about the Jacobites, of whom he wrote:

> The superstition of the Jacobites is more abject, their fasts more rigid, their intestine divisions more numerous, and their doctors (so far as I can measure the degrees of nonsense) more remote from the precincts of reason.

Another religious curiosity in the area are the Yezidis, those cosmic neutralists who worship God and the Devil. Most of the Yezidis live in northern Iraq, but there are quite a few in Turkey too. They are said to practise Christian rites such as baptism, and the drinking of sacred wine. Yezidi infants are dedicated to both God and Satan. They have certain strange beliefs: they never eat cabbage, because the Devil inhabits the leaves, and they abominate the colour blue. It is also said that if you draw a circle in chalk around a Yezidi, he will not dare to move out of it, and will remain there docilely till you release him.

There was a case, when I was in Turkey, of two criminals who were being pursued by the police in south-east Turkey, both of whom were Yezidis. According to the Turkish press, the police succeded in drawing a chalk circle round the area where the fugitives were, and captured them with the utmost ease. On one occasion, in Ottoman times, when there was no room in the local gaol for two hundred Yezidi prisoners, the authorities apparently did the same thing, leaving them in the open till other arrangements could be made. Like Herodotus, I pass this story on for the benefit of the credulous.

*   *   *   *   *

Gaziantep is the first town one comes to in the south-east. It used to be called Aintab. This became Antep in modern Turkish, and it got the honourable addition 'Gazi' (warrior for Islam) for its heroic resistance to the French invasion of southern Turkey in 1921. It is a very alive, industrious, sophisticated town, with whole streets of craftsmen banging and hammering away like in an oriental Nuremberg. It is a centre for pistachio-growing, and a great place for the smuggling of opium and cattle to the Middle East. The old gag was to float the opium down the Euphrates in tins so weighted that they stayed just below the surface of the water, and were fished out in Syria. Alternatively it was flown across the frontier by children in toy aeroplanes.

Personally I shall always remember Gaziantep for the unparalleled hospitality I received there on a visit in 1966 from Mr. Orhan Barlas, a leading barrister of the city, and one of the nicest men of any nationality it has been my good fortune to meet.

Urfa, the Roman Edessa, is another interesting old city. It is associated with Abraham, who is said to have been born in a cave in the neighbouring region. According to tradition Abraham, when a young man, refused to bow down to the Assyrian gods, and was ordered by Nimrod, King of Assyria, to be launched by a catapult from the citadel into a burning fiery furnace kindled in the plain below. The order was carried out. The future patriarch, after describing a graceful parabola through the air, landed accurately on target, but lo!, as he touched the furnace, a miracle occurred. The flames turned to water, and the logs to fish.

This is said to be the origin of the sacred carp of Urfa, one of the oldest cults of Anatolia, which attracts many pilgrims. For a few coins you can feed the fish. As they are sacred, and can never be killed, they grow to immense sizes and ages. They are the biggest, ugliest, most voracious creatures I ever set eyes on, and the pool swarms with them. When you throw food in, there is a horrible swirling of the water as they tumble over each other to get it. I was terrified of falling in: I am sure they would have eaten me immediately, like those horrible little South American fish which rip the flesh from your bones in a matter of seconds.

Amongst other things at Urfa, there is a building known as the 'Red Church', in which tradition has it that a handkerchief belonging to Jesus Christ in person was piously preserved for many centuries.

The two finest cities of the Turkish east are Diyarbakir and Van. Diyarbakir was the Roman Amida. It stands magnificently on a long hill above the Tigris, and is one of the most perfect walled cities in the world. The walls, made of black basalt, were built in the fourth century AD by the Roman emperor Constantius. Like all these places, it has a most confused history, having been occupied at one time or another by at least twenty-two different states and peoples, among other Hurrians, Mitannians, Assyrians, Urartians, Medes, Persians, Scythians, Macedonians, Armenians, Romans, Byzantines, Mongols, Turcomans, Arabs, Seljuks, and Ottomans. Most of them left inscriptions on the old black walls. There is a very pretty museum in Diyarbakir in an arcaded courtyard, where one sees relics of many of these peoples. Kurdish nationalists also consider Diyarbakir as capital of their autonomous 'Kurdistan'.

But the most beautiful place of all is Van, situated at nearly 6000 feet on the huge remote lake of the same name, fifty miles from the Persian frontier. 'Van in this world, Paradise in the next', is what the Armenians used to say about it, and they should know, because it was their capital for hundreds of years. Before that it was under the Medes and Persians. On the citadel there is a tremendous trilingual cuneiform inscription – in Babylonian, Persian, and Medic – in praise of Xerxes, 'King of Kings, King of the provinces of many languages . . . .' Before that again it had been the chief city of the mysterious kingdom of Urartu, a state contemporary with Assyria. The Urartians seem to have been neither a Semitic nor an Indo-European people, and their secret has not yet been completely elucidated.

The best approach to Van is by air. In this way you get the full impact of the first sight of the lake – an immense turquoise jewel ringed by snow mountains. The most important monument of the area, apart from the citadel, is the remarkable little Armenian church of Aghthamar, on an island in the lake, built in the tenth century by the Ardzrouni dynasty. Its walls are decorated with extraordinary three-dimensional reliefs of birds, beasts, and Biblical scenes, said to be of high importance in the history of oriental art. The colour of the church, a rich chocolate brown, strikes a spectacular chromatic chord with the turquoise glory of the lake.

About eighty miles north of Van, where the frontiers of Turkey, Persia, and the Soviet Union meet, but entirely on Turkish soil, stands Mount Ararat – a shade under 17,000 feet high – on which the Ark of Noah is supposed to have rested after the Flood (Genesis 8.4.). Some sceptics have questioned how even so extraordinary a deluge as this could have reached this height while others have queried where Noah's dove found the olive-leaf, seeing that from time immemorial no olive trees have grown anywhere near the mountain. But many devout people believe that the Ark is somewhere near the top of Ararat. Year after year, parties of Seventh Day Adventists, and other hopeful persons, usually from the United States, make pilgrimages towards the summit, braving ice and snow, bears and Kurds, in search of the holy relic. But none has yet found it.

Ararat is a fascinating mountain, which has always drawn men to it. It is not easy climbing, and has taken a number of lives. It stands alone, dazzlingly high, in the plain through which the tired stream of the Araxes crawls towards the Caspian, looking as if it were the model for Swinburne's lines:

> That even the weariest river
> Winds somewhere safe to sea.

From a river's viewpoint, presumably, even so unsatisfactory a sea as the Caspian is better than none.

Ararat is so high, and has such a magnificently commanding position close to the Soviet frontier, that many people are convinced that it is used by the Americans, with the connivance of the Turkish government, for espionage over parts of Russia, and that the pious American expeditions which are constantly searching for Noah's Ark are really agents of the CIA. This story, whatever the truth of it may be, is sedulously fostered by the Russians; but many Turks fall for it, and there has been a call for an end to the expeditions. The Kurds, on the other hand, regard Ararat as 'their' mountain. One of the great Kurdish rebellions in the time of Mustafa Kemal actually made its headquarters on the Peak.

Westwards from Ararat, along the old caravan route which once linked Persia with the West, stands the rugged fortress of Erzurum,

Konya: Serafettin Camii, the interior of the mosque

Ankara: Ulus Meydani, a view of modern Ankara

Ankara, the Ataturk mausoleum

formerly outpost of the Byzantines against the Turks, and today of the Turks against the Russians. Erzurum is headquarters of the Turkish 3rd Army, and uncrowned capital of the east. There is a university there, 6000 feet above sea level, wonderfully situated amid high mountains. It is a wild place in winter. Wolves have been seen prowling on the university campus.

From Erzurum one can strike northwards over the Zigana pass, near the place where Xenophon's Ten Thousand first sighted the sea, to Trabzon (Trebizond) on the Black Sea coast. This is one of the finest drives in Turkey. Trabzon is another interesting old town. Sheltered behind its mountains, it held out as the last refuge of the Greek culture eight years after the capture of Constantinople, and long after the whole of Anatolia had been engulfed by the Turks. In the Church of St. Sophia, wall paintings of exceptional quality have been uncovered in the last few years by British Byzantinologists. From Erzurum, alternatively, one can push straight on west to Sivas and Ankara. This road is famous for something in more recent Turkish history. It is the route followed by Mustafa Kemal in 1919, at the start of his historic struggle for the independence of Turkey.

This drive takes one over typical Anatolian plateau country: great sun-drenched shimmering plains punctuated by compact villages of mud houses with flat roofs, each roof with a stone roller on top to roll it smooth after the rain. Poplars are the most common trees here, tall and lissom against a summer sky as blue as a Perugino Virgin's robe. There are fierce dogs with spiked collars (against wolf-bite) and clipped ears (said to make them fiercer). Ponderous geese patrol the village squares, water-buffaloes walk with sublime dignity towards streams, and storks strike attitudes on the tops of Roman ruins, as if the Roman empire had risen and declined for them to nest on.

And so to Ankara, Ataturk's new capital, now fifty years old. The approach is striking, because it is unexpected. One rounds a corner in the waste and sees a city, rather as Burckhardt must have seen Petra. The first glimpse of Ankara is through a gap in the Galatian hills – it lies below you in a broad, shallow plain – very bright, new, and far-flung, its buildings sprinkled over the lowish tea-coloured slopes as if out of a gigantic pepper pot.

Ankara is an important centre of archaeology. The museum

contains finds from at least eight different civilizations: Neolithic, Bronze Age, Hittite, Phrygian, Urartian, Persian, Greek, and Roman. Ankara has been a natural stronghold since Hittite times. It was an important place when Anatolia was under Persian rule, because the Royal Road, that famous highway of the Persian kings, ran right past it on the way from Susa to Sardis. Relics of the Roman period include a Temple of Augustus, and baths of the time of Caracalla. The citadel resisted the armies of Tamerlane. But Tamerlane trounced the Ottoman Sultan Bayazid at a great battle outside Ankara in 1402, and this defeat delayed by fifty-one years the Turkish capture of Constantinople. Of the modern monuments, the mausoleum of Ataturk is the finest, and has been spoken of in the same breath as the Parthenon.

Ankara suffers inevitably from comparison with Istanbul, but the new capital has its own beauty – a beauty made of sun, pale earth, and almost limitless space. This is a straightforward, optimistic city, quite different in character to the devious, pessimistic, cynical, older capital. It is expanding fast; houses, hotels, and apartment blocks go up almost while you watch. The population is over a million. Ankara's two best seasons are spring and autumn, above all autumn, which is blessed by warm sun and blue skies almost into December. Ankara is particularly fine at night, especially seen from the hill to the south where the President's Palace and the British Embassy stand. As dusk falls, the gaunt plain lights up and sparkles like a sea of jewels.

I have hardly mentioned Izmir (the ancient Smyrna), which Strabo thought the most beautiful of all the world's cities, and which is associated with so many famous names from Homer to Ataturk. Homer is thought to have lived there, and one is shown a place in town where he may have written his great epics. Though shorn of its past glory, Izmir is still a thriving, sophisticated city. It has a wonderful climate, surroundings of sensational beauty, and all the best sites of classical antiquity within easy reach. It is one of the chief centres of Turkish tourism.

Izmir has all the attractiveness of a big port, with ships tying up along the front, taking on cargoes of tobacco, dried figs, raisins, and cotton, the produce of the region. Horse-drawn phaetons trot through the streets. There are few things more delightful than to stroll along the water-front in Izmir on a spring day, sniffing the ambrosial mixed scent of horse-manure and tobacco, to which may occasionally be added, if the Imbat* is blowing on shore, a potent whiff of drains. This Aegean metropolis is a lodestone for peasants from the remotest parts of Turkey, who trek westwards in search of a better life, perhaps with the obscure instinct of their ancestors that civilization is to be found on the shores of the sea. Only one city of the area outshines Izmir: one can guess which.

★　　★　　★　　★　　★

So much has been written about Istanbul, alias Byzantium, alias Constantinople, in the 2700 years of its existence that one wonders whether anything can usefully be added. Still, in a book about Turkey, one can hardly leave it out. In writing about this marvellous city, so stocked with treasures, it is difficult to tread the path between a pretentious rhapsody and an arid guide. Even the sardonic Gibbon becomes dithyrambic at moments in the *Decline and Fall*: 'The incomparable situation which marks her out for the metropolis of a great empire', 'the genius of the place', which 'will ever triumph over the accidents of time and fortune'.

Gibbon has little use for the folly of the Byzantines who lost their capital to the Turks in 1453, or for the Grand Duke who was heard to exclaim, shortly before the fall of the city, that he would rather see the turban of Mahomet in Constantinople than the tiara of the Pope. The Duke's words were quickly fulfilled. Gibbon does not refer to the apocryphal story that the Byzantine leaders, when the Turks were at the gates, were debating the vexed question of whether angels were male or female. That discussion has been regarded by posterity as the *ne plus ultra* of all irrelevance, though one might add that the problem is of obvious importance to anybody who one day expects to meet an angel.

Istanbul is a very great city; but if you were blindfolded and dumped in the middle of it, you would never think so. There is no proper main street or central square, almost no fine modern buildings, no form, plan, or concept to the urban structure. At first sight there seems nothing but a thousand twisting streets curling up and down the hills above the Golden Horn, a jumble of jerry-built houses, a hideous cacophony of horns, and an undisciplined mass of pedestrians who encroach ever further on the

* Izmir's local wind.

narrow streets, making traffic jams ever more frequent and more impossible to disentangle. Anybody dumped in such a place, after enduring its din and frustration for a time, would probably shout: 'Get me out of here – and quickly!'

But everything is changed from the moment that one sees the sea. Istanbul is more than a city, it is a marine agglomeration. Venice used to be married to the sea; to pursue the metaphor, Istanbul has with it an even more intimate relationship. It is less that of husband and wife, than of body and soul. The city bestrides the triple confluence of the Bosphorus, the Marmara, and the Golden Horn,* and extends along the shores of all three. This makes the water not the fringe, but the centre, of the urban area. The Bosphorus, the sixteen-mile strait which winds north-eastwards to the Black Sea, is really like a main street – a street of salt water, traversed by ocean-going liners, and by the fast efficient steamers which daily transport a quarter of a million people between the suburbs and the nodal centre of the Galata Bridge.

Near the point where Bosphorus and Marmara converge, on the Anatolian side, stands the suburb of Uskudar (Scutari), within the confines of the municipality and part of the modern city. From here thousands of men and women cross daily to work in Europe – perhaps the only place in the world where people live in one continent and work in another. In Uskudar stands the colossal Selimiye barracks, where Florence Nightingale worked, amid scenes of filth and horror, during the Crimean War. So huge is the building that two brothers who did their military service there for eighteen months are said to have never met.

From here one gets a spectacular view of the city, with its mosques, domes, towers, and palaces so wonderfully banked up on the hills above the Golden Horn. Below them, the Marmara stretches westwards in a silken sheen of water – a small, almost private, Turkish sea, though it can be whipped to frenzy by sudden terrifying storms, and people have sometimes been drowned within yards of the shore. Twelve miles to the south, the archipelago of the Princes Islands relieves the emptiness of the Marmara, and, by giving the eye something tangible to rest on, completes the almost oppressive splendour of the well-known scene.

* A strait, a sea, and a river.

The Bosphorus, which also starts from this point, is a most attractive stretch of water. It is narrow, often no wider than a broad river, and is bordered on both shores by charming villages and by the wooden waterside mansions (known as *Yalis*), where famous families of the Ottoman past live in minor palaces so flush with the water that their lawns can be flooded by the wash of a passing ship. The Bosphorus is not straight, but sinuous. Trapped in summer in its blue folds you might think for a moment you were on Lake Maggiore or Como, till you see a Russian tanker steaming past you at close quarters.

It is a fast-flowing strait, the current reaching seven or eight knots in places. This is known as the 'Devil's current'. The prevailing flow through the Straits is from Black Sea to Mediterranean, but there is a reverse undertow of saltier water flowing in the opposite direction, which makes swimming or boating in the Bosphorus a curious experience. Sometimes, when bathing, one is carried upstream against the surface current. Under the influence of strong southerly winds, which often blow in the area, the normal flow in the Bosphorus may be temporarily reversed, and there can be very sudden changes of current, which may oblige ships entering the Straits to take on a Turkish pilot.

Istanbul, being situated at a highly exposed geographical intersection-point, in touch with the Mediterranean, Balkan, and Anatolian climates, and within feeling-distance of the Russian and Siberian steppes, is renowned for its formidable winds. There are at least nine winds which blow round Istanbul, all of which have names. The fresh north-easterly is called the *Poyraz* (a corruption of Boreas), and this tends to be the prevailing wind in the Bosphorus. The due-north wind is the *Yildiz*, or 'star', because it blows from the pole-star. The *Karayel*, or 'black wind' is a bluff and blustery affair which comes in from the Balkans in winter, and in past days, it is recorded, could freeze up the Bosphorus. The *Meltems* are a series of light pleasant breezes which blow offshore in summer. The *Keşişleme* or 'intersecting wind' comes from the south-east and the mountains of Bursa.

The worst of all Istanbul winds is the *Lodos*, from the south-west, a sort of hot fug which constricts the veins and dries up the lymphatic ducts. It can also be extremely violent, uprooting trees and paralysing shipping in the Marmara. Most people hate the

Lodos. So trying is this particular wind on the temper that in past times judges were not allowed to give judgement when it was blowing, for fear it would make them vindictive, and extenuating circumstances were found for crimes of violence committed under its influence.

The great 'sight' of Istanbul is, of course, the basilica of St. Sophia ('Church of the Holy Wisdom'), built in the sixth century by the Byzantine emperor Justinian. Ten thousand men are said to have laboured on its construction, and temples all over the east were pillaged to add to its splendour. Justinian in person supervised the work each day, dressed in a linen tunic. When finally the edifice was complete, the emperor raised his arms to heaven and exclaimed excitedly: 'O Solomon, I have outdone you!' And in fact the new church was much larger and more sumptuous than Solomon's temple.

In view of the extravagant praise lavished on Justinian's church by people from all parts of the globe in the last 1400 years, it is curious to recall the sarcastic, indeed venomous, judgement passed by Gibbon on the celebrated building:

> A magnificent temple is a laudable monument of national taste and religion, and the enthusiast who entered the dome of St. Sophia might be tempted to suppose that it was the residence, or even the workmanship, of the Deity. Yet how dull is the artifice, how insignificant is the labour, if it be compared with the formation of the vilest insect that crawls upon the surface of the temple.

For the historian, it seems, Justinian's masterpiece was literally not worth a fly! But no writer has done greater justice to Istanbul than Gibbon. In that rich prose the history of the city lies, as it were, embalmed; and the massive architecture of the *Decline and Fall* rivals that of St. Sophia itself.

Ataturk, though he did as much as any man, at Gallipoli and elsewhere, to preserve Istanbul as a Turkish possession, moved his capital inland to Ankara. Probably he did so with a good instinct. For all that, Istanbul remains the magnet to which Turks of all classes are irresistibly drawn, not only because it is their largest and most famous city, but because, in some almost mystical way, it represents their link with the western civilization itself.

And it is true that, by capturing the city, the Sultans became the successors of Constantine, and the Turks, by a sort of post-facto graft, heirs to the Roman empire. In this sense they feel, not imitators, but inheritors, of the civilization which is based on Greece and Rome. Philhellenes may laugh, but this is what many Turks sincerely believe.

And what of Istanbul today? Everything is jumbled together: past and present, beauty and ugliness, treasures and rubbish. Around and about the antiquities swirls the life of the modern city: masses of humanity pouring in and out of ships, buses, or *dolmush** taxis, on their way to the villages of the Bosphorus, across to the Anatolian shore, out to the islands, along the Marmara, up to the strangely-named suburbs behind the Golden Horn, or further afield to the resorts of the Black Sea coast. What with the surging population (3 million), the narrow serpentine streets, the encroaching pedestrians, the inextricable traffic, the over-crowded steamers, and a municipal council which is perpetually bankrupt, there are naturally acute problems. Some of these may be relieved by the new bridge over the Bosphorus, when it is finished in 1973; though there are people who argue that the bridge will only make things worse.

Istanbul has been beautifully depicted in the short stories of ~~Sait Faik~~, that most gifted of modern Turkish writers, who died in 1954. It is a shame that these fine stories, some of them perfect works of art of their kind, have not yet been translated into English.** They give better than anything else the flavour of everyday life in the old sea-city.

* Taxis which fill up with passengers before moving off, then pick up and drop them along the route.
** There is an excellent French translation of Sait Faik, *Un Point sur la Carte*, by Professor Sabri Esat Siyavuşgil. A. W. Sythoff, Leyden, 1962.

16 ❊ *Byzantium, Kurdistan, Armenia*

CERTAIN PROBLEMS are perennially connected with the Turks and their occupation of Anatolia, which are best not mentioned because the Turks are highly sensitive about them, but which are part of the tangled web of historical fact and prejudice colouring our view of the Turks and equally their view of the western world.

I am referring particularly of course to the Kurds and Armenians. One cannot travel for long in eastern Turkey without becoming acutely aware of the existence, or one-time existence, of these peoples, and similarly one cannot spend much time in Istanbul without feeling the still partly Greek atmosphere of that city which was for so long capital of the Byzantine empire. There is also the curious anomaly that the highest spiritual office of eastern Christendom, the Oecumenical Patriarchate of Constantinople, should be situated in a Muslim city, and that the Patriarch himself should be a Turkish subject.

I am putting Greeks, Kurds, and Armenians in the same bracket, not merely because they are, or were, minorities in the Turkish state, but because I am trying to convey the atmosphere inside Turkey, and the phobias and complexes which affect the Turks in their relationship with the outside, especially the western, world. It is a delicate matter to write about these questions, and I shall certainly offend many Turks, even perhaps my friends, by doing so; but these things have to be mentioned, provided one tries to be fair and objective, in any 'warts and all' account of the problems of the Turks in the modern world.

★   ★   ★   ★   ★

Despite the strong westernizing current in Turkey, the Turks still have in them a certain apprehension about the West and a deep subconscious suspicion of western motives. There are good historical reasons for this. The Ottoman empire was on the defensive during the last two hundred years or so of its existence, and the West made an attempt as recently as 1918 to reverse 1453 and get back Constantinople. Anatolia has been Turkish territory for some nine hundred years, but it is only fifty years since a Greek aggression and occupation of large parts of Anatolia (backed by a British government and many Hellenophils in the West) had to be beaten off at the cost of a tremendous and exhausting struggle. Other Western powers, such as France and Italy, tried at this time to carve off pieces of Anatolia for themselves.

It is hardly likely that another Western attempt on this scale to win back Constantinople and parts of Anatolia will be made in the foreseeable future, but fifty years is not a long time in the history of nations, and Turkish suspicion of the West is an inevitable consequence. This was the light in which the Turks saw, and still see, the Cyprus problem, and which makes it so much more than just the affair of who owns a small island: it is rather the extension of Greek power, backed by Europe. The Turks feel the West will always prefer the Greeks to them, and, when the opportunity presents itself, will try to regain territory historically lost to the Turks. The fact that the Greek Cypriot leader, Archbishop Makarios, was a Christian priest moreover aggravated the issue by evoking Turkish memories of a Western onslaught headed by a crafty Byzantine prelate.

This being so, the presence of the Oecumenical Patriarchate in Istanbul is a constant source of trouble. At the Conference of Lausanne in 1923, which led to the Treaty that ratified Ataturk's victories in the field, an attempt was made by the Turkish delegation to have the Patriarchate removed from the city; but such an idea so horrified Lord Curzon and the Greek leader Venizelos that it was abandoned. The Turks finally agreed that the Patriarchate should remain in its traditional location provided that it gave up all pretensions to temporal power and limited itself exclusively to spiritual functions. Despite this, the Patriarchate today has no clear juridical status in Turkey, and merely depends on the verbal assurances given at Lausanne by Mr. Inönü, leader of the Turkish delegation.

This arrangement, because of the difficulty of defining 'spiritual functions', has caused acute problems for the Patriarch and his staff, particularly at moments of tension between Turkey and Greece, or during the many Cyprus crises. The popular Turkish view of the Patriarchate, perhaps inevitably, is that it is a fifth column, a 'nest of spies', a Trojan Horse for the revival of Hellenism, and the thin end of the wedge for a reconquest of Constantinople and the re-establishment of the Byzantine empire. All this is perfectly ridiculous, of course, as anybody who has been inside the dilapidated precincts of the Patriarchate, and has observed its real functions, can see. Even in spiritual matters, the Oecumenical Patriarch is relatively powerless, due to the peculiar structure of the Greek Orthodox church, and to such thorns in his flesh as the intrigues of the Patriarch of Moscow.

Although the Patriarchate is a perpetual target for popular abuse inside Turkey, and has repeatedly been threatened with expulsion at moments of crises, no Turkish government since Lausanne has made a serious attempt to remove it from the country, and in my view it would be unwise (and unnecessary) for the Turks to do so. Possession of the Patriarchate, though it often causes political trouble, is a feather in Turkey's cap (as well as an invaluable bargaining counter), and although the Patriarchate, in its atmosphere, is itself a very oriental institution, it continues to be Turkey's historic link with Greece, Christendom, and the West, so long as the Turks judge it to be in their interests to preserve that link.

*   *   *   *   *

The Kurds are a far more serious problem for the Turks because the Kurdish minority in Turkey is the largest of its kind in the East – much bigger than the Kurdish minorities in Iraq, Iran, Syria, or the Soviet Union, the other countries which have Kurds. The total number of Turkish Kurds is almost impossible to assess (it is probably somewhere between 3 and 5 million). Officially in Turkey there is no such thing as a 'Kurd': there are only 'eastern compatriots' or 'mountain Turks'. In fact 'calling a spade a spade' in Turkey today usually means calling a Kurd a Kurd. Repression of Kurdish nationalism in any form has been complete under the Republic, and anybody who even refers to it is regarded as 'dividing the Turkish nation'.

It is difficult to say how much Kurdish nationalism there is in Turkey. There are noisy Kurdish students in the universities, and if one goes to the south-east, especially Diyarbakir, one finds a few restless Kurdish intellectuals who speak with surprising openness about Turkish repressive measures. This is true to the extent that south-east Turkey has been governed traditionally in an almost colonial manner, with officials receiving special training for 'service in the East', as British civil servants used to have for service in the colonies. It is largely because of the linguistic problem: Kurdish is a completely different language to Turkish, and east of the Euphrates many Kurdish peasants, especially the women, cannot speak Turkish.

The Kurdish war in northern Iraq, which went on intermittently for about eight years from 1963 to 1970, has caused periodic anxiety in Ankara, even more so the recent agreement between the Kurdish insurgents and the Baghdad government, which seems likely to lead to some kind of Kurdish autonomy in north Iraq. How will this affect the Kurdish population in Turkey? There are various influences acting on the inhabitants of these areas. The Soviet Union has, of course, been engaged for years in subverting the Turkish Kurds, and there is little sign that the recent rapprochement between Ankara and Moscow has altered this situation. Any secession movement among the Turkish Kurds would, of course, involve a vast area of south-east Turkey. It is a different matter for the Iraqis, who have a numerically smaller Kurdish minority in a secluded mountainous area of north Iraq.

It is all very well for Turkey to refer officially to the Kurds as 'mountain Turks', but there seems no question that the Kurds are ethnically a different people to the Turks, even if their genealogy is obscure. According to the Jews, the Kurds are sprung from four hundred virgins who were raped by devils while on their way to King Solomon's court. As might be imagined, not many Kurds subscribe to this theory of their own origin. The Kurds claim to be Aryans, are classified as a white race, and speak an Indo-European language. They have inhabited eastern Anatolia, so far as one knows, since about the seventh century BC. They look back on such heroes as Saladin (probably the most famous of historically known Kurds), and there are mystical prophecies about a great Kurdish leader who will one day arise and throw off the multiple oppressors' yoke.

The Kurds are a gay, colourful, intelligent, poetic, and rather extravagant people, who often make preposterous claims to be the originators of other ethnic strains, as is seen in the old Kurdish saying:

> Kurds who have seen the sea are Lazes.
> Kurds who ride a horse are Circassians.
> Kurds who are stupid are Turks.

which, of course, is rubbish. Many Kurds in Turkey (though their Kurdish origin is never publicly referred to) have reached high positions in the Turkish state, and enriched many walks of Turkish life, in the same sort of way, it seems to me, as Scotsmen, Welshmen, or Irishmen have done in Britain.

In the case of the Kurds, as with the Circassians and Lazes in Turkey, there is no problem of religion, as there is with the Christian or Jewish minorities, because the Kurds are Muslims, and mostly Sunni Muslims at that. There were at least three great Kurdish rebellions in the time of Ataturk, all of which were firmly repressed. (Most Turks still suspect the British of having been behind these revolts.) These insurrections were not purely nationalistic, but partly religious revolts by the Sheikhs and Dervish leaders in the east against the policies of the Kemalist secular state.

Kurdish nationalism – what there is of it in Turkey – is very mixed with social and economic questions. As we have already said, the part of Turkey where the Kurds live is the most backward. The Kurds feel that nothing is done for eastern Turkey, and that they tend to be treated as second-class citizens. Personally, I have come across little Kurdish nationalism as such in Turkey, but have often found resentment among the Kurds that their part of Turkey is treated as a semi-colonial area, and that legitimate grievances in the Kurdish regions are ignored by Ankara, which according to them, merely sends the dreaded gendarmerie to the villages and deals out repression. There were a number of riots and disorders in eastern Turkey during the period when I was there, especially in the last few years.

Since about 1950 efforts have been made by various Turkish governments to assuage Kurdish feelings by programmes of public works in the east and schemes such as the new health service based on Mush, the Keban dam on the Euphrates (which, if rightly applied, should help the industrialization and electrification of the east), and the Ataturk University in Erzurum. There is also the CENTO railway connecting Turkey and Persia via Lake Van, and the fine CENTO motorway being built through tremendous mountain country to link the Tigris valley with western Iran. Kurdish nationalists maintain that these roads and railways have a military purpose – an agreement between Turkey and Persia to keep the Kurds down – but there is no obvious evidence that this is so.

In March 1970 a new holding company for economic development of the east was formed, founded by a number of big Turkish banks and private firms. It seems a hopeful idea. If these various projects succeed, Kurdish arguments that there is discrimination against the part of the country they live in will gradually lose force. At all events, there is no sign that Ankara would ever try for anything other than an economic and social solution to the Kurdish problem. Any sort of Kurdish autonomy, even of the mildest kind, is unthinkable in Turkey, nor, so far as I have been able to see, is there any real popular demand for it.

In general, Turkish governments since the Republic have pursued a policy of assimilation, repression, or dispersal of the Kurds. Over the last fifty years for example, large numbers of Kurds have been transferred from the eastern provinces to other parts of Anatolia. One sometimes comes across almost pure Kurdish villages in central, or even western, Turkey. When I was there, moreover, a whole series of secret military trials of leading Kurdish personalities were in almost constant session in Ankara, presumably as a form of political pressure.

The military government, after 1960, caused something of a sensation by uprooting fifty-five of the biggest Kurdish sheikhs and landowners and sending them to live in western Turkey. The purpose of this seems to have been, not so much to deprive the Kurdish populations of their potential leaders, as to disrupt the feudal regime in eastern Turkey. But the idea was not carried through. Even the military government wilted under the strain of so revolutionary a measure. Soon the great lords were back on their lands, and are today more powerful than ever. In parts of eastern Turkey the writ of Ankara hardly runs, and brigandage has increased in recent years. Meanwhile the Turks remain more than ever hypersensitive to the Kurdish issue, and perennially suspicious of foreign intervention or influences which might inflame it.

* * * * *

As for Armenia, it is altogether different, because Armenia is a ghost, or perhaps more aptly a skeleton in the Turkish cupboard. It is a body whose flesh was long since picked clean. In all that beautiful country between Van and Ararat, where the Armenian kingdom once flourished so brilliantly, there is today only a memory – and a terrible one. Few peoples, not even the Jews, have had a more ghastly history than the Armenians. The massacres and holocausts within living memory were only the last in a whole chain of disasters which befell this extraordinary people, of whom their own historian, John Katholikos, wrote as early as the tenth century AD: 'We are like a harvest reaped by bad husbandmen, amidst encircling gloom and cloud.'

The Armenians were, and are, a most talented and cultured race, gifted for commerce and the arts, refined craftsmen, solid and imaginative builders, and not unaware, as a people, of their own superior qualities. They also had characteristics which others found irritating. Armenia was the first country in the world to adopt Christianity as its state religion, but the Armenians infuriated other Christians by arrogating to the Armenian church all sorts of special virtues, such as that it was founded by Jesus Christ in person. They embraced the Monophysite heresy, which was proscribed by the Council of Chalcedon; for this they were much disliked by the Greeks. It is a sad fact of history that the mutual antipathy of Greeks and Armenians finally exposed the whole of Asia Minor to the Muslim deluge. Furthermore, when the turn of the Armenians came to be slaughtered in horrifying numbers at the end of the nineteenth century and beginning of the twentieth, the Orthodox Church did little or nothing to help its fellow-Christians in distress.

Nearly a million Armenians were killed or deported from Turkey at the end of the Ottoman empire, on the orders of the Young Turk dictatorship, until the moment came when Talat Pasha could announce proudly: 'We have done more to solve the Armenian problem in three months than Abdul Hamid did in thirty years.' The purpose of the Young Turks was to exterminate or remove the whole two million or so Armenians living in the empire at that time

(1915), but in fact they liquidated less than half that number. Armenians who were neither killed nor deported were converted to Islam, and their children brought up as Muslims and Turks. How many of these crypto-Armenians there are in Turkey today is difficult to estimate, but their number must be considerable. They are usually recognizable by their physiognomy, and often, it seems to me, by a more subtle and flexible mind. But they would never admit that they are anything but Turks and Muslims, and today what is left of Armenia is merely merged into the infinitely complex racial stock of Anatolia. Over all this a veil of complete ethnic homogeneity is drawn, which no outsider can easily penetrate. (In Istanbul, of course, there is a recognized community of about fifty thousand Armenians – Christians, but Turkish citizens – and an Armenian patriarchate.)

At regular intervals the Armenians in the outside world (numbering some four million) organize demonstrations to remind people of the atrocities, and to lay claim to an Armenian national home in eastern Turkey. (The only 'Armenia' left in the world now is the Soviet republic of that name.) The chances of their ever achieving such an aim are remote. These demonstrations, though they keep anti-Turkish feeling alive in the outside world, have little practical effect except to annoy the Turks, because all Turks, so far as I have been able to judge, are adamant on the Armenian question. No Turk I have ever met, however sophisticated and westernized, or however well I personally knew him, has ever in my hearing shown a sense of guilt about the fate of the Armenians, or admitted moral responsibility for it. Divided on most other questions, the Turks seem united on this.

The Turkish view of the matter is that the Armenians were a disloyal minority, who worked actively with foreign powers for the defeat of Turkey, intrigued with Turkey's enemies, the Russians, to partition Turkey and set up a separate Armenian state, and who, as traitors to their country in wartime, and at a moment of great national danger for Turkey, deserved their fate, however cruel, shocking, and barbaric that fate may have been.

What has been the verdict of history on the Armenian atrocities? Most objective western historians appear to agree, now, that the Turkish charges against the Armenians, though of course they could never justify the liquidation of nearly a million people, were at least partially true. Many Armenians had in fact been disloyal to the Turkish state, which was, after all, their country. They had worked with the Russians; some Armenians had even deserted to the Russian army. They had rejoiced openly, in a most imprudent fashion, at the long series of Turkish defeats in the Balkan wars. They had been encouraged in this by outside countries – especially the western powers and Russia, which were in no position, when it came to the crunch, to do anything to protect this unfortunate people.

For about forty years before 1915 the Armenians, as an unprotected Christian minority living among Muslims, had been in a desperately dangerous situation. They acted rashly, many of them openly banking on an allied victory over Turkey. As Aubrey Herbert put it: 'Though the Armenians had a future before them in the development and improvement of Turkey, they were seduced by Europe and flattered to suicide.' Herbert was a Turcophile, but he expressed a truth which has to be taken into account in considering those terrible events. The curious fact was that in Ottoman times the Armenians, of all the mixed bag of nationalities which composed the empire, were the most loyal and the most trusted. They were known by the Turks as the 'faithful nation'. Perhaps for this reason the Turks turned on them all the more savagely once they started to suspect them.

There was, of course, a history of jealousy between the two peoples – the Turks, who were the rulers and soldiers, and the gifted, industrious, commercially-minded and more prosperous Armenians. The Armenians did not live only in the cities, but in small towns and villages all over Turkey. They were not all in one block, but mixed with the Turks through Anatolia like pepper and salt. Apart from the difference of religion, there had grown up something of the same network of jealousy and envy which in other countries had surrounded the Jews, so that when the order came from above to 'eliminate' the Armenians, it unchained in the Turks the same sort of dreadful passions which Hitler evoked in the Germans nearly thirty years later. The Turks in 1915 were on the verge of defeat, and in one of the acute crises of their history; in blind rage they turned on a minority they suspected of working against them, driven mad by the thought that the people they had most trusted were traitors.

In the Turkish case it was not the cold efficiency of the gas-chambers, carried out on the principle that the Jews, like vermin, had to be exterminated for the greater good of the German nation. It was rather insensate killing by a people driven to desperation, so that, once started, the Turks went on and on with the slaughter, as Alan Moorehead well expresses it in his *Gallipoli*: 'with a crazed and guilty logic . . . until the very enormity of their cruelty was its own justification'. They might have said, with Macbeth:

> . . . I am in blood
> Stepp'd in so far that, should I wade no more,
> Returning were as tedious as go o'er.

I am not trying to palliate what was done to the Armenians, because, even if the Armenians *had* proved traitors in wartime, one does not simply deport or massacre nearly a million people. The Turks did a terrible thing, which can never be forgotten, but (to repeat) one must remember these two somewhat mitigating facts: first, that a series of disastrous wars and defeats had driven the Turks to desperation, and the last straw was the apparent betrayal of the Armenians; secondly, the Turkish population had not only been encouraged, but actually ordered, to carry out the massacres by the odious Young Turk triumvirate (with Talat Pasha as the man chiefly responsible), and the killings and deportations were conceived by that government, coldly and deliberately, as a 'solution' to the Armenian problem. Some enlightened Turks, at considerable risk to themselves, protected the Armenians, such as Rami Bey, the governor of Smyrna, or the Mevlevi convents, which hid and sheltered many of the wretched victims. But, as has been seen in other countries, brutal and ruthless leadership brought out the worst in human nature, giving opportunities to the scum of society to pay off personal scores, or indulge hideous passions.

Why bring up the Armenian massacres at all, one may ask? Why drag this particular skeleton out of its cupboard? What was done was done, and can never be undone. Most books about the Turks, for obvious reasons, avoid the subject. But I feel that any serious consideration of the Turks, and the contribution they can make to Europe, must face up to the Armenian question, if only because its shadow passes inexorably between us and them, and is an unspoken thought in dealings with the Turks. It was a horrific episode, even in the context of the great welter of blood of which so much of human history consists. For we have all massacred, at one time or another, some more wholesale and with less justification than others – but all peoples have done it, some many times.

We must also consider the question of historical prejudice, in that we are taught to hold such episodes more against some peoples than others. The exterminations carried out by the Russians in central Asia at various times over the last hundred years were almost on a par with the Armenian massacres, but the latter were given infinitely more publicity in the West than the former, because the Turks, ever since the Crusades, had been regarded as the enemies of Europe. Anything the Turk did was automatically an atrocity in European eyes, almost before it was done. In the context of the innumerable massacres carried out by other peoples throughout history (including, I regret to say, ourselves), it is fair to consider whether the peculiar horror aroused by the Armenian atrocities in Europe was not due, at least in part, to an anti-Turkish prejudice rooted very much deeper in the past.

Though the Turks have never openly repented of the slaughter and deportation of the Armenians, it seems to me that the Turkish Republic has, at least by implication, turned its back on the regime which perpetrated them, through the liquidation of the Sultanate and Caliphate, and the extraordinary emphasis laid by Ataturk and his collaborators on the concepts of 'secularism' and 'civilization'. Both Abdul Hamid and the Young Turks had played on religious fanaticism in ordering the wholesale liquidation of a Christian minority – fanaticism of a kind which had been only too familiar in Europe at the time of the Inquisition and Counter-Reformation. Ataturk wanted to destroy religious fanaticism, one of the most dangerous of human emotions, because it seems to those who indulge in it to justify all crimes.

The new emphasis in Turkey was on the secular ideal – which meant in this case religious toleration. Reason and conscience should tell you what was right, not what some fanatical priest or imam or Dervish sheikh told you, not even necessarily what some holy book told you. This was secularism, this was civilization, and this was what the new Turks wanted. That is why the Islamic reaction in Turkey – because it means the revival or continuance of fanaticism – remains a desperately important issue for the Turks.

17 ❋ *How Westernized are the Turks?*

WHERE have the Turks got to in their long saga? They have been 'westernizing' slowly for some two hundred years. Ataturk gave them the biggest push in that direction. How far has the process gone? How westernized are they? Has Ataturk's dream come true? Is Turkey part of the West, and is the Turk a European? Is it possible to answer these questions?

There were westernizers before Ataturk, but they never went the whole hog like he did. They wanted to borrow from Europe while remaining part of Islam – in other words they tried to be western while remaining eastern. This would not work. Ataturk was the first Turkish leader to realize that to be properly western the Turks must be prepared to a large extent to jettison even Islam. He went to a logical extreme, making Turkey a secular state, which no other Muslim country to this day has done. By so doing he prepared the ground for the entry of the Turks to Europe. How far has this succeeded?

Actually, in his speeches Ataturk did not talk about 'westernization', but rather 'civilization'. For most people, it is true, this amounted to the same thing, because in their minds there was only one civilization in the twentieth century, and that was the civilization of the West. This was of course rejected by Muslims, who maintained that Islam, even today, was a civilization which rivalled, if not outshone, that of the West, while extreme Muslims maintain that the Islamic World is infinitely superior to the West.

In the minds of the Kemalists 'westernization' was roughly equated with civilization because they did not believe that Islam could equal the West, or, to be more specific, they did not believe that it had succeeded in civilizing the Turks. Ataturk's aim, which he constantly repeated, was to raise the Turks 'to the level of contemporary civilization'. This was the phrase he consistently used during his lifetime, and which his followers use today.

Many people think the word 'westernization' has a trumpery and superficial sound about it, as if it implied mere imitation of the

West, which of course to a large extent it does. You can make a man wear a hat instead of a fez, or write in the Latin instead of the Arabic script, or give him parliamentary democracy on the western model and make him vote in elections. But how far, in so doing, do you change the basic man? The leftists in particular avoid the word 'westernization', which they associate with American capitalism and the supremacy of the bourgeois class. In their eyes 'civilization' means quite different things to hats and alphabets – it means 'radical reforms', social justice, and for many of them, no doubt, Communism itself.

But westernization is the main issue in Turkey, because it is assumed that the whole purpose of the last two hundred years, and the last fifty in particular, has been to raise Turkey to the cultural and technical level of Europe. This is what causes the interminable discussions and dissensions about the religion, since in the minds of the westernizers Islam is associated with the East, and westernization is measured in inverse ratio to the hold Islam still has on the people. No other wholly Islamic people has tried to pass into Europe. The result is that there is a perpetual debate in Turkey as to what westernization and civilization mean, how far the two things are identical, and how far the Turks have succeeded in attaining either.

A few years ago a professor at the University of Istanbul wrote a controversial little book called *Where have we got to in our Westernization?*, which shocked a lot of people because it suggested the Turks had not got very far. It dismissed such things as the hat and script reforms as virtually meaningless in any profound sense, arguing that westernization meant something much deeper than this. He defined the word as meaning in particular the acquisition of the scientific and technical mind of the West. He said it was very difficult for the Turks to westernize, because they had been outside the pale of the Graeco-Roman and Christian traditions which were assumed to be the basis of the western civilization. He maintained that this could only be remedied by acquiring the mental attitudes of the West, something the Turks had not yet succeeded in doing.

It is a debateable question how far Ataturk's changes were merely superficial and imitative, and in fact one can argue about how far imitation itself, if prolonged over a long period, can ultimately change the substance. Making people wear hats instead of fezes and western instead of oriental clothes may not change them in any fundamental sense, but perhaps it does so more than one thinks. Clothes are very important, and in a way they make one feel part of the rest of the community which wears them. This was especially true of the Turks and the hat, because the fez symbolized Islam, whereas the hat symbolized Europe. If one is obliged by law for long enough to adopt the manners of another civilization, as the Turks have been, it is possible that one to some extent becomes identified with that civilization.

This raises the question of how far the Turks themselves feel European. I think the answer is: more than one might expect, especially the younger generation. On a recent visit to Turkey I was struck by the remark of a young peasant in a remote village of Anatolia, where I had stopped in the coffee-house for a chat. The talk turned to football, and to the World Cup final between Italy and Brazil which was due to be played in a few days time. The peasant youth, who was keen about football, said in passing: 'Italy represents *us* in this match.' 'How do you mean, represents us?', I asked. 'Yes,' he said 'Italy represents Europe.' This remark would have been of no interest if it had been made by an educated westernized Turk, but was striking coming from an Anatolian peasant.

*   *   *   *   *

Many people today take the line that Ataturk merely demolished the Islamic and oriental superstructure in preparation for 'real westernization, which was to follow, but which he himself (dying at 57) did not live to achieve. He closed the windows to the east, as it were, and opened them to the west. Since his death many of the eastern windows have been reopened. On the other hand one cannot say that the western windows have been closed. The Turks are now exposed, in a rather extraordinary fashion, and to an extent few other peoples are, to the influences of two completely different cultures. To give a concrete example: new editions of both Shakespeare's plays and the Mesnevi, the mystical work of the mediaeval Muslim poet Mevlana Jelaluddin el-Rumi, were published a few years ago almost simultaneously. It has to be admitted that the sales of the Mesnevi went much quicker than those of Shakespeare, which just goes to show what a difficult process westernization is. On the other hand, in many Turkish intellectual circles, the works of Marx, Lenin and Mao sell far faster than those of Rumi.

Ataturk may have 'cleared the site' for new building, but many of his recommendations for westernizing Turkey have never been carried out. Two examples are statues and music. Statues are frowned on by orthodox Islam as idolatrous. Ataturk's idea was to have, all over Turkey, statues of past Turkish worthies, as one does in European countries. In Europe one is constantly coming across monuments to obscure national figures in odd corners, and this is an excellent thing, because one is reminded of their contribution to history. In Muslim countries this was not so, because of the religious ban. Unfortunately, in Turkey today, Ataturk's advice has not been carried out: there are merely ubiquitous statues and photographs of himself, either in uniform (hammering the Greeks), or resplendent in western clothes.

In the town of Afyonkarahisar, in western Turkey, there is one of the most savage pieces of statuary I have seen anywhere in the world. It shows a gigantic naked Turk, of superhuman stature, a pair of vast hands raised above his head like predatory claws, trampling underfoot an unfortunate Greek who is depicted as writhing and squirming on the ground. One has to remember that this part of Turkey suffered terribly in the Greek invasion of Anatolia in 1919. But this statue has a barbarizing rather than a civilizing effect.

Apart from this there are only a few statues here and there in Turkey today. There is one of the great architect Sinan, in a turban, outside the University of Ankara, and in Istanbul another of the liberal reformer Midhat Pasha, in spectacles and a fez, somewhere near St. Sophia. There are a few (very few) monuments to Inönü in various parts of the country. Some years ago a bust of Ataturk's mother, Zubeyde Hanim, was erected in the main boulevard in Ankara – an event which was doubly horrifying for good Muslims, first because it was a statue, secondly because it was a woman.

Music is even more difficult. Ataturk informed his people that western classical music was better than oriental music, but even he hardly expected them to take to it very easily. Admittedly Turkey's excellent Presidential Symphony Orchestra (based in Ankara) tours the remote provinces of Anatolia once a year, playing Beethoven and Mozart to packed though somewhat baffled-looking audiences in such places as Erzurum and Van. These large audiences are probably due less to an appreciation of the classics, than to the exquisite boredom of life in these faraway places, and the need for any diversion, however incomprehensible.

The number of people who genuinely enjoy western music is still a handful. The ordinary Turk loves to sit by the radio listening to his own music – hopeless, formless, repetitive, fatalistic – or to the mournful songs of unrequited love of which so much of Turkish folklore seems to consist. Such music can become attractive; but, listening to it, one feels it induces a condition of utter resignation which is hardly compatible with progress.

As for the old Turkish music, it is difficult for us to grasp or enjoy it, though clearly the soul of the Turk is expressed in his music. As the Turkish poet Yahya Kemal wrote:

> Most people don't understand our old music,
> Yet if they don't understand our music,
> They understand nothing of us.

.*   *   *   *   *

Some people have claimed that Ataturk's transformations were too rapid and drastic and caused a trauma from which the Turks have never really recovered, furthermore that the Islamic reaction which followed has left the Turks as oriental as before. This is not true. The westernization of Turkey in the last forty years, though slower than the Kemalists hoped for, is very striking even if it is not always easy to pin down its exact nature.

There are ways, of course, in which every country in the world is becoming westernized. Industrialization is a form of westernization, since industry started in the West. Things like tourism, hotels, good roads, banking systems, trades unions, the right to strike, and parliamentray democracy, are all forms of westernization. The list of criteria can be vastly extended, on almost any level: from Bikinis, mini-skirts, long hair, drugs, and glossy magazines, to deeper things such as logic, fatalism, the degree of bribery and corruption, frankness, technical efficiency, and the 'western' attitude of mind. Where does superficial westernization end and real westernization begin?

There are certain tangible forms of westernization in Turkey, which are interesting to observe: the shape of Turkish women, for example, and men's taste in female beauty. The two things, of course, interact. In former times female corpulence was much admired in Turkey. There was an old Ottoman saying: 'She is so beautiful that she has to go through the door sideways.' This idea has gone by the board today. Turkish women, having been released from the harem and the veil, have taken to a much more outdoor life. They go in for sport, and such things as ballet-dancing, which formerly was taboo. There has been an astonishing change in only two generations, for example, in the shape of girls' legs. Even female forearms, it seems to me, are less oriental than they used to be.

An interesting series of articles appeared recently in the Istanbul mass-circulation newspaper *Hurriyet*, which gave figures documenting the extent to which Turkish women have become slimmer and taller, so that western European ready-made clothes now fit them without alteration. No woman I saw during my time in Turkey had to go through the door sideways, and I doubt if many Turkish men today would want them to do so.

In trying to measure the degree of westernization in a country like Turkey one tends to seize on small but tangible things of this kind, such as the shape of girls' legs, how far people still squat on their heels instead of sitting on chairs, whether lavatories have seats, and the extent to which toilet paper is used. Most Turkish grocers still stock the latter commodity at an almost inaccessible point on their shelves, showing that it is in small demand among the common people. One could perhaps get a rough yardstick of westernization by enquiring at a toilet-paper factory about how far sales have gone up or down in recent years.

Even the number of camels can be seen as an indicator. The camel, being a non-European animal, gives a country an oriental flavour. When I first went to Ankara, during the Second World War, I remember seeing large numbers of camels in the market-place there, but the building of roads has made them unnecessary, and one never sees them now. In fact the number of these animals has enormously diminished in Turkey in the last twenty years.

These are minor but tangible sophistries with which to measure visual westernization, only because the deeper criteria – the replacement of fatalism by reason, the capacity for dispassionate judgement, the nature of the logic, the attitude to the truth, the degree to which, say, political parties are founded on principles and not mere personalities, the ease with which feudal chieftains control the vote in elections, even such things as the continued prevalence of polygamy, and the patriarchal dominance which is so characteristic of the East – are all difficult to gauge accurately.

I should perhaps mention again at this point the distinction Ataturk himself made between westernization and civilization. The former is obviously easier to define because it is a matter of *fact*: what the West in practice does – whereas the latter is a matter of opinion. A toilet without a seat is un-westernized, but it is not necessarily uncivilized; in fact many hygiene experts might argue that it is more civilized. A camel is not a western animal, but can one argue that it is not a civilized animal? Yet Ataturk, in making his reforms in Turkey, seems to have known clearly what he meant when he talked about civilization in the Turkish context: he was talking to a large extent about relations between the sexes and the general attitude of his people to women. It was not merely a matter of polygamy or monogamy; it was more a matter of the wild, almost insane jealousy and sense of honour which most ordinary Turks have about women, which means that it comes far more natural to them to kill than to go to law.

A Turkish shopkeeper whom I used to talk to from time to time in the town where I wrote this book, a most enlightened man, once summed up very briefly and vividly what civilization, in his view (i.e. in the Turkish context), meant. He expressed it succinctly thus: 'You look at my woman, I look at your woman. Bang! Bang!', and he made a gesture imitating one man shooting another. This was exactly it. I have in front of me as I write this chapter a newspaper cutting about a Turkish worker who came home one day and found his wife in bed with another man. Without a moment's hesitation he fetched an axe from the wood-shed, killed them both by smashing their heads in as they actually lay on the pillow, then with the utmost calmness gave himself up to the police, saying 'I have cleared my honour'. This incident is typical, and happens from time to time in many parts of Turkey. Civilization means going to court for one's rights, not to the wood-shed for one's axe.

Both civilization and westernization can be measured in Turkey by the degree to which polygamy, bride money, the abduction of girls, and the blood feud, though all exist still in various parts of Turkey (less in the west and more in the east), are slowly diminishing. The idea of Kemalism, as explained to me by one of its leading exponents, was that westernization would gradually be achieved by what he called 'the pressure of the superstructure on the infrastructure' – which meant, put in other words, that the force of the secular laws, and more especially that of the Swiss civil code, would ultimately change the habits, and even the nature, of the people.

The key thing was, and is, the Swiss code. The code, as my Turkish lawyer friend portentously but rightly expressed it, 'draws our people upwards to civilization'. The Kemalist idea, not yet realized, was that the Turks should change their nature to conform to the code, not that the code should be changed to fit the Turkish nature. If and when the civil code is fully applied in the last Anatolian village, my friend envisaged, the Turks would be Europeans. This was, and is, the ideal; but it has not yet happened.

At the moment there are not sufficient inducements for the Turkish peasantry to conform to the code. For a peasant a legal marriage is a bore. He has to complete all sorts of formalities, and to have a medical inspection. He may walk ten miles to the nearest town, only to find the doctor is not at home. It is far easier in these circumstances to have an imam marriage – a form of union which has the added charm, from the male viewpoint, that divorce is even easier than it was under the Koranic law. The religious marriage is certainly on the decline in Turkey, but it is by no means eradicated, as we have seen, and so long as it exists, polygamy can exist. To this extent, on one of the most essential criteria, Turkey is not yet fully westernized.

I don't want to paint too pessimistic a picture. Many people coming from Europe find Turkey and the Turks far more westernized than they expect. It is indeed partly a matter of where you come from. Approaching from Europe, the mosques and teeming bazaars of Istanbul seem like the beginning of the east; entering from Persia or the Arab countries, the Latin script and the dignified serious comportment of the Turk himself, make Turkey seem like the antechamber to Europe. People who have lived in Persia and other oriental countries often say they find the Turks much more western, partly because bribery and corruption (though not non-existent in Turkey) are much less there than in the countries further east, and several people who have lived in Persia told me they found the Turks more frank and direct in their dealings – usually a 'western' characteristic. It is possible that the racial factor we mentioned in the first chapter, which seems to present the Turks as a more western mixture than had been thought, partly accounts for this.

One of the biggest westernizing reforms, as far as appearances are concerned, was the change of the script in 1928, so that Turkey has at least the same alphabet as Europe. This has caused the need to transliterate most of the old Ottoman literature into the new writing. It is a double process, because it means not only transliteration, but translating from the Ottoman language into modern Turkish. Ottoman literature is gradually being rendered into the new alphabet and the new language, but it is a gigantic task. In the meantime most Turks below the age of forty are cut off from 90% of their own classical literature.

There have also been persistent attempts to teach Latin and Greek in Turkish schools, though up to now it has not been a great success. Most determined westernizers advocate that such teaching should be expanded, as a means, so to speak, of grafting Turkey *post facto* onto the Graeco-Roman civilization. Latin and Greek, to some extent, are replacing Arabic and Persian. There are Turkish scholars who have mastered a truly extraordinary assortment of eastern and western languages, both classical and living.

Another question is how far Islam has an 'orientalizing' effect on the Turks. Obviously it has to a considerable extent. The very word 'Islam' means surrender or resignation of everything to Allah. This is the source of 'Muslim fatalism'. There is also no doubt that, apart from Islam, the Turks have in them a strong dose of 'Asiatic' resignation. On the other hand, the genuine freedom of the remarkably liberal regime of the last twenty years may to a large extent be breaking this resignation down, by making the ordinary Turk feel that the established order of things can be changed by his own acts.

One 'oriental' feature in the Turks, as I see it, is their tendency to deal in personalities rather than principles, and the difficulty they find in making dispassionate judgements which are not coloured by personal likes and dislikes. These are mental attitudes which can hardly be overcome in a few years. But I get the impression that the younger generation of Turks are more 'western' in this way than their parents and grand-parents, while preserving the extreme courtesy which is one of the best features of oriental societies. In this sense westernization is almost visible as one generation succeeds another.

*　　*　　*　　*　　*

There is also the vexed question of nomadism, which constantly crops up in any discussion of the Turks, as well as other Turanian peoples, such as the Finns and the Magyars. This is obviously a complex subject, but it is relevant to the question of westernization among the Turks, if only because sedentarization and the practice of agriculture by settled communities is simply taken for granted among western peoples, who – perhaps quite wrongly – tend to think of nomads as uncivilized. The real question, probably, is whether any residual nomadic instinct among the Turks is a psychological barrier to 'westernization'.

A great deal has been written about the Turks having been nomads in central Asia, and there has been much speculation as to how far the nomadic instinct is one of the fundamental traits of the Turkish character, or indeed of all the Turanian peoples. There are few, if any, true nomads in Turkey today, though there are still semi-nomads, such as the Turcomans and *Yürüks*, who make seasonal migrations to the high plateaux in summer, but usually reside in villages in the winter. The *Yürüks* are a rather mysterious people, with their own customs and religion, and not much loved, it seems, by the Turks.

There are also many seasonal migrations for purely economic reasons, such as the mountain dwellers of south Turkey who go down annually to the Cilician Plain for the cotton-picking, leaving whole villages empty – nobody would dream of robbing them. This has been beautifully described by Yashar Kemal in 'The Wind from the Plain'.

Modern Turkish historians claim that many of the Turkish

peoples in central Asia before the Turks came to Anatolia were not nomads at all, but lived in cities and practised trade, as is recorded in the Orkhon inscriptions (in what is now Mongolia), which date from the eighth century AD, and the older Yenisei inscriptions in Tannu Tuva. Despite this, many of the Turkish peoples undoubtedly were nomads before the conquest of Anatolia, but became sedentarized over the centuries during their residence in the latter country and by intermingling with the native peoples. The sedentarization of nomads is, it seems, a difficult process. As Ramsay puts it: 'It is a hard experience for a nomadic people to settle down to agricultural life. The life of the nomad, is in a sense, a continual holiday. Looking after sheep or goats requires little physical toil and no hard manual labour . . . but to the nomad the agricultural life presents itself as one of hard, never-ending and uncongenial toil.'

Some authorities on the mediaeval history of Anatolia think that a sort of double process went on in the peninsula after the first Turkish incursions: first, a 'nomadization' by the Turks of the settled indigenous peoples, which helped to break up the solid and stable structure of the Roman-Byzantine society, to weaken and finally subdue it; secondly, that the invading nomads, by a long and difficult process, were themselves sedentarized, and have over the centuries become more and more so, until there are no more real nomads left today in Turkey.

Anatolia is in many ways a wild and mysterious place, and what has gone on in its recesses in the past is something historians are only now unravelling. In the sixteenth and seventeenth centuries there were constant confused movements of people in the peninsula, great popular rebellions against the established power, and almost a state of anarchy, which sometimes lasted for years on end, and the meaning of which is difficult now for anybody to understand.

It is possible that the Turks still have in them, to some extent, the instincts of a once-nomadic people. Observers have expanded on the peculiarity of their dwellings, which often appear flimsy when compared with those of more sedentary peoples, and with very little furniture, as if a sudden move on camel or horseback might have to be considered. One of the things that strike one on arriving in Istanbul from the west is the insubstantial appearance of the buildings (apart from the great mosques and palaces), compared with the solid cities of Europe – even of the Balkans. Many of the Istanbul houses look as if they were made of paper or cardboard, and a single stiff puff would blow the lot down.

The modern Turks are indignant at being described as nomads, since nomads are associated with Asia. For all that, the ordinary Turk always seems to me to be the type of fellow who, more than most, is mentally prepared to strike camp at short notice and wander forth hopefully in search of greener pastures. This may partly explain the extraordinary internal migrations which are constantly in progress all over Turkey. If this is atavistic nomadism, it is an attractive trait, though it causes difficult social problems.

* * * * *

The social reformers take the line that Ataturk would have done better if, instead of changing the fez and the script, forcing Turks to take surnames, and so on, he had abolished such things as bride price, kidnapping, and blood feuds, and had sharpened the penalties for evading the civil law which allows polygamy to continue. In this way he would really have 'changed the social infrastructure'. But it seems that Ataturk was unwilling to do things of this kind. In particular he refrained from interfering directly in family life (he never actually banned the veil, for example).

Ataturk was not a brutal dictator, and his acts were not arbitrary edicts. Most of them were long thought-out and exhaustively discussed decisions. In family life, because of the long traditions of the Turks, he judged it out of the question to interfere with drastic prohibitions. His idea was to leave this sort of thing to the combined influence of literacy, secular education, and better economic conditions gradually to civilize his people. He may have been right, because that is what has been happening, but it has been happening far too slowly for most of the Angry Young Turks, who see the social condition of the villages virtually as primitive as ever.

In their eyes the reforms needed – social, economic, agrarian, administrative, cultural, political, and religious reforms – are so numberless that they hardly know how to describe them. They have no faith in gradualism. They blame the whole trouble on the democratic system. Only a single-party regime, dedicated to pressing home what Ataturk started, can achieve what they want. Only rule by a Kemalist élite (in practice the army) can change the social realities which even Kemal left untouched – such as the complete enforcement of the civil law. But this would seem to demand a form of totalitarian regime which would make Ataturk's look mild.

So in practice it all comes back to the question of the political regime, and here you have the arguments fairly evenly balanced. Those who stand staunchly for democracy, of whom Inönü and his associates are the protagonists, argue that the regime is in itself a civilizing influence, the best of all civilizing influences, because in the long run nothing is more educative than freedom. The peasant is waking up, and as he awakes he will gradually become aware of what the rest of the world is doing, and how primitive his own condition still is. It is useless to force a man to be civilized or westernized; he must find his way there himself. Moreover, political freedom is something of absolute value, which Turkey, after a century of struggles, has attained, and which must at all costs be preserved.

The opponents of democracy reply that this argument is a fake. No particular form of political regime can be regarded as an end in itself: regimes are a means for achieving progress. Democracy cannot be regarded as Turkey's ultimate goal. Turkey's goal, as Ataturk put it, was civilization, and, as he made clear, the western civilization. To get there, many things would have to be drastically changed, and no democratic government had done this, or looked likely to do so. Democracy in Turkey was a disguise for conservatism and reaction. Ataturk's own type of regime had not been western democracy, and his experiment with it in 1930 had patently failed. Inönü had made an error of judgement in 1945 which had cost Turkey twenty-five years progress, and this error must now be corrected.

So argue the two sides in Turkey. Which will win? Even for the Kemalists, unless they are extreme leftists, it is difficult to abandon democracy, because to do so, since it would oblige Turkey to leave the Council of Europe, would work against the very westernizing ideal which Ataturk aimed at. It was one thing for Greece to quit the Council; Greece, whether under democracy or dictatorship, would always be part of Europe. But if Turkey left the European forum, would she ever get back?

Yet how, under the present form of democracy, can the Turks make the drastic and long-overdue changes which progress in their country demands? It is a curious dilemma, where one form of westernization negates the other. The Turks, in their present series of political crises, are grouping for a solution.

For the pursuit of their European ideal they must have democracy – and not just a fake, like the 'popular' democracies and 'guided' democracies of other developing countries. They need the real thing, at least in form. Equally, for the solution of their desperate problems they need dictatorship, or at least strong leadership. Perhaps they will succeed in establishing a regime which combines both. Already their present system virtually reconciles parliamentary government with military rule. It is difficult to know what name to give to this regime. Will 'democtorship' perhaps be the contribution of the Turks to the history of political science?

18 ❋ *Conclusion*

IN TEN YEARS TIME, at the present rate of population-increase, the Turks of Turkey will be 50 million – a fair-sized nation! What will happen to this 50 million? The Turks, as I see them, are a *poised* people: poised, that is, to move in several different possible directions. To the west is Europe; to the south, Islam; to the north, Communism (social revolution); to the east, finally, the great belt of Turkish peoples which stretches through the southern confines of the Soviet Union into China. The Turks, inhabiting a geographical fulcrum, are in an important central position in the emerging world of the super-states. What will they do? With whom will they link up? They are no longer nomads in the physical sense, but they are cultural or spiritual nomads, who can choose to move wherever the ideological pastures seem greenest.

Will they press on westwards into Europe, their old love, following in Ataturk's footsteps? I started this book with the question: Is a Turk a European? I have not answered the question. I cannot answer it – nobody can – but I can get nearer to an answer than I did at the beginning. I would say that the Turk is a 'potential European' (which an African or a Japanese is not), and that if the Turk presses on into Europe, and if Europe welcomes him, there seems no reason why a Turk should not be as European as any of us.

Personally, I think the Turks ought to be in Europe, because I am convinced that they have something to contribute. They know Europe; they lived for centuries within its boundaries, and gradually absorbed much of its civilization. They could make at least as great a contribution as their relatives, the Finns and Magyars; because the Turks are a creative, not a destructive people. I mean this not merely in the sense of establishing and maintaining a great empire – but creative also in art. They are quite different (though they claim kinship with them) to the Huns, Mongols, and other cataclysmic peoples, who have behaved historically more in the manner of whirlwinds and earthquakes than branches of the human race, flowing and ebbing like tides which leave a trail of desolation. The Turks added something creative to the lands they conquered, as the Ottoman and Seljuk monuments in Anatolia, and the famous skyline of mosques, minarets, domes, towers and palaces in Istanbul, bear eloquent witness.

Furthermore the Turks have human qualities which in my view would be of value to Europe. By virtue of being still in part an oriental people, they have in them that intuitive intelligence, that deep understanding of the fundamental facts of the human situation, which the orientals (perhaps because they are less blinded by materialism and money) possess. The touch of the eastern mind the Turks could bring into Europe would be a valuable complement to the dynamic, Cartesian, straightforward intellect of the West.

Added to this, as his own peculiar characteristic, is the aristocratic mentality of the Turk – a man who has always been the ruler, never the ruled. This has, of course, its drawbacks: it accentuates the natural negligence and indolence of the Turk, his relative ignorance of preservational techniques. He constructs, typically, a series of stupendous edifices, but expects others to maintain them. If those others do not exist, his grandiose constructions fall to pieces. But the Turk today, by *force majeure*, is doing many things he never did before, rather in the way the aristocracy in Europe has learnt to do the washing-up.

But will the Turk go for Europe? Westernization may be official doctrine in Kemalist Turkey, but is that the will of the Turks? Despite democracy, I have the feeling that the national will of the Turks has not yet really been expressed. If, say, the armed forces took over Turkey in some new political upheaval or transformation, where would the Turks go? Not, presumably, back towards Islam. Might it be northwards: Communism, or some kind of extreme Socialism? It cannot be ruled out. The problems of Turkey are as acute now as those of Russia before 1917, or China before 1949. The Turks, under Ataturk, were inured to a single-party regime, and before that, of course, to the personal autocracy of the Sultans.

Yet for all that I cannot quite see Turkey as Communist. There is a strong sense of both freedom and equality in the Turks. The peasants, because of their peculiar past, are not even a potential proletariat. There is a long tradition among the Turks, at all social levels, of government by discussion and not by edict (T. E. Lawrence and H. A. L. Fisher were wrong about this). It seems doubtful whether totalitarian methods are fundamentally suited to the Turkish nature. Some kind of dictatorship there may well be; but pure Communism? – I doubt it. I hope I shall not prove mistaken. Certainly there is no likelihood of Communism being imposed on Turkey from outside.

A more likely trauma may arise from the conflict between the vision of Turkey as part of Europe and the suppressed dream, entertained perhaps by more Turks than one thinks, of a greater Turkey to the East, as ultimate head of some vast confederation of Turkish peoples stretching from Bulgaria to the Gobi. Pan-Turkism, apart from minor outbreaks, has been taboo for fifty years in Turkey, and is commonly dubbed (mainly by the leftists) 'racist', 'chauvinist' or 'Fascist'. But there are signs that this attitude is changing. It is becoming increasingly fashionable today to take an interest in the 'outside Turks' (as they are called in Turkey).

One should remember that, in addition to the 40 million-odd Turks in central Asia, there are Turkish minorities in Greece, Bulgaria, Yugoslavia, Roumania, Cyprus, Iraq, Iran, and the Crimea. Cyprus apart, these are not especially important minorities; but they could perhaps become important, given sufficient interest from the 'homeland'.

Recently a big Istanbul newspaper published a prominent article by a very level-headed, intelligent Turk, who was formerly an officer in the armed forces and very close to the revolutionary group of 1960. He claimed that the 'outside' Turks, living under the rule of other governments, looked openly to republican Turkey, the only independent Turkish state in the world, as their 'leader' and their 'dawning hope'. This is rather apocalyptic language. If so balanced a man feels that way, it is probable that many others do too. I would not exclude the possibility of a Pan-Turkist revival in Turkey.

Throughout history, as we know, there have been great shifts of geographical emphasis. The trade of the Mediterranean city-states dwindled to unimportance when the Cape route to India was discovered. If, in the coming epoch, the conflict between the Soviet Union and China is to dominate the scene, central Asia might become a pivotal area. Those strange places, known only to travellers and explorers, will then be in the news: the Caspian and Aral seas, the Pamirs, the Yenisei and the Lena, the Takla-Makan and the Gobi, such romantic names will be in the front line. If this happens, the Turks will be living in one of the hottest spots on earth. Furthermore if ever there were to be any disintegration of the Soviet or Chinese empires, it is the Turks, on the principle of self-determination, who should rightfully inherit the vast spaces of the earth which were, and are, their homeland.

The 'north-east-south-west' alternatives I have mentioned are not, of course, mutually exclusive. Among Turks, almost anything is compatible. I see no reason why a Turk should not be simultaneously a Communist and a Pan-Turkist, a Pan-Turkist and a Muslim, a Communist and a Muslim, or a Muslim and a European. What does seem difficult, even for the Turks, those arch-combiners of the uncombinable, would be an 'east-west' combination: that they should be united with the West, yet linked to the broad band of their kinsmen living to the East. It would be difficult for the Turks to be *closely* integrated simultaneously with Europe and with Asia.

But the Turks, being of all peoples the most perfectly poised between East and West, need at this critical point in their history some decisive influence which can determine their future course. Forty years ago Ataturk gave them a great shove westwards. His followers are equally convinced Europeans. It is up to us westerners now to receive them, if not with open arms, at least with open minds. The Turks have always been extremely sensitive about their relationship with Europe. If Europe blocks them, or turns a deaf ear to their wishes, they might react angrily, instinctively, towards Islam, Pan-Turkism, and Asia. Blood might prove stronger than culture. We should encourage their westernism, accepting them as fellow-Europeans. Personally I hope that the Turks will be with us in the new Europe.

✳ *The Ritual of The Whirling Dervishes*

THE MAIN LINES of the ritual, as performed at Konya, are as follows. Sixteen Dervishes, wearing the traditional tall hat, like an elongated flower-pot, known as the *zikke*, and the black voluminous gown called the *hirka*, enter the arena, led by the Mevlevi Shaikh. Music accompanies the rite, played by an orchestra of some 20 musicians in Dervish garb.

The main instrument is the *ney*, a reed pipe originally from Persia, which has a long association with Islamic mysticism. There is also the *rebab*, a violin with one string and a kind of drum, the *kudum*. The music, repetitive and slightly hypnotic, in modes and rhythms unfamiliar to the west, is well calculated to heighten the mystical atmosphere of the strange ritual.

At first the Dervishes sit motionless on the floor, their heads bowed in prayer or profound contemplation, while a recitative is chanted by one of the musicians. Then comes a piercing solo from the *ney*, which seems to act like a summons. The Dervishes rise, and led by the Shaikh, perform three complete circles of the arena, walking in an oddly halting gait. Completion of the third circle leads almost directly to the essential feature of the rite. The Dervishes throw off their gloomy cloaks, emerging, like butterflies from the cocoon, in flowing robes of glistening white, with full skirts which reach almost to the ground. They are now ready for the *sema*, or sacred dance.

Although this is the moment one has been waiting for, when it comes it is unexpected. The first Dervish kisses hands with the Shaikh, then crosses his arms over his chest and hugs his shoulders. At the moment that he makes this gesture, almost imperceptibly, he begins to turn, slowly at first, and in an anti-clockwise direction. The other Dervishes follow suit.

One has the curious impression that the turning movement begins, not as an act of the Dervish's will, but really as if he were spun by some higher power – a human top. As they gather speed their arms, as though by centrifugal force rather than their own volition, unfold gradually to their full extent, and remain outstretched throughout the dance, the palm of the right hand facing always upwards, that of the left hand downwards to earth.

The 16 Dervishes now rotate evenly, some fast, some slower, always in an anti-clockwise direction, with absolute order and precision, without apparent effort or exhaustion, their tall-hatted heads inclined at a slight angle, their brilliant skirts flared by the circular motion. It is a movement of great beauty, strangeness, and originality. A practised adept can whirl, it is said, for one and a half hours without breaking off.

The symbolism, as explained to me by the Mevlevi Shaikh, is as follows. The black outer garments symbolize the tomb; the tall hats, tombstones. The white dancing robes represent the shroud. The Dervish is at first dead to the divine power. The halting walk is the walk of human life. The casting-off of the black gowns, the rising from the tomb. The hugging of the shoulders, the gesture of absolute surrender to the will of God.

The turning movement itself, the climax of the rite, is the means by which, in the Mevlevi belief, mystical union can be achieved with the Absolute. The anti-clockwise motion conforms with the rotation of the sphere. The upturned right palm receives God's mercy from Heaven and transmits it by the down-turned left palm to Earth.

In performing the dance the Dervish pivots on his left toe. The left leg is known as the 'pillar', while the right leg, which revolves round it, is called the 'wheel'. Much training is needed to become an adept. Apprentice Dervishes practise whirling round a nail set in the floor, which is held between the first and second toes of the left foot. To avoid giddiness they are taught to keep their eyes fixed on their left thumbnail.

✳ Bibliography

ABADAN, NERMIN. *Social Change and Turkish Women.* Ankara 1961.
ABEGG, Lily. *The Mind of East Asia.* Thames & Hudson. 1952.
ACIPAYAMLI, Orhan. *Customs and Beliefs of Anatolia.* Ankara 1963.
AKURGAL, Ekrem. *Ancient Civilisations and Ruins of Turkey.* Istanbul 1969.
ALTAN, Çetin. Onlar Uyanırken. Letters and articles. Ararat 1967.
AND, Metin. *Dances of Anatolian Turkey.* 1959.
ARMSTRONG, Harold. *Grey Wolf.* Arthur, Barker 1934.
ATATURK, Mustafa Kemal. Speech delivered at Ankara, 15–20 October 1927. English translation Leipzig 1929.
ATATURK, Mustafa Kemal. *Atatürk'ten Düşünceler* (Thoughts of Ataturk's). Ankara 1956.
ATAY, Falih Rıfkı. *Çankaya.* Istanbul 1958.
AVCIOGLU, Doğan. *Türkiye'nin Düzeni* (Turkey's Regime). Bilgi 1968.
AYDEMIR, Şevket Sureyya.
—— *Suyu Arayan Adam* (The man who searched for water). Autobiographical. Öz Yayınları. Ankara 1959.
—— *Tek Adam* (The One Man). Biography of Ataturk. 3 vols. Remzi Kitabevi, Istanbul 1965–66.
—— *Ikinci Adam* (The Second Man). Biography of Inönü. 3 vols. Remzi Kitabevi, Istanbul 1966–68.
—— *Inkilap ve Kadro* (The Revolution and Kadro). Remzi Kitabevi, Istanbul 1969.
—— *Menderes'in Dram* (The Drama of Menderes). Remzi Kitabevi, Istanbul 1969.
BARTHOLD, W. *Histoire des Turcs d'Asie Centrale.* Adrien Maisonneuve. Paris 1946.
BAYKURT, Fakir. *Yılanların öcü* (The Snakes' Revenge). Remzi Kitabevi 1959.
BAYNES and MOSS. *Byzantium.* Clarendon Press 1948.
BENOIST-MECHIN. *Mustapha Kemal, ou la mort d'un Empire.* Editions Albin Michel 1954.

Bibliography

BERKES, Niyazi. *The Development of Secularism in Turkey*. McGill U.P. 1964.

BOLITHO, William. *Twelve against the Gods*. Heinemann 1930, Penguin 1939.

CAHUN, Léon. *Introduction a l'Histoire de l'Asie*. Paris 1896.

CERAM, C. W. *Narrow Pass, Black Mountain :* the discovery of the Hittite Empire, transl. from German. Gollancz 1956.

COLES, Paul. *The Ottoman Impact on Europe*. Thames & Hudson 1968.

CREASY, Edward S. *History of the Ottoman Turks*. [1854–56.] Oriental reprints. Khayats, Beirut 1963.

DAVER, Bulent. *Türkiye Cumhuriyetinde Laiklik* (Laicism in the Turkish Republic). Ankara 1955.

DEMOMBYNES, Maurice Gaudefroy. Muslim Institutions. Allen & Unwin 1950.

DODD, C. H. *Politics and Government in Turkey*. Manchester U.P. 1969.

DURRELL, Lawrence. *Bitter Lemons*. Faber & Faber 1957.

EDIP, Halide. *The Turkish Ordeal*. John Murray 1928.

EREN, Nuri. *Turkey today and tomorrow*. Pall Mall Press 1963.

ERKIN, Feridun Cemal. *Les Relations Turco-Sovietiques et la question des Détroits*. Ankara 1968.

FAIK, Sait. *Stories. Un Point sur la Carte*. French translation by Sabri Esat Siyavuşgil. 1962. A. W. Sythoff-Leyde. Leyden 1962.

FRAZER, J. G. *The Golden Bough*. Macmillan 1936. 13 vols.

GABRIEL-LEROUX, J. *Les Premiers Civilisations de la Méditerranée*. Presses Universitaires de France. Paris 1961.

GIBB, H. A. R. *Mohammedanism*. Oxford U.P. 1953.

GIBBON, Edward. *The Decline and Fall of the Roman Empire*. [1776–1780.] 1971. Dent Everyman. 6 vols.

GÖKALP, Ziya. Writings of. *Turkish Nationalism and Western Civilisation*. Translated by Prof. Niyazi Berkes. Allen & Unwin 1959.

GROUSSET, René. *L'Empire des Steppes*. Payot, Paris 1939.

GUILLAUME, Alfred. *Islam*. Penguin 1954.

GURNEY, Oliver. *The Hittites*. Penguin 1952.

HARRIS, George. *Communist Movements in Turkey and the Formation of the First Turkish Republic*. Stanford U.P. 1967.

HASLIP, Joan. *The Sultan*. Cassell 1958.

HASLUCK, F. W. *Christianity and Islam under the Sultans*. 2 vols. Clarendon Press 1929.

HERODOTUS. *The Histories*. Tr. A. de Salincourt. Penguin 1954.

HEYD, Uriel. *Foundations of Turkish Nationalism*. Harvill. Luzac 1950.
—— *Language Reform in Modern Turkey*. Jerusalem 1954.
HIKMET, Nazım. *Selected poems* (Turkish). Ararat Yayınevi 1969.
HILLS, Denis. *My Travels in Turkey*. Allen & Unwin 1964.
HÖPKER, Wolfgang. *Wie rot ist das Mittelmeer?* Seewald 1968.
HOSTLER, C. W. *Turkism and the Soviets*. Allen & Unwin 1957.
HUXLEY, Julian. *From an Antique Land: Ancient and Modern in the Middle East*. Max Parrish 1954.
ISLAM. Encyclopedia of. Article on Ataturk, etc. Luzac 1954.
JÄCKH, Ernest. *The Rising Crescent*. Farrar, Straus. 1944.
KARAOSMANOGLU. *Yakup Kadri*. Yaban. Remzi Kitabevi. Istanbul 1960.
—— *Zoraki Diplomat*. Inkilap Kitabevi. Istanbul 1955.
KAPANI, Münci. *Kamu Hurriyetleri* (Public Liberties). Ankara 1964.
KARPAT, Kemal. *Turkey's Politics: The Transition to a Multi-Party System*. Princeton U.P. 1959.
KEMAL, Yaşar. *Memed, my Hawk*. Collins 1961.
—— *The Wind from the Plain*. Collins 1963.
—— *Anatolian Tales*. Collins & Harvill Press 1968.
KEMALISM. *Atatürkçülük nedir?* Collection of essays on Kemalism by prominent Turkish intellectuals. Varlık Yayınları. Istanbul 1955.
KEYSERLING, Count Hermann. Europe. Cape 1928.
KINROSS, Lord. *Ataturk:the Rebirth of a Nation*. Weidenfeld & Nicholson 1964.
KIRK, George. *A Short History of the Middle East*. Methuen 1960.
KITSIKIS, Dimitri. *Propagande et Pressions en Politique Internationale*. Presses Universitaries de France 1963.
LAQUEUR, Walter. *Communism and Nationalism in the Middle East*. Routledge & Kegan Paul 1956.
LENCZOWSKI, George. *The Middle East in World Affairs*. Cornell U.P. 1952.
LEWIS, Bernard. *The Emergence of Modern Turkey*. Oxford U.P. 1961.
LEWIS, Geoffrey. *Turkey*. Ernest Benn 1955.
LERNER, Daniel. *The Passing of Traditional Society*. Free Press of Glencoe. (Collier-Mac) 1958.
LLOYD, Seton. *Early Anatolia*. Penguin 1956.
LOTI, Pierre. *Turquie Agonisante*. Calmann-Levy 1913.
—— *Les Désenchantés*. Calmann-Levy 1906.
MAKAL, Mahmud. *A Village in Anatolia*. Vallentine, Mitchell 1954.
MANGO, Andrew. *Turkey*. Thames & Hudson 1968.

Bibliography

MOOREHEAD, Alan. *Gallipoli.* H. Hamilton 1956.

MORTON, H. V. *In the Steps of St. Paul.* Methuen 1936.

MULLER, Herbert J. *The Loom of History.* Harper 1958.

NESIN, Aziz. *Stories* (Turkish). Düşün Yayinevi. Istanbul 1964.

OLIVERO, Luigi. *Turkey without Harems.* Macdonald 1952.

ORGA, Irfan. *Portrait of a Turkish Family.* Macmillan 1957.

—— *Phoenix Ascendant.* Robert Hale 1958.

ORGA, Irfan and Margarete. *Ataturk.* Michael Joseph 1962.

OTYAM, Fikret. *Gide gide* series of books on Anatolia. Ankara Gazeteciler Cemiyeti 1964.

RAMSAUR, E. E. *The Young Turks.* Princeton 1957.

RAMSAY, Sir W. M. *The Historical Geography of Asia Minor.* John Murray 1890.

ROBINSON, Richard D. *The First Turkish Republic.* Harvard U.P. 1963.

RUMI. Poet and Mystic. *Selections from Mevlana Jelaluddin el-Rumi* by Reynold A. Nicholson. Allen & Unwin 1950.

RUNCIMAN, Sir Steven. *A History of the Crusades.* 3 vols. Cambridge U.P. 1951.

RUSTOW, Dankwart A. *The Army and the Founding of the Turkish Republic.* World Politics, XI (1949), 513–52.

ŞAPOLYO, Enver Behnan. *Mezhepler ve Tarikatlar tarihi.* (History of the Dervish sects and orders in Turkey). Türkiye Yayınevi. Istanbul 1964.

SCHUON, Frithjof. *Understanding Islam.* Allen & Unwin 1963.

SMITH, Elaine. *Turkey: Origins of the Kemalist Movement.* 1919–23. Judd & Detweiler 1959.

SPECTOR, Ivan. *The Soviet Union and the Moslem World.* Univ. of Washington Press 1956.

STARK, Freya. *Alexander's Path.* John Murray 1958.

—— *Riding to the Tigris.* John Murray 1959.

STIRLING, Paul. *Turkish Village.* Weidenfeld & Nicholson 1965.

TAHIR, Kemal. *Devlet Ana.* Bilgi Yayınevi 1967.

TOKER, Metin. *Ismet Paşayla 10 yıl* (10 years with Ismet Pasha). Akis Yayınları Ankara 1965.

TOYNBEE, Arnold. *The Western Question in Greece and Turkey.* Constable 1922.

—— *A Study of History.* passim (R.I.I.A., O.U.P.).

TUNAYA, Tarık. *Türkiye'de Siyasi Partiler* (Political parties in Turkey). Istanbul 1952.

TURHAN, Mumtaz. *Garplılaşmanın Neresindeyiz?* (Where have we got to in our Westernization?). Istanbul 1959.

TÜRK HALK EDEBIYATI. *Anthology of Turkish Folk Poetry.* Chosen by Dr. Ilhan Başgöz. 1956. Yaşaroglu Istanbul 1956.

VALLOIS, Henri. *Les Races Humaines.* Presses Universitaires de France. Paris 1956.

WEIKER, Walter. *The Free Party of 1930 in Turkey.* Princeton 1962.

—— *The Turkish Revolution 1960–61.* The Brookings Institute, Washington D.C. 1963.

XENOPHON. *The Persian Expedition.* Penguin 1967. Tr. Rex Warner.

YALMAN, Ahmed Emin. *Turkey in my Time.* Oklahoma U.P. 1956.

* Index

213

Index

Army revolution of 1960, 21, 33 ff., 55, 105; restores parliamentary rule, 33; 'fourteen' radical reformists, 33, 99; legalistic justification, 34; trials of deposed leaders, 34, 37, 43–4, 117; causes, 34–7, 64; published accounts, 39; choice of leader, 39–40; military skill, 41; numbers in the dock, 44; proceedings, 45–7; attempt to commute death sentences, 48; passing of power to 'real Junta', 48; and leftism, 87, 89

Aspendos, classical theatre, 163–4

Assyrians, 164, 167

Ataturk, Mustafa Kemal, 38, 55, 169; and revolt against the West, 6, 23; and westernization, 6, 17–20, 22, 187, 188–9; abolition of the fez, 17, 24, 31, 189; and the call to prayer, 26; abolishes religious education in schools, 17, 31; language and civil law changes, 18–19, 80, 106, 139, 195; monotheistic cult, 21–2, 51; character as a dictator, 23, 60, 61, 198; concern with civilization, 23–4, 59, 186; abolition of the *Tekkes*, 28; army based power, 56; and democratic rule, 61, 62–3; abolition of the Sultanate, 61; opposition parties, 61–2; and birth control, 69; public works, 71–2, 76; and land reform, 83; flirtation with Communism, 91–4, 114; compared with Gökalp, 102–3, 106; and Turkish morale, 104, 106, 123; and the peasantry, 139; unfulfilled recommendations, 190; distinguishes between westernization and civilization, 193

Attila, Turkish 'hordes', 53

Avcioglu, Dogan, 88–9; *Turkey's Regime*, 89, 97

Aydemir, Sevket Sureyya, 95

Aydemir, Colonel Talat, leader of 'real Junta', 48; and 1962, '63 revolts, 49–52, 88–9; trial and execution, 51–2; cause of his failure, 58

el-Azhar, and Turkish unorthodoxy, 17 and n.

Baku, 93

Barlas, Orhan, 166

Bashol, Salim, judge, 46

Bayar, President Celal, 56, 64; character, 37; and 1960 coup, 37, 38, 41; trial and sentence, 37, 38, 45; and Inönü, 37–8; audience with the Pope, 105

Bayazid, Ottoman sultan, 170

Bean, G. E., *Turkey's Southern Shore*, 164

Belge, Burhan, 95 and n.

Berkes, Niyazi, 27, 104 n.

Black Sea, 94, 119, 142, 144; Eregli steel works, 67; coast, 80, 81, 111, 155, 169; Caucasian peoples, 127

Bodrum, 120

Bolitho, William, on Mahomet, 14

Bolsheviks, 87, 91, 98, 114

Bosphorus, 67, 119, 156, 175; Galata Bridge, 172; *Yalis*, 173

Bozkurt, Mahmut Esat, and Swiss legal code, 140

Brusa (Bursa), Ottoman capital, 160, 162

Buddhism, 15, 16; Turks and, 16–17, 27

Bulgaria, 6, 9, 66, 111; Turkish minorities, 203

Byzantium, 5, 123, 138, 167, 171; empire, 7, 22, 159–60

Cahun, Leon, Pan-Turkist, 103

Caliphate, 13 n., 93; abolition, 17, 103, 186; possible restoration, 98, 100

Carlyle, Thomas, on the Koran, 13

Cebesoy, General Ali Fuad, 93

Celts, 7, 8, 157

Central Treaty Organization, 79, 181

China, 87, 91, 96; Turkish peoples, 7, 9, 15, 16, 101, 107, 122; surviving influence, 16, 123; conflict with USSR, 204

Christianity, 10, 16, 110; contrasted with Islam, 2, 10, 12–15; coterminous with westernization, 6, 17; breakaway sects, 15; Turkish converts, 16, 27; office of Oecumenical Patriarch, 176, 177–8

Christians, 13; identified as 'Infidels', 15, 17; isolated communities, 164

Index

Greek Orthodox Church, 176, 177–8, 182
Greeks, 8, 67, 135, 170, 203; compared with Turks, 4–5; mutual antipathy for Armenians, 182
Green army, secret communist, 92, 93
Grousset, René, 81
Gulek, Kasim, 3
Gumuşova, 156
Gurcan, Major Fethi, trial and execution, 51–2
Gursel, General Cemal, leader of 1960 revolution, 21, 33, 40, 41, 105
Guventurk, Lt.-Col. Faruk, 40

Hakkari, 156
Halicarnassus, 157
Hattusas, Hittite capital, 158
Hellenism, 110, 178
Hellenophils, 177
Herbert, Aubrey, on Turks, 124–5; on Armenians, 184
Hikmet, Nazim, Communist poet, 89–90
Hinduism, polytheistic, 15
Hittites, 71, 104, 106, 107, 170; Anatolian empire, 7, 8, 158–9
Hodja, Nasreddin, mythical hero, 124, 149–51
Huns, 104, 105, 106, 201
Hurrians, 164, 167
Hurriyet, 192

Injirlik, U.S. air base, 120
Inönü, Ismet, President, 33, 51, 60, 134, 177; and Menderes, 35–6, 37; and Bayar, 37–8; political expertise, 38–9; appeals for clemency, 48; army based power, 56, 58; inauguration of democracy, 60–1, 62, 65, 199; and land reform, 83; and rapprochement with USSR, 112, 115
Ipekci, Abdi and Coşar, Omer Sami, *The inside story of the Revolution*, 39 and n.
Iran, 81, 178, 203; opium smuggling, 71
Iraq, 178, 179, 203; cattle smuggling, 71
Iskenderun, steel complex, 68, 112

Islam, contrasted with Christianity, 2, 10–11, 11–12; Turkish adherence, 2–3, 8, 9, 17, 19, 27, 29, 31; fatalism, 12–13; Sunni – Shi'i split, 13 n., 28; obstacle to westernization, 17, 187, 188; 195; and Kemalism, 24, 25; fusion of religion and state, 26; priesthood (hodjas), 26, 31; identified with backwardness, 32, with conservatism, 98; and birth control, 69; sacred colour, 92; Jewish converts (*Dönmes*), 136; and statuary, 190
Issus, Battle of, 159
Istanbul, 3 n., 120, 155, 197–8; Eyub mosque, 47–8; army headquarters, 54–5; 'night-built' districts, 75; destruction of Greek property, 116, 136; goal of Turks, 156, 174–5; jewel of Turkey, 157, 161, 171–5; Golden Horn, 171, 172; winds, 173–4; St. Sophia, 174; today, 175; Armenian community, 183
Italy, Zanardelli code, 44 n.
Izmir (Smyrna), 120, 134, 147; association with Homer, 170; water-front, 170–1
Janissaries, Christian origins, 28, 53
Jenghis Khan, Turkish 'hordes', 53
Jews, 7, 15, 67, 135, 136, 185; isolated communities, 164
Johnson, President, letter to Inönü, 117, 118
Judaism, 27
Justice party, 30, 48, 52, 98, 112
Justinian, emperor, 174

Kadro, periodical, 95
Kaldor, Nicholas, and a tax on agriculture, 84
Kaptan, Yahya, 94
Karaosmanoglu, Yakup Kadri, 95; *Yaban*, 138–9
Kars, 71
Katholikos, John, historian, 182
Kayseri, 162
Kemal, Yaşar, leftist novelist and poet, 88, 191, 196
Kemalism, and civilization, 23–4, 187, 194; secret enemies, 24–5; 'six principles', 25, 71, 84, 95; and

216

Index

Muslims – *cont.*
14, 26; and women, 14; taboo on painting, etc., 18; religious unorthodoxy, 27; migration into Europe, 74; Imam marriages, 141

Nationalism, definition, 25, 87; and population control, 69–70; Bolshevik support, 91, 113; importance today, 100

National Order party, 98, 99

National Security Council, 57

National Unity Committee, ousting of the 'Fourteen', 33, 48; and parliamentary rule, 33, 34, 48; trials of deposed leaders, 43–8; military revolts (1962, '63), 48–9

Nationalist Action party, 98, 99; 'Grey Wolves' commandos, 99; anti-semitism, 135

NATO, 87, 117, 119, 120; Turkish membership, 3, 5, 19, 54, 110–11, 112, 119, 120–1

'Neo-Kemalists', 97

Nesin, Aziz, humourous writer, 153

Nestorians, 15; and Jacobites, 165

Nur movement, 92–3

Omar Khayyam, *Rubaiyat*, 160–1, 161 n

Okyar, Fethi, 62

Okyar, Prof. Osman, 72 and n.

Ottoman empire, 17, 167; period of military service, 54; foreign technicians and entrepreneurs, 67; land ownership (the Derebey's), 78; and word 'Turk', 104; toleration of minorities, 135–6; magical practices, 145; expansion and duration, 160; mosques, 161–2; opposition to the West, 176–7; literature, 195

Pan-Turanianism, 106; aims, 101

Pan-Turkism, 98; 'right-wing' doctrine, 100, 101; confusion with racism, 101; latent existence, 101–2, 203; ideology, 102–5; semi-mystical concepts, 105

Peasantry, 72, 73; migrations abroad and into cities, 74, 138, 139; conditions, 79–80, 138; seizure of land,

88; and Russian Revolution, 91; incidence of murder, 133–4; % of population, 138; intellectuals and, 138–9; love, marriage and sex, 140–3, 194; blood feuds, 143–5, 194; unwanted girls, 145–6, 146 n.

Penal code, 44 and n., 86

People's Houses, 76

People's Participation party, 93

Perga, 160; St. Paul and, 157

Pergamum, 157, 159

Persia, Shi'i sect, 13 n., 28; and Turkish arts, 148; conquest of Asia Minor, 159; Royal Road, 179

Persians, 7, 135, 159, 164, 167

Petrof, Grigori, *Country of the White Lilies*, 55

Phrygians, 7, 8, 107, 158, 159, 170

Pir Sultan Abdal, folk poet, 148

Polatkan, Hasan, trial and execution, 44 n., 46–7

Plaza, Galo, UN mediator, 116

Populism, definition, 25, 84

Progressive Republican party, 61–2

Protestantism, Gökalp's thinking, 103

Rami Bey, and Armenians, 185

Ramsay, Sir W. M., on the nomad, 197

Reaction, the, against Kemalism, 29–30, 32, 35, 186; and use of *charshaf*, 30–1

Reformism, definition, 25

Republican People's party, 62, 131; political programme, 25; rivalry with Democrats, 36, 76; and army coup, 38; secular character, 64–5; internal division, 95, 98; and Turco-Soviet rapprochement, 112

Romans, 8, 167, 170

Rome, 5, 138, 159; struggle with Persia, 159, 164

el-Rumi, Jelaluddin, 148, 189–90

Russia, 106; central Asian extermination, 186

St. Jerome, 157

St. Nicholas of Myra, 164

St. Paul, Asia Minor journey, 157

Sakarya, Battle of, 22

Saladin, 179

218

Index